Apparatus for Salvation, Renewal & Maturity

*A Revolutionized View of Scripture Will
Renew Minds, Restore the Church,
Revive Society*

By Galyn Wiemers

Last Hope Books and Publications
A division of Generation Word Bible Teaching Ministry

The Word: Apparatus for Salvation, Renewal and Maturity
Copyright 2011 by Galyn Wiemers. All rights reserved.
Printed in the United States of America by
Signature Book Printing, www.sbpbooks.com

Last Hope Books and Publications
A Division of Generation Word Bible Teaching Ministry
P.O. Box 399
Waukee, Iowa 50263

Visit www.generationword.com

Unless otherwise indicated, all scripture passages are from the
New International Version, 1985

Cover design by Clint Hansen
Editing by Tim Vaniman

ISBN-13: 978-0-9794382-4-0
ISBN-10: 0-9794382-4-1

*This book is dedicated to the pastors,
authors and Bible teachers who
have presented themselves to God
as approved workman who correctly
handled the Word of Truth.*

*Thank you for setting the Word of God
before my eyes and placing the voice of
the Spirit in my ears.*

TABLE OF CONTENTS

Preface

Section One: An Overview of the Salvation Process

Section Two: Ten Concepts for Reaching Spiritual Maturity

Section Three: The Ten Concepts in Scriptural Context

Preface

The Word of God reveals the great salvation for mankind which is available in Jesus Christ.

This same Word also communicates the truths that believers must understand in order to renew their minds to the plan and will of God, thereby enabling them to produce fruits of righteousness in their lives, and in the end, receive a rich inheritance into the eternal Kingdom of our Lord.

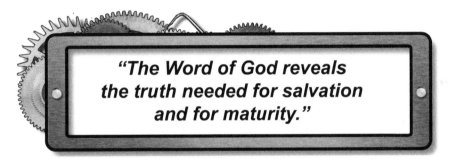

"The Word of God reveals the truth needed for salvation and for maturity."

This book emphasizes the crucial importance of the teaching ministry in the church. Simply put, the temporal and eternal relevance of faithful teaching look like this:

1. Teaching provides the opportunity for believers to grow in their knowledge and understanding of God, his revelation, plan, will, character, etc.
2. This understanding is both the seed of faith and the light of the Spirit which shine into the heart of the believer, leading to maturity.
3. Maturity produces good deeds, righteous acts, and fulfilled ministries – the fruit of believers' lives.
4. This fruit will be rewarded in eternity at the Judgment Seat of Christ.

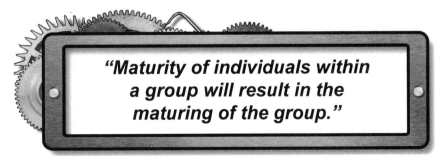

"Maturity of individuals within a group will result in the maturing of the group."

Not only is the individual believer built up and blessed by faithful teaching, but the local church and the universal church benefit as well. The maturity of individuals within a group will result in the maturity of the group. In other words, a majority of mature individuals within a church will produce a mature local church. And, it goes without saying but still needs to be said, a majority of mature local churches will result in a mature universal church, extending across denominational lines.

In Ephesians chapter 4, Paul talks about "unity of the faith" and "maturity" in the same passage. This indicates that when the Faith is clearly and accurately taught, there will be unity and maturity in the church at the highest possible level on this side of eternity.

If the ideas presented in this book are true, churches should be holding Bible studies constantly – each day and every night of the week. Obviously, not everyone can afford (financially, socially, emotionally or time-wise) to attend every single class. Nevertheless, they ought to be offered. Churches should be teaching the Word of God in class form, or by any other method they can manage, to help facilitate this renewal and growth.

Paul's words to Timothy from 63 AD ring throughout the Christian world today:

Until I come, devote yourself to the public reading of Scripture, to preaching and to teaching. Stop neglecting your gift! – 1 Timothy 4:13

These are the words of him who holds the seven stars and
walks among the seven golden lampstands…
who is the First and the Last,
who died and came to life again…
who has the sharp, double-edge sword…
whose eyes are like blazing fire and whose feet are like
burnished bronze…
who holds the seven spirits of God and the seven stars…
who is holy and true, who holds the key of David,
what he opens no one can shut and what he shuts
no one can open…
the Amen, the faithful and true witness,
the ruler of God's creation…
I know your deeds…
I know where you live…
I know your afflictions and your poverty…
I know your deeds, your love and faith,
your service and perseverance, and that you are now
doing more than you did at first…
I know your deeds, that you are neither cold nor hot.
I wish you were one or the other…
I know your deeds,
you have a reputation of being alive, but you are dead.
WAKE UP!…
He who has an ear,
let him hear what the Spirit says to the churches.

– Revelation 2, 3

Section One
An Overview of the Salvation Process

Saved by the Word, Mature through the Word, Continue in the Word

The Three Phases of Salvation

The Role of the Word of God

Will of God vs. Will of Man

Seeking God

Pagan Principles, Spiritual Ignorance, or Christian Truth

Phase Two and the Word of God

Chapter One:
Saved by the Word, Mature through the Word, Contin

The importance of the Word of God (the Bible, the Scriptures) can
overstated. We are saved by our faith in the gospel that is recorded in
Word, and our spiritual maturity is only possible as we renew our minds t
the Truth that is reveled in those same Scriptures.

The writers of the New Testament knew that the Word of God is the
foundation for the whole Christian life. Beginning with the new birth
and continuing through spiritual growth to maturity, a knowledge and
understanding of the Word is crucial. Without it, the believer cannot
produce the fruit of the Spirit or the good works which will result ultimately
in victory (rewards, crowns, praise, etc.) at the bema seat of Christ.

That is why all of the New Testament writers referenced below vowed to
their readers that they would not only preach and teach the Word of God,
but when they had finished, they would go back to the beginning and start
reminding them of what they had already preached and taught.

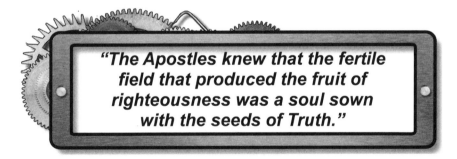

> *"The Apostles knew that the fertile field that produced the fruit of righteousness was a soul sown with the seeds of Truth."*

They knew that a fertile field, capable of producing good deeds,
godliness, holy character, the fruit of the Spirit, etc. was a soul sown with
the seed of Truth from the Word of God.

Paul wrote to Timothy in 2 Timothy 2:14:
Keep reminding God's people of these things.

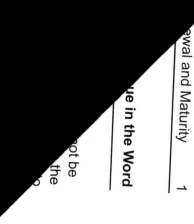

...iis readers in 2 Peter 1:13:
...your memory as long as I live in the tent of ...ery effort to see that after my departure you ...ember these things.

...tter to you. I have written both of them as ...u to wholesome thinking. I want you to recall ...ast by the holy prophets and the command given by our Lord and Savior *through your apostles.*

Jude did it in Jude 5:
Though you already know all this, I want to remind you.

John did it in 1 John 5:13:
I write these things to you who believe in the name of the Son of God so that you may know that you have eternal life.

The writer of Hebrews warned in Hebrews 2:1:
We must pay more careful attention, therefore, to what we have heard, so that we do not drift away.

And Paul wrote in 1 Corinthians 15:1:
I want to remind you of the gospel I preached to you, which you received and on which you have taken your stand. By this gospel you are saved, if you hold firmly to the word I preached to you. Otherwise, you have believed in vain.

Considering all this, what should we do today other than constantly teach, explain, communicate and present the Word of God? And then, when we have exhausted the entire text of Scripture, we should do nothing except return to it again and remind everyone of what has already been taught.

As I stated before, everything in our Christian life is built on the foundation of an understanding and knowledge of the truth. As you read this book, which explains the salvation process and God's purpose for the teaching ministry in the church in greater detail, I believe that *"if on some point you think differently, that too God will make clear to you"* (Philippians 3:15). To this end, these claims will be supported by over three hundred references from the New Testament.

Chapter Two:
The Three Phases of Salvation

You are already clean because of the word I have spoken to you (phase one). *Remain in me* (phase two)....   – John 15:3

How great is the love the Father has lavished on us, that we should be called children of God! And that is what we are! ...now we are children of God (phase one), *and what we will be* (phase three) *has not yet been made known. But we know that when he appears, we shall be like him* (phase three).... *Everyone who has this hope in him purifies himself* (phase two), *just as he is pure.*   – 1 John 3:1-3

The Christian life can be divided into three phases: past (relating to the spirit), present (relating to the soul) and future (relating to the body).

Phase One (Past)

The salvation of our spirit known as the new birth, or being "born again", begins the Christian life. For Christian believers this event occurred in the past, when they first believed the message. Paul writes to the Ephesians: *"You also were included in Christ when you heard the word of truth, the gospel of your salvation. Having believed, you were marked in him with a seal, the promised Holy Spirit"* (Ephesians 1:13). Theology calls this first phase "justification" for by it we are saved from the penalty of sin and made just (or righteous) in the eyes of God. It is the victory of the Cross over sin applied to our lives, and by it we receive the new nature and the Holy Spirit. This phase also includes redemption and positional sanctification.

Phase Two (Present)

The salvation of the Soul (Mind) is referred to by Paul as *"the renewing of your minds"* (Romans 12:2). For Christian believers, if this phase two process is happening, it is happening now, in the present time, during their life on earth. Paul writes to believers in Philippi who have already been saved (phase one) by believing the message and trusting in Christ for their salvation: *"Continue to work out your salvation with fear and trembling"* (Philippians 2:12). To the believers in Corinth Paul writes: *"For the message of the cross is foolishness to those who are perishing, but to us who are being saved it is the power of God"* (1 Corinthians 1:18).

Theology calls this second phase "sanctification", for in it we are rescued from the power of sin in our lives (i.e., we are sanctified). This is the practical victory over sin that takes place in our lives. This is maturity, which is the goal of our faith in this lifetime.

Phase Three (Future)
The salvation of our bodies occurs at the physical resurrection, which was referred to by Paul when he said, *"We wait eagerly for our adoption as sons, the redemption of our bodies"* (Romans 8:23). And again, *"Our citizenship is in heaven. And we eagerly await a Savior from there, the Lord Jesus Christ, who, by the power that enables him to bring everything under his control, will transform our lowly bodies so that they will be like his glorious body"* (Philippians 3:20-12). The writer of the book of Hebrews says that *"(Christ) will appear a second time, not to bear sin, but to bring salvation to those who are waiting for him"* (9:28). Theology calls this third phase "glorification" and "complete sanctification", for it is the process by which we are delivered completely from the presence of sin in our lives. This is the final victory over sin.

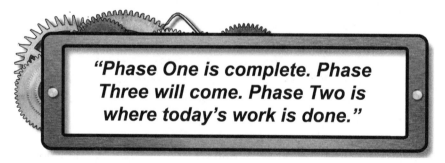

"Phase One is complete. Phase Three will come. Phase Two is where today's work is done."

If you are a believer (a Christian, a saint, a born-again person), then phase one is a finished work. Your spirit has been saved in the past. You are complete in Christ.

You cannot lose this salvation or undo it, and you cannot bounce back and forth between being saved and unsaved. You either are saved or you are not. If you are, then it is time to move on in your spiritual growth. If you are not, then it is time to consider placing faith in the work of Jesus on the cross, which is able to deliver you from sin and the penalty of sin, and enter once and for all into God's plan of salvation. John writes:

Whoever believes in the Son has eternal life.   – John 3:36

SALVATION
For Regeneration to Glorification

1 **PHASE ONE - Spirit**
Justification -Removal of Penalty of Sin

PAST
FINISHED,
Completed

2 **PHASE TWO - Soul**
Sanctification -Removal of Power of Sin

PRESENT
We work here. This is the
labor of our Christian life.

3 **PHASE THREE - Body**
Glorification -Removal of Presence of Sin

FUTURE
Not Yet Available,
Waiting For God

Whoever hears my word and believes him who sent me has eternal life and will not be condemned; he has crossed over from death to life.
— John 5:24

He who believes has everlasting life.   *— John 6:47-48*

God has given us eternal life, and this life is in his Son. He who has the Son has life.   *— 1 John 5:11-12*

And just as phase one is past, phase three is coming. Your body will be saved in the future. You will be physically resurrected with a body that has been delivered from death, decay, mortality, corruption, sin, etc.

This deliverance has not yet happened, nor can you make it happen. The event is out of human control. All we can do is wait for it. We cannot believe strongly enough, work hard enough, be good enough, or pray long enough to cause this phase of salvation to occur. It will happen when it happens, and that will be in God's perfect time. Paul writes of this eventful day when he says:

...in a flash, in the twinkling of an eye, at the last trumpet. For the trumpet will sound, the dead will be raised imperishable, and we will be changed. For the perishable must clothe itself with the imperishable

Not that I have already obtained all this,
> (i.e., the goals of phase two; full maturity based on what Paul refers to when he says, *"I want to know…"* in Philippians 3:10)

or have already been made perfect,
> (i.e., the completion of phase three; *"the resurrection from the dead"* from Philippians 3:11)

but I press on to take hold of that for which Christ Jesus took hold of me.
> (service, good works, the apostolic ministry, etc.)

Brothers, I do not consider myself yet to have taken hold of it.
> (it = completion of service and good work; full maturity; completion of phase two)

But one thing I do: Forgetting what is behind
> (past mistakes, failures, sins occurring in the battle fought during phase two)

and straining toward what is ahead, I press on toward the goal to win the prize (eternal rewards and honor for rich service; not salvation,
> which is a free gift)

for which God has called me heavenward in Christ Jesus. All of us who are mature should take such a view of things. And if on some point you think differently, that too God will make clear to you. Only let us live up to
> (apply to our lives)

what we have already attained.
> (the understanding of the knowledge we have heard)

> – Philippians 3:12-16

Ultimately, success in phase two will result in *"a rich welcome into the eternal kingdom"* (2 Peter 1:11) and *"praise, glory and honor when Jesus Christ is revealed"* (1 Peter 1:7).

THREE PHASES OF SALVATION

PHASE #	THEOLOGICAL TERM	TIME IN BELIEVER'S LIFE	EFFECT ON HUMAN CONDITION	RESULTS	DELIVERANCE FROM SIN
ONE	Justification	Past	Spirit	Born Again	Penalty of Sin Removed
TWO	Sanctification	Present	Soul (Mind)	Renewed Mind	Power of Sin Removed
THREE	Glorification	Future	Body (Flesh)	Resurrected Body	Presence of Sin Removed

Chapter Three:
The Role of the Word of God

God is in every facet of his creation. And in turn the whole Creation declares his glory, his work, his voice and his knowledge (Psalm 19:1-4). Theology calls this fact "general (or natural) revelation". God also reveals his nature, character, will, and power in words. This type of manifestation is known as "special revelation" and refers to the written Word of God (the Bible) which was revealed to his prophets and apostles.

The etymology of the Hebrew word for "word" (dabar) traces back to the concept of "what is at the back" or "behind." The meaning of this Hebrew term includes connotations of the thought and the power inherent in a word. In other words, the acts or deeds which occur both before and after the thought or expression of the word, are included in dabar (The Zondervan Pictorial Encyclopedia of the Bible, vol. 5, p.956).[1]

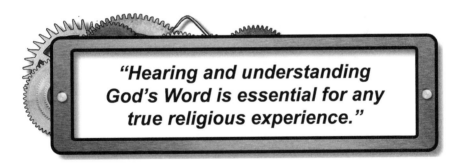

"Hearing and understanding God's Word is essential for any true religious experience."

[1] Two Greek terms are translated "word" in the New Testament and the Septuagint (the Greek translation of the Hebrew Old Testament, referred to as LXX). First is the Greek word logos, which means "the rational expression" or "the expression of thought". The second is the Greek word rhema, meaning "statement." Rhema first referred to "words" in contrast to "deeds," yet kept the meaning of the active power inherent in the "words." It appears that logos and rhema are used as synonyms in the LXX and the New Testament. However, in the New Testament logos (300 times) is used more than four times as often as rhema (70 times). (The Zondervan Pictorial Encyclopedia of the Bible, vol. 5, P.956)

The Word of God is so important because it is the supreme way that the Creator makes himself and his will known to the created world. God, the creator of the universe, expresses himself in his Word, and from it we learn about his character, his will, his plans, his views, his values and his opinions. Thus, hearing and understanding this Word from God is the most important part of any religious experience in biblical Christianity.

God has even exalted his Word to equality with his own name and nature.

I will bow down toward your holy temple and will praise your name for your love and your faithfulness, for you have exalted above all things your name and your word.   – Psalm 138:2

In the beginning was the Word, and the Word was with God, and the Word was God. He was with God in the beginning…. The Word became flesh and made his dwelling among us.   – John 1:1-2, 14

This is what the Lord says –
Israel's King and Redeemer, the Lord Almighty:
"I am the first and I am the last;
Apart from me there is no God.
Who then is like me? Let him proclaim it.
Let him declare and lay out before me what has happened since I established my ancient people,
And what is yet to come – yes, let him foretell what will come.

Do not tremble, do not be afraid.
Did I not proclaim this and foretell it long ago?
You are my witnesses.
Is there any God besides me?
No, there is no other Rock;
I know not one."

                                                      – Isaiah 44:6-8

This Word of God is more than mere talk. The words of God can be easily contrasted with the vain, empty words of idols and the idle, false words of man. This is because God's Word directly creates the reality of our universe and expresses the thoughts, attitudes and plans of God himself. Jesus called God's Word truth (John 17:17); and truth, simply

Sin
- *"sin is lawlessness"* (1 John 3:4)
- *"Scripture declares that the whole world is a prisoner of sin"* (Galatians 3:22)
- *"everything that does not come from faith is sin"* (Romans 14:23)

Love
- *"Love does no harm to its neighbor. Therefore love is the fulfillment of the law"* (Romans 13:10)
- *"Love is patient…kind…does not envy…does not boast…is not self-seeking…always protects…trusts…hopes…perseveres…never fails"* (1 Corinthians 13:4-8)

God
- *"God is love"* (1 John 4:16)
- *"God is light; in him there is no darkness"* (1 John 1:5)
- *"Eternal God"* (Deuteronomy 33:27)
- God fills heaven and earth (Jeremiah 23:24)
- *"God is spirit"* (John 4:24)
- *"God, who does not lie"* (Titus 1:2)
- *"The same yesterday and today and forever"* (Hebrews 13:8)
- *"The Word was with God, and the Word was God"* (John 1:1)
- *"…immortal, invisible, the only God…"* (1 Timothy 1:17)

Spiritual
- *"I could not address you as spiritual but as worldly – mere infants in Christ. I gave you milk, not solid food, for you were not yet ready for it. Indeed, you are still not ready. You are still worldly. For since there is jealousy and quarreling among you, are you not worldly?"* (1 Corinthians 3:1-3)
- *"The spiritual man discerns all things"* (1 Corinthians 2:15)[2]

---

[2] The Greek word for "discerns" is anakrinei which means "to scrutinize." The spiritual man examines, investigates, interrogates and determines all things. This word is translated in the New Testament as "examine", "judge", "ask questions", "search" and "discern". The spiritual man is a mature man with a renewed mind who can discern and appraise all things because he has been equipped with a standard of evaluation which comes from knowing the Word of God. Biblically, a spiritual man is not a dreamy-eyed mystic who teaches from visions he sees while being led through life by the "voice of God". That sort of mystic needs to be constantly judge and discerned by the mature spiritual person, not the other way around.

- *"The spiritual man makes judgments about all things, but he himself is not subject to any man's judgment."* (1 Corinthians 2:15)
- *"Two or three prophets should speak, and the others* (meaning the mature, spiritual congregation) *should weigh carefully* ("diakrinetosan" – meaning, "to separate, to make a distinction, to pass judgment on, to test, to discern") *what is said."* (1 Corinthians 14:28)
- *"Do not treat prophecies with contempt. Test everything. Hold on to the good. Avoid every kind of evil."* (1 Thessalonians 5:19-22)

- *"Dear friends, do not believe every spirit* (mystic, prophet, or man), *but test the spirits* (mystic, prophet, or man), *to see whether they are from God, because many false prophets* (mystic, prophet, or man who is deceived or deceiving), *have gone out into the world."* (1 John 4:1)

Another benefit comes from the blessings that God's Word provides:
- **Empowerment** – *"Become blameless and pure, children of God without fault in a crooked and depraved generation, in which you shine like stars in the universe as you hold on to the Word of life."* – Philippians 2:15
- **Direction** – *"All Scripture is God-breathed and is useful for teaching, rebuking, correcting and training in righteousness."* – 2 Timothy 3:15
- **Enlightenment** – *"We have the word of the prophets made more certain, and you will do well to pay attention to it, as to a light shining in a dark place, until the day dawns and the morning star rises in your hearts."* – 2 Peter 1:19
- **Encouragement** – *"For everything that was written in the past was written to teach us, so that through endurance and the encouragement of the Scriptures we might have hope."* – Romans 15:4
- **Doctrine** – *"they received the message with great eagerness and examined the Scriptures every day to see if what Paul said was true."* – Acts 17:11

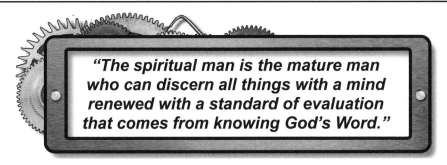

"The spiritual man is the mature man who can discern all things with a mind renewed with a standard of evaluation that comes from knowing God's Word."

We should also be aware that the Word of God reveals God's will for us, and thus helps us set goals for our lives, because truly godly goals can only be set once the purpose, plan and desire of God is known. For example, the Word of God not only tells us that we must be born again, it also tells us how to be born again. It does not merely give a list of things we are to do – such as become Christ-like, mature, do good works, evangelize, guard the good deposit, etc. – it also tells us how to successfully accomplish these commands. So, if the Word of God were ever replaced with the views and teachings of imposters (men merely posing as Bible teachers), we would have no way of knowing how to accomplish things of spiritual importance, and we might not even know this kind of potential and responsibility exists.

The Word of God explains process. It answers the question: Why? Through God's revelation in his Word we understand why evil exists. We understand why we exist. We understand where we came from, where we are, and where we are going. In the Word of God, natural history (which comes to us by general revelation) becomes enlightened through the lens of the divine special revelation. We see God's plan, God's will, man's purpose, and the ultimate future as all things work together.

Finally, the Word of God is productive in the believing human heart. The Word of God:

- **Gives us hope** – *"Remember your word to your servant, for you have given me hope."* – Psalm 119:49
- **Produces faith** – *"Faith comes from hearing the message, and the message is heard through the word of Christ."* – Romans 10:17
- **Guards our heart** – *"For wisdom will enter your heart, and knowledge will be pleasant to your soul. Discretion will protect you, and understanding will guard you."* – Proverbs 2:10-11
- **Renews our mind** – *"Do not conform any longer to the pattern of this world, but be transformed by the renewing of your mind. Then you will be able to test and approve what God's will is – his good, pleasing, and perfect will."* – Romans 12:2
- **Keeps us from being deceived** – *"I tell you this so that no one may deceive you by fine-sounding arguments."* – Colossians 2:4
- **Produces fruit** – *"All over the world this gospel is bearing fruit and growing, just as it has been doing among you since the day you heard it and understood God's grace in all its truth."* – Colossians 1:6

Let the word of Christ dwell in you richly as you teach and admonish one another with all wisdom.   – Colossians 3:16

Chapter Four:
Will of God vs. Will of Man

Human beings have a will that must be brought into line with God's will if we are to manifest the fullness of what God desires for us. To do this, we must respond to God's will as it is revealed in both natural and special revelation.

God has revealed himself in written form through the Christian Scriptures, but God, the creator and ruler of the universe, has also revealed himself through natural phenomena and events such as the character of the world around us, mankind, and history – and through sciences such as math, music, and chemistry. His divine character, power and desires are revealed in nature and can thus be seen, known and understood by all men.

> *What may be known about God is plain to them, because God has made it plain to them. For since the creation of the world God's invisible qualities – his eternal power and divine nature – have been clearly seen, being understood from what has been made so that men are without excuse.*   – Romans 1:19-20

> *The heavens declare the glory of God; the skies proclaim the work of his hands. Day after day they pour forth speech; night after night they display knowledge. There is no speech or language where their voice is not heard. Their voice goes out into all the earth, their words to the ends of the world.*   – Psalm 19:1-4

Even today, God's creation is explored and studied as man continues unraveling what God has revealed to all of humanity through general revelation. We find that, at times, our ideas and opinions are locked in with God's ideas and opinions. Things like gravity, the need for food and the need for sleep are universally followed either willingly or by the pressure of sheer natural force. Man follows these "rules" – which are part of the natural will of God – whether he wants to or not. But, there are also aspects of God's natural revelation (e.g., laws of cause and effect, wise principles, common sense, etc.) that man can choose to live in harmony with or rebel willfully against.

God has given every person his or her own personal will (Genesis 2:16), but since the fall of Adam, man's will has persisted in rebellion against God's will, having been corrupted by the sin nature (Ephesians 2:1; Romans 5:12). At times, our human will follows God's natural order by its own free volition, but often (very often), we rebel against what God has established by nature: institutions like marriage, a strong work ethic, civil obedience – and moral behavior such as honesty, courage, respect, generosity, kindness, etc. In fact, the Bible tells us that the sin nature in man joins with Satan and the world system (kosmos) in rebellion toward God.

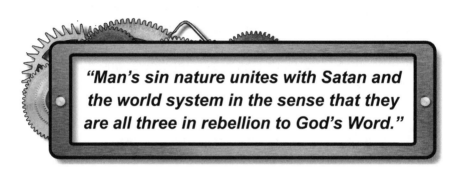

"Man's sin nature unites with Satan and the world system in the sense that they are all three in rebellion to God's Word."

But even with the burden of a sin nature, man is still responsible to know, understand and follow God's general revelation as seen in the natural world.

> *When Gentiles (Pagans) who do not have the law (the written Word of God), do by nature things required by the law, they are a law for themselves, even though they do not have the law, since they show that the requirements of the law are written on their hearts (by creation; created in the image of God), their consciences also bearing witness, and their thoughts now accusing, now even defending them.*
> *– Romans 2:13-15*

While the creation itself teaches us much about God, God has also chosen to reveal himself through prophets and apostles. These prophets and apostles came primarily from Israel, and later through the church. He also speaks to us through Jesus Christ.

In the past God spoke to our forefathers (Israel) *through the prophets at many times and in various ways, but in these last days he has spoken to us by his Son* (Jesus Christ).... *This salvation, which was first announced by the Lord* (Jesus), *was confirmed to us by those who heard him* (Apostles of the church).   – Hebrews 1:1-2; 2:3

Our human wills must respond positively toward the message provided by the special revelation recorded in the written Word of God. The Apostle Paul writes concerning this revelation, specifically in the New Testament:

I have become its servant by the commission God gave me to present to you the word of God in its fullness – the mystery that has been kept hidden for ages and generations, but is now disclosed to the saints. To them God has chosen to make known among the Gentiles the glorious riches of this mystery, which is Christ in you, the hope of glory.
                                                                  – Colossians 1:25-27

This grace was given me: to preach to the Gentiles the unsearchable riches of Christ, and to make plain to everyone the administration of this mystery, which for ages past was kept hidden in God, who created all things.   – Ephesians 3:8-9

Peter confirms the apostolic revelation given to Paul and recorded in his letters, when he writes:

Bear in mind that our Lord's patience means salvation, just as our dear brother Paul also wrote you with the wisdom that God gave him. He writes the same way in all his letters, speaking in them of these matters. His letters contain some things that are hard to understand, which ignorant and unstable people distort, as they do the other Scriptures, to their own destruction.   – 2 Peter 3:15-16

The means of salvation and deliverance from sin, death, and eternal damnation are not revealed through general revelation, but only in the special revelation we call the Word of God (the Bible). The gospel (literally, "good news") of salvation through faith in Jesus Christ is not seen by mankind in the study of math, chemistry, psychology, geology or history. These areas of study can reveal God's character, power and his general will, but the gospel of salvation is found clearly only in God's Word.

You also were included in Christ when you heard the word of truth, the gospel of your salvation. Having believed, you were marked in him with a seal, the promised Holy Spirit.   *– Ephesians 1:13*

We have heard of your faith in Christ Jesus and of the love you have for all the saints – the faith and love that spring from the hope that is stored up for you in heaven and that you have already heard about in the word of truth, the gospel that has come to you.
                                                   – Colossians 1:3-5

I want to remind you of the gospel I preached to you, which you received and on which you have taken your stand. By this gospel you are saved.   *– Romans 15:1-2*

This grace was given us in Christ Jesus before the beginning of time, but it has now been revealed through the appearing of our Savior, Christ Jesus, who has destroyed death and has brought life and immortality to light through the gospel. And of this gospel I was appointed a herald and an apostle and a teacher…. What you heard from me, keep as the pattern of sound teaching, with faith and love in Christ Jesus. Guard the good deposit that was entrusted to you.
                                                  – 2 Timothy 1:9-14

Once we hear, understand and believe the special revelation, we must carefully discipline ourselves to continue in it. Our progress into spiritual maturity as believers is based on our remembering and doing (walking in) the words of special revelation. The same Word of God that showed us the means of salvation through faith in Jesus Christ will lead us into a mature, productive life in him. Mature believers in Christ will live lives filled with fruits of righteousness that will not cause us shame when we stand blameless before Jesus on the Day of Judgment.

The necessity of continuing in the Word of God, in which we began, can be seen in John 8:31:

To the Jews who had believed him, Jesus said, "If you hold to my teaching, you are really my disciples. Then you will know the truth, and the truth will set you free." [3]

Paul and John also emphasized the importance of continuing in the same Word that saved the believer's spirit for the "salvation" (i.e., renewal) of the believer's mind:

> *So then, just as you received Christ Jesus as Lord, continue to live in him, rooted and built up in him, strengthened in the faith as you were taught.*   – Colossians 2:6

> *I want to remind you of the gospel I preached to you, which you received and on which you have taken your stand. By this gospel you are saved, if you hold firmly to the word I preached to you. Otherwise, you have believed in vain.*   – 1 Corinthians 15:1-2

> *Evidently some people are throwing you into confusion and are trying to pervert the gospel of Christ.*   – Galatians 1:7

---

[3] In John 8:31, the words "believed him" indicate that those Jews had placed faith in Jesus. In the Greek, the words translated "believed him" are in the perfect active tense. The perfect tense suggests "the lasting effects of a past action" (Linguistic Key, p. 202-203). The active voice means these Jews had, of their own volition, chosen to believe Jesus' words. The phrase "hold to" is the aorist subjunctive active tense of the Greek word meno, which means "to remain". The aorist tense here indicates a point of action**; the subjunctive is the mood of potential; and the active voice, once again, means that these Jews themselves will be the ones who make the decision to continue in the Word of God.

So, if those who had believed in Jesus wanted to continue their spiritual growth, they would have to take advantage of the potential they were given of choosing to always continue in Jesus' Word. If they did that, then they could know the Truth and, by that Truth, they would be set free.

** "For instance, outside of the indicative mood it is often customary to use the tense that implies a 'simple occurrence', the aorist tense. The aorist places no emphasis on the progress of the action, but only shows a simple occurrence (or summary occurrence), the action viewed as a whole. If the writer does not wish to emphasize or focus on the progress of the verb's action (whether continuous or completed) he will use the aorist tense. The term 'aorist' means 'unspecified' or 'unlimited'. It signifies nothing as to the progression or completeness of an action, it just indicates 'happenedness' or simple occurrence. If one has the mistaken concept that aorist tense means past time, many passages of the New Testament will be very confusing if not altogether nonsensical. Only in the indicative mood does the aorist indicate past time. Many times the action of a verb in the aorist subjunctive or aorist imperative forms, for instance, will actually take place at a future time, not a past time."
(Quoted from: http://www.ntgreek.org/learn_nt_greek/inter-tense.htm)

That, however, is not the way of life you learned when you heard about Christ and were taught in him in accordance with the truth that is in Jesus.   – Ephesians 4:20-21

As for you, see that what you have heard from the beginning remains in you. If it does, you also will remain in the Son and in the Father.   – 1 John 2:24

After being saved (phase one) we must continue (phase two) in the same word that provided the knowledge and understanding that led us to salvation. At the same time, we must avoid the counterfeits and false teaching that can lead us away from the source of salvation. Losing salvation (phase one) is not possible, but failing to grow and produce the fruit of that salvation is a daily danger. Good deeds, godly character and the fruit of the Spirit are products of the seed of the Word of God, the same seed that produced the new birth.

For you have been born again (phase one)*, not of perishable seed, but of imperishable through the living and enduring word of God…. And this is the word that was preached to you…. Like newborn babies, crave pure spiritual milk, so that by it you may grow up in your salvation* (phase two).[4]   – 1 Peter 1:23-2:2

In this verse, Peter encourages the early Christians to realize their salvation is a result of the Word of God being planted in their lives. These believers had heard and believed "the word that was preached." And now that they have been born into the kingdom of God ("newborn babies") by the seed of the Word of God, he explains that they should "crave" more of that same Word. The Greek word for "crave" is epipothesate (in the aorist imperfect active tense) and means "to long for, to desire, to crave". This preposition in compound indicates intense desire directed toward an

---

[4] The word translated as "pure" in First Peter 1:23-2:2 is adolos which means "without deceit, unadulterated, uncontaminated". The Greek word is commonly used to describe the quality of corn, wheat, barley, oil, wine, and other farm products. (Linguistic, p570)

The term "may grow" is the Greek auxethete. It is rendered in the aorist subjunctive passive tense, and means "to cause to grow." These words could be translated "in order that you might be nourished up."

object (Lingustic p. 570). The active tense means that the subject does, or causes, the craving. A good image of this kind of desire can be seen in Psalm 42:1-2:

As the deer pants for streams of water, so my soul pants for you, O God. My soul thirsts for God, for the living God.

The verse from 1 Peter ends by assuring the readers that this craving for the pure spiritual milk of the Word of God will result in believers making progress in their salvation. It is helpful to note that it is the healthy baby who hungers, and even cries, for milk. So it is with the Christian. A spiritually healthy Christian hungers for the hearing, teaching and instruction that come from the Word of God.

Also important is the fact that, although the use of the word "milk" in 1 Corinthians 3:2 and Hebrews 5:12-13 is a metaphor for the basics of faith, in 1 Peter it is a metaphor for the nourishment that comes from the Word of God. It therefore has no negative connotation of immaturity here, as it does in the other passages, which are aimed at believers who had entered into salvation (phase one) but had not progressed in their salvation (phase two). The believers being addressed in Corinth and in the book of Hebrews where quenching their spiritual hunger on things that were not the Word of God. Like children who eat candy before dinner, they had ruined their appetites, and their growth had been stunted by false teaching, legalism, worldly philosophies, religious rituals and mysticism. The very fact that these believers were not seeking God, nor craving his Word, was a symptom of an unhealthy spiritual life.

Brothers, I could not address you as spiritual but as worldly – mere infants in Christ. I gave you milk, not solid food, for you were not yet ready for it. Indeed, you are still not ready. You are still worldly.
– 1 Corinthians 3:1-2

These Corinthians were producing the fruit of the worldly religious life: jealousy and quarreling (3:3).

The author of Hebrews was equally disappointed in the believers he was addressing when he wrote:

And so, they became nothros, and their lives reflected a lack of spiritual vigor and competitiveness. This is the two-fold problem of cause and effect. The failure to "inhale" Bible doctrine is followed naturally by the inability to "exhale" a mature spiritual life. These Hebrew believers were not hearing or believing the Word of God, which meant their faith was not growing. The result of this spiritual malnutrition is the collapse of their confidence and the loss of their hope. This same problem is reflected throughout the book of Hebrews.

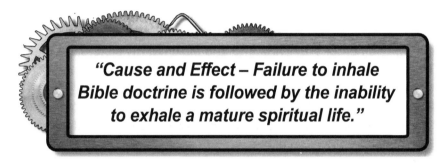

"Cause and Effect – Failure to inhale Bible doctrine is followed by the inability to exhale a mature spiritual life."

The diagnosis of the Hebrew's problem then leads the author to prescribe "someone to teach you the elementary truths of God's word all over again." He told them, "You need milk." The milk here symbolizes the elementary truths of God's word that are so necessary we should never lose track of them nor allow them to escape from our understanding. The author had wanted to build on these foundational truths, but could not. Instead, he tells the Hebrews that they must not only know these truths but become skilled in using them in their daily lives to make decisions and determine right from wrong and good from evil. Study his words:

> *Solid food is for the mature who by constant use have trained themselves to distinguish good from evil.*   – Hebrews 5:14

"Solid food" is teaching that is built on the basic elementary truths of God's Word. In order to properly mature, it is necessary for Christians to progressively hear, learn and understand this solid food – and then use it to guide their lives, make decisions, motivate good behavior, produce good works, and determine a correct worldview. By doing this consistently over a long period of time, the believer will find that he has trained himself in the acquired technique of distinguishing good from evil.

The ESV translation captures the meaning of the Greek words better than the NIV does:

Solid food is for the mature, for those who have their powers of discernment trained by constant practice to distinguish good from evil.
                                                              – Hebrews 5:14 (ESV)

In order to better understand the full meaning of this verse, we need to look more closely at the meaning of the individual words within it.

"Mature" is teleion, meaning "perfect or mature", referring in this case to those who are able to assume adult responsibilities and produce the fruits of righteousness.

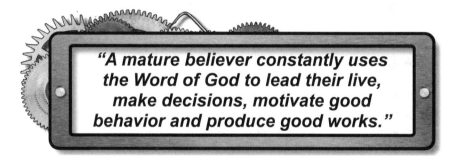

"A mature believer constantly uses the Word of God to lead their live, make decisions, motivate good behavior and produce good works."

"Their powers" is hexin and means "habits", referring to a finished skill developed from experience and practice, such as those used in crafts, sports or dance routines. Hexin is the final product of hours, days and years of practice and drills. It is the result of past exercise that trains the body to perform consistently in a certain way. In this case, it refers specifically to the disposition of the character.

The word "discernment" is from the Greek aistheteria and describes an "organ of perception or faculty" – i.e., the organs of the senses and perception, such as sight, taste, smell and the ability to hear.

"Trained" (gegumnasmena – "having been trained") is the perfect passive tense of gumnazo, which means "to practice naked in the gym or during games", the main idea being exercising or training by exercise. It was originally an athletic term referring to training and practicing in the Greek gymnasium. Later, it began to take on a connotation of training and exercising the mind. Paul uses the word in this way in 1 Timothy 4:7 when warning Timothy to avoid false doctrines and distracting philosophies, and to continue in the Word of God:

If you point these things out to the brothers (teaching of the Word of God)*, you will be a good minister of Christ Jesus, brought up* (nourished) *in the truths of the faith and of the good teaching that you have followed. Have nothing to do with godless myths and old wives tales; rather, train yourself to be godly.*

The writer of Hebrews uses this same word again in Hebrews 12:11:

No discipline seems pleasant at the time, but painful. Later on, however, it produces a harvest of righteousness and peace for those who have been trained by it.

Peter also uses it in reference to false teachers having exercised their hearts in covetousness:

They have eyes full of adultery, insatiable for sin. They entice unsteady souls. They have hearts trained in greed.   – 2 Peter 2:14 (ESV)

The word "distinguish" is from diakrisin and means "distinguishing, deciding, making a judgment between two things". One of the main points of the book of Hebrews is that its readers should have been able to discern the fact that returning to temple worship instead of continuing to grow in Christ was a bad choice. The fact that they turned away from New Testament revelation to resume the practice of the Old Testament law indicated that they could not yet discern right from wrong or good from evil.

"Good" (kalou or kalos) means good in the sense that something is beautiful, valuable, virtuous or useful. It refers to something that is beautiful to see; something excellent that suits its purpose. It is the word used by John the Baptist and Jesus to define the good fruit produced on good trees (Matthew 3:10 and Matthew 12:33). Jesus used it again when he called the ground which produced the thirty, sixty and a hundred fold crop good (Matthew 13:8). Other uses of the same word include these examples: good fish are separated from bad fish at the judgment

(Matthew 13:48); every creature of God is good and should be received with thanksgiving (1 Timothy 4:4); and, the minister of the word and his doctrine are good (1 Timothy 4:6).

"Evil" (kakou or kakos) means "worthless". Just as the word "good" above indicated something that was useful for its purpose, this word means that something is useless. Kakos indicates the lack of something that should be found in a person or a thing (Strongs Dict., p.1160), and because it is lacking, the person or thing is now worthless to such a degree that it has actually become potentially dangerous and destructive. It is like driving on bad tires that are lacking in quality and so become a liability. A similar situation occurs when using a dull chisel or a dull saw blade. The dullness makes the tool dangerous, and thus evil. The bad tires and blade are evil because they cannot produce the good they were intended to, and will instead produce the opposite.

When taken all together, Hebrews 5:14 is saying something like this:

> *Bible teaching is pursued, understood and believed only by the man who has proven he is living responsibly based on the Truth he already knows. Drilling faithfully, he has trained himself to apply the Word to his daily habits and reasoning, so with skillful separation he can discern between his own productive actions and attitudes, and any behaviors, words and opinions that are worthless, empty or destructive.*

So, we see that to be spiritually mature, we must not only know but also carefully live by the Word of God. And to do that, we must be very diligent.

The revelation from God found in the written Word is contrary to the wisdom of the world. That is why it is called a "revelation". It is revealed only from God and it is not found in the wisdom, philosophies or religions of the world. When natural men agree with and embrace the wisdom of the world, it is no surprise. We are merely witnessing the fact that, like the world (kosmos) all around them, man is also in a state of rebellion toward God's Word.

Paul's ministry was focused on teaching the Word, and he often prayed that his hearers would seek and understand it, because the Word of God reveals both the means of salvation and the means of spiritual

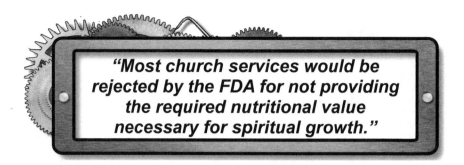

"Most church services would be rejected by the FDA for not providing the required nutritional value necessary for spiritual growth."

To borrow an image, most church services would be rejected by the FDA for not providing the basic nutritional value required for normal, healthy Christian development. The level of teaching from the pure spiritual Word of God in today's Western church is similar to dining out at a gas station convenience store – what we get has almost no nutritional value, and is overloaded with spiritual additives, philosophical enhancements and artificial sweeteners:

1. Messages of encouragement and comfort
2. Topics that are culturally relevant
3. Sermons that avoid shocking or confusing the seekers
4. Entertaining presentations to keep the tax exempt dollars rolling into the offering bucket
5. Attacks from a bully pulpit intent on indoctrinating people into whatever the preacher's pet doctrine happens to be:
   a. Baptism
   b. Healing
   c. Predestination
   d. Prosperity
   e. Spiritual gifts
   f. The evils of public school
   g. End times
   h. Etc.

The church needs to be as clear in identifying the means of spiritual growth in phase two of salvation as it is in identifying the means of spiritual salvation in phase one: Teach the Word of God!

Like newborn babies, crave pure spiritual milk (the Word of God), *so that by it you may grow up in your salvation.*   – 1 Peter 1:23-2:2

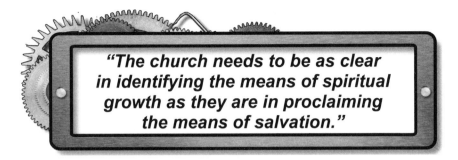

"*The church needs to be as clear in identifying the means of spiritual growth as they are in proclaiming the means of salvation.*"

So then, just as you received Christ Jesus as Lord (phase one), continue to live in him (phase two), rooted and built up in him, strengthened in the faith (the body of doctrinal truths, the Word of God) as you were taught…. see to it that no one takes you captive through hollow and deceptive philosophy…   – Colossians 2:7, 8

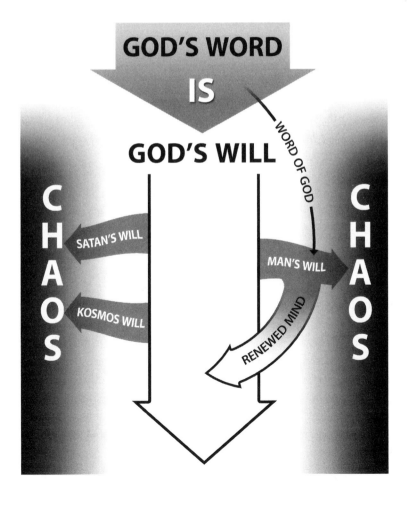

Chapter Five:
Seeking God

Our wills can seek God:

"If from there you seek the Lord…"	– Deuteronomy 4:29
"If you seek him, he will be found."	
	– 1 Chronicles 28:9 and 2 Chronicles 15:2
"Those who seek the Lord lack no good thing."	– Psalms 34:10
"Those who seek the Lord rejoice."	– Psalm 105:3
"Blessed are those who… seek him with all their heart."	– Psalm 119:2
"Those who seek me find me."	– Proverbs 8:17
"Those who seek the Lord understand."	– Proverbs 28:5
"Seek the Lord while he may be found."	– Isaiah 55:6
"You will seek me and find me…"	– Jeremiah 29:13
"For it is time to seek the Lord."	– Hosea 10:12
"Seek me and live."	– Amos 5:4
"Seek the Lord, all you humble."	– Zephaniah 2:3
"Seek first his kingdom."	– Matthew 6:33
"Seek and you will find."	– Matthew 7:7
"He who seeks finds."	– Matthew 7:8
"He rewards those who earnestly seek him."	– Hebrews 11:6

Our wills can seek God, but without the opportunity to hear and understand the Word of God (first for salvation and second for maturity) we would be left helpless to pursue some cheap substitute for God's glorious Truth.

Thus, if our wills can indeed seek God (hunger for God, pursue God, etc.) then one of the steps toward that goal must include an intimate encounter with his Word. And so, God's Word must be made available. Making the Word of God available is one of the reasons the Church was instituted by God on earth. As Paul wrote in 1 Timothy 3:15: "…the church of the living God, the pillar and foundation of the truth." We have been entrusted with the Word of God, to make it available and teach it clearly to men.

I had to write and urge you to contend for the faith that was once for all entrusted to the saints.   – Jude 3

This grace was given me: to preach to the Gentiles the unsearchable riches of Christ, and to make plain to everyone the administration of this mystery…. His intent was that now, through the church, the manifold wisdom of God should be made known to the rulers and authorities in the heavenly realms….   – Ephesians 3:8-10

If the church fails to read, preach and teach the Word of God that was entrusted to them, it will not be readily available to anyone. And, understandably, if the Word of God is not set before people as a thing of the greatest importance, they will readily replace it with something artificial.

A man in a church where reading, preaching and teaching the Word of God is not the principal purpose will be forced to embrace some other form of spiritual nutrition, and that will prove destructive to his spiritual maturity. The New Testament identifies and even warns against pseudo-nutritional additives that threaten to replace the pure Word of God:
- Traditions of men
- Myths
- Hollow and deceptive philosophies
- Empty rituals
- Religious regulations
- Every wind (fad) of teaching
- Deceit and scheming of men
– Ephesians 4:14; Colossians 2:8, 21-23; 1 Timothy 1:3-4; 4:1-3, 7

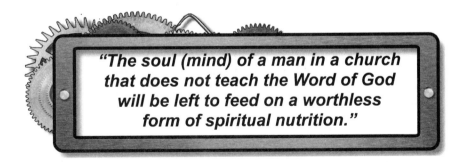

"The soul (mind) of a man in a church that does not teach the Word of God will be left to feed on a worthless form of spiritual nutrition."

False teaching that comes from the worldly philosophies of vain human imagination, and demonic doctrines that come from deceiving spirits, have been available since Satan first questioned and misquoted the Word of God in the Garden of Eden (Genesis 3:1). The very first act of evil and betrayal recorded in Scripture was an attack on the veracity of the Word of God and a denial of its accuracy. This happened when Satan added to the Word and claimed that what God had said did not accurately reflect the true character of God (Genesis 3:4-5). Then, centuries later, the very first time Jesus encountered Satan in his earthly ministry, he quoted verses from the Word of God three times to counter Satan's twisted use of Scripture and his warped will (Matthew 4:1-11). When Jesus publicly taught about the importance of the seed of the Word of God, he was quick to point out that Satan comes immediately to steal that seed (Matthew 13:3-9; 18-23). Satan knows that if the Word is allowed to grow up to fruition it will produce thirty, sixty and one hundred fold in a believing heart (Matthew 13:28).

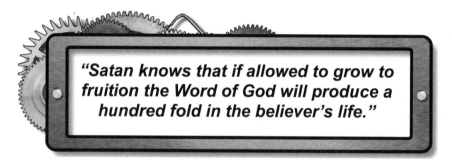

"Satan knows that if allowed to grow to fruition the Word of God will produce a hundred fold in the believer's life."

If these philosophies and doctrines of men and demons are allowed to replace the Word in the mind of believers their spiritual growth will be stunted, and their potential of producing eternal rewards will be squelched; they will have lost their inheritance (rewards) in the Kingdom of God. Even though they may have a true understanding of salvation through faith in Jesus – and so be saved from eternal damnation – they will be spiritually unproductive during their time on earth. They may be very religiously busy, but they will, nonetheless, lead a life of vanity and emptiness.

Scripture identifies several imitations, alternatives and artificial sources that replace the Word of God in the pulpits of the church and in the heart of a believer:

1. **"Weak and miserable forces… observing special days and months and seasons and years"** (Galatians 4:9, 10)

This verse refers to some form of asceticism that is perceived as spiritual to people watching and feels spiritual to those who are ignorant of the Word of God as they participate in it, refraining from basic functions of life. In reality, though, it amounts to nothing. There is nothing spiritual here and carefully following its dictates is not a sign of maturity. Instead, it is a sign of ignorance and immaturity.

9. **"false doctrines"** (1 Timothy 1:3; 2 Timothy 2:18)
In 1 Timothy 1:3 Paul writes:

> *As I urged you when I went into Macedonia, stay there in Ephesus so that you may command certain men not to teach false doctrines any longer, nor to devote themselves to myths and endless genealogies. These promote controversies rather than God's work....*

The word "urged" is parakaleo. It is a strong word that means "to beg or entreat" (Wuest, v. 2, p.27). Apparently, Timothy had wanted to go to another location (possibly with Paul) or had a different plan for his ministry. But Paul wanted him to stay in Ephesus and "command" certain men to stop teaching. The word for "command," paraggeiles, is a technical military term that referred to the passing on of orders understood to have come from a superior authority and were to be obeyed without question. By choosing this word, Paul makes it clear that he has given Timothy apostolic direction to demand this false teaching cease immediately. These "certain men", who had caused doctrinal confusion and been identified by Paul as a problem, where to be commanded to no longer teach false doctrine (heterodidaskalein) and to stop paying attention to tales (muthois) and unending genealogies (genealogiais aperantois).

The men in question most likely included Hymenaeus and Philetus *"who have wandered away from the truth"* and who taught *"that the resurrection has already taken place"* and *"destroy the faith of some"* (2 Timothy 2:17-18). Two other men from Ephesus that Paul wanted ordered to stop teaching could be Alexander (who probably was not a Christian and who Paul warns Timothy to *"be on your guard against...., because he strongly opposed our message"* and caused Paul *"a great deal of harm"*) and Demas, who *"deserted"* Paul *"because he loved this world"* (2 Timothy 4:14-15 and 4:10).

Some of the men in question were Christian teachers who taught Christian doctrines, such as the resurrection and eschatology, but they did it in such a way that their teaching conflicted with the Truth of the Word of God. Indeed, they used Christian terms and Scriptural references, but they did something to them that resulted in a "Christian" teaching of a different kind.

The Greek word that captures the thought of "another of a different kind" is heteros. This word is part of another word that was translated as "false doctrine" – heterodidaskalein. It is made up of two Greek words heteros and didasko (meaning "to teach"). The word therefore means "another teaching of a different kind". The word does not refer simply to any religious teaching other than Christianity – such as the teachings of Buddha or of atheism – but specifically to twisted Christian doctrine. In fact, this is where we get our English word heterodoxy.

10. **"devote themselves to myths"** (1 Timothy 1:3)
The word "myths" is preceded by the Greek word prosechein, which has a literal meaning of "to hold to" and means here "to give assent to" or "believe" or "put their trust in". These false teachers were basing their Christian doctrine on "myths". The Greek word muthos, which is translated as "myths", has a general meaning of "word, speech, conversation", but as the Greek language developed, muthos began to connotate fictional talk as opposed to historic fact (Wuest, v.2, p. 27). Thus, muthos could also be translated "fable, legendary stories, fiction" (Lingustic, p. 187). It may be worth mentioning that Paul refers to "Jewish myths" in Titus 1:14, which was written to Titus on the isle of Crete between 12-36 months after 1 Timothy. These myths appear to have had two possible sources:
   a. Fictional Jewish legends built around the scriptural account and written down around 150 BC in the Jewish Book of Jubilees (NAC, Lea, 1, 2 Tim., p. 67). These entertaining legends would easily capture the minds of the listeners, but the sensational speculation could provide no basis for spiritual growth.
   b. Cultural Greek legends that explained the origins of men and their ancient history. These eventually contributed their philosophic seed and became the gnostic heresies of the second century AD. These pagan myths easily adjusted to Christianity and were bent to form false Christian teaching.

11. "devote themselves to...endless genealogies" (1 Timothy 1:3)
The use of speculation in the teaching of the myths, combined with the allegorical practice of interpretation, created an endless flow of new ideas. Many people enjoy teaching allegorically, because they are free to spiritualize all historical facts and terminology as symbolizing some deeper and mysterious hidden meaning.

In Ephesus during Paul and Timothy's day (62 AD), the false teachers were spiritualizing the Truth of God's Word, but even more, they were incorrectly developing allegorical insights from genealogical records taken from Jewish documents, or even from fables, myths and legends that had been made up by men. It is ignorance to teach myth as truth, but to use the allegorical approach of interpretation to explain the myth only adds chaos to it.

The word "devote", prosechein, literally means "to hold to". But as it is used here, it means "to give assent to". So, these teachers actually believe and follow the allegorical interpretations of the fables they make up. "Endless" is from the word aperantos, a compound word made up of peras ("a limit or terminus") and the negative prefix a– ("not"). Thus, to describe these "genealogies" as aperantos, or "without limits", means the false teachers' lists of genealogies never ended. This confirms the erroneous concept of spiritualizing, or allegorizing, the Word of God in order to reveal some supposedly deeper truth.[5]

The "genealogies", which are described as "endless", come from the word genealogiais, referring to genealogical lists that are traced back through history. It appears that the myths and their endless allegorization had long lists of genealogies to fuel their teaching. Paul ends this comment

---

[5] It is important to note that allegory is a legitimate form of writing, so when the writers of the Bible say they are using allegory, or that their writing is allegorical, then it is appropriate to interpret that portion of Scripture allegorically. But, even then, we must keep in mind that most of the symbolism of Scripture is repeated and consistent in its interpretation. There is still no room for endless chaos in interpretation. When a portion of the Bible is written historically to communicate doctrinal truths, there is no need to dip into the method of imaginative allegorical interpretation

by saying that this kind of teaching does not promote the Word of God, but instead produces "controversies" (ekzetesis). Ekzetesis is from zeteo meaning "seek" and the prefix ek– meaning "out". Together they mean simply "seek out", but as it is used here, it more specifically means "useless speculation, out-of-the-way-research, seeking out" (Linguistic, p.487) and "an investigation, a laborious inquiry or dispute, an exhaustive investigation" (Wuest, v.2, p.28). The result of this false teaching based on the allegorical interpretation of myths is ekzeteo, because it produces questions and opinions based on endless speculation that lead people to even more questions and controversial opinions. There is no growth from this kind of teaching since there is no truth to understand. As mentioned before, it is hollow.

12. **"Deceiving spirits and things taught by demons...forbid people to marry...order them to abstain from certain foods."** (1 Timothy 4:1-3) Paul also writes to Timothy:

Some will abandon the faith and follow deceiving spirits and things taught by demons. Such teachings come through hypocritical liars, whose consciences have been seared as with a hot iron. They forbid people to marry and order them to abstain from certain foods.

Again we see the two options: The first is faith based on the collection of true doctrine from the Word of God; the second is deception which originates in the spiritual realm (just like the Word of God does) but in this case comes from deceiving spirits and demons. These deceptive doctrines and teachings are eventually disseminated by hypocritical, lying men, but they originate in the demonic realm. The evil spirits work through men who speak for them.

Paul says that some people will abandon the faith. The word abandon comes from the Greek word apostesontai and means "to go away, to withdraw, to fall away, to become apostate". The evil spirits' doctrine establishes religious regulations that project an evil image to marriage and certain foods. While the Word of God attributes good things, such as marriage and food to God, the demonic doctrine leads men away from the goodness of God into mere ascetic religious observance. Notice which side is devoted to religious ritual and "morality" in this case – the deceiving spirits.

It is worth mentioning that these false teachers, who are the human agents of evil spirits and are called hypocritical liars, are men who know what is true, but choose to speak the lie instead. They are not called "deceived liars" which would indicate they have been taken captive to do Satan's will (2 Timothy 2:26), but "hypocritical liars" – people who willing follow the practice of lying. Their consciences have been "seared" and hardened with scar tissue, which make them insensitive to the urging and calling of the Holy Spirit. "Sear" is from the Greek word kekausteriasmenwn in the perfect passive form, which means "having been branded on" (Wuest, v.2,p.67) or "to brand with a red hot iron" (Linguistic, p493). This is the word used to refer to the branding of slaves as property or of criminals who were branded on the forehead (Wuest, v.2, p.67). The word being used here could refer to Satan branding them as his own slaves. Or it could mean that the sensitivity of their conscience has been seared, resulting in total insensitivity. Either way, something outside of them has branded or seared them to finalize the hardening process. The perfect tense means this branding or searing is a completed action with lasting results. The passive tense means it has been done to them, not by them. What these men had done to themselves before they were branded is identified in Scripture as *"hardening of their hearts. Having lost all sensitivity, they have given themselves over to sensuality"* (Ephesians 4:19), and then *"grieved the Holy Spirit"* (Ephesians 4:30), which resulted ultimately in putting out the Spirit's fire (1 Thessalonians 5:19).

13. "a form of godliness but denying its power" (2 Timothy 3:5)
Already in the book of 2 Timothy, Paul has mentioned false teachers who "want to be teachers, but they do not know what they are talking about (2 Timothy 1:6-7), and those who practice a religious form of asceticism even as they follow demons (2 Timothy 4:3). Now, Paul says they have a "form of godliness but deny its power". This "form of godliness" probably referred to the fact that they had all the trappings of the Christian religion – like teachers, doctrine, regulations, and self-denial (as seen above), but no real power. Why? Because true power comes only from the Truth, the Word of God.

The word "form" is morphosis and can be translated as "bringing into shape, embodiment, outline, outward form, resemblance". "Godliness" is not the same thing as "godlikeness" (which could indicate a holy, righteous character), but instead refers to a reverence for God. These false teachers have an outward appearance of reverence for God, but in reality, it is hollow and void of any power. In fact, the word "deny" (ernemenoi from arneomai) means "disavow, reject, abnegate", and is used of the act of disowning Jesus in Matthew 10:33, Luke 12:9, Acts 3:14, 2 Timothy 2:12, 2 Peter 2:1, Jude 4, etc.

In Romans 1:16 the gospel is said to be "the power of God for salvation". The false teachers, then, have an appearance of reverence for God, but in actuality have denied that there is any hope of saving people or empowering them for productive lives through the teaching of the God's Word. Thus, they create the impression of power, but actually have no Truth and thus no power to help.

Timothy is finally told to *"have nothing to do with them"* (2 Timothy 3:5). They are a waste of time – and also, dangerous!

14. **"destructive heresies"** (2 Peter 2:1)
Peter wrote in 65 AD:

> *There will be false teachers among you. They will secretly introduce destructive heresies, even denying the sovereign Lord who bought them.*

The word "heresies" here is the Greek word hairesis, which has the basic meaning of "choice". Here it refers to the particular teaching of a school of thought within the larger body of teaching it is associated with. A heresy is a choice, or a new opinion, on points of doctrine within the larger body of Christian truth. Simply put, a heresy is "the choice of an opinion contrary to that usually received" (Vincent, v.1, p. 689). This new choice is then transferred into the accepted doctrines of a certain sect. The introduction of these new choices and opinions, which come from the false teachers, will challenge the established doctrine revealed by the apostles. These false opinions (heresies) will not go away, but will instead "spread like gangrene (or, cancer)" (2 Timothy 2:17) and harm the reputation of the Truth.

> *Many will follow their shameful ways and will bring the way of truth into disrepute.* – 2 Peter 2:2

The word "destructive" is apoleias in the genitive of product form, which indicates that it is the heresies that produce the destruction. Peter is referring to the destruction of the Truth, unity, maturity and fruit of righteousness in the individual believer and in the church universal, caused by the presence of these heresies. False teaching and heresy are the church's biggest problem today – no, throughout the entire 2,000 years of church history. So, how can we successfully identify it, isolate it and remove it?

Chapter Six:
Pagan Principles, Spiritual Ignorance, or Christian Truth

When Paul addressed the Thessalonian and Corinthian churches in 51 and 55 AD respectively, he indicated that there are two faulty points of view from which a believer can function – and only one position of truth. First, Paul warned those believers against thinking like a pagan, and then he made it very clear that he did not want them reasoning as ignorant Christians who allow their own opinions and interpretations to create some kind of personal theological belief system. Instead, Paul taught them the doctrinal system revealed in God's Word. These three positions (two faulty, one true) can be identified in Paul's words to the Thessalonians regarding the death of their fellow believers, the Resurrection, and the return of Jesus:

> *Brothers, we do not want you to be* **ignorant** (Christians with no Bible teaching) *about those who fall asleep, or to grieve like* **the rest of men** (pagans)*, who have no hope. We believe* (doctrine based on Bible teaching) *that Jesus died and rose again and so we believe that God will bring with Jesus those who have fallen asleep in him.* **According to the Lord's own word** (the Word of God)*, we tell you....*
> — 1 Thessalonians 4:13-15

The three views that Paul addressed in this verse are bolded above:

1. **Ignorance** – This describes the ignorant Christian – the untaught believer who is living the Christian life but is illiterate concerning the doctrinal truths revealed in God's Word. These believers still have questions and are still seeking hope and encouragement, and they will still answer spiritual questions and try to instill hope in fellow believers with words of encouragement. The problem is, their answers are likely not based on God's Word, but instead, on human reasoning, wishful thinking, and personal preferences. And their answers are then evaluated based on what seems reasonable to normal human understanding.

2. **"The rest of men"** – This refers to the typical pagan worldview, which is based on cultural norms and mythical religious standards. The answers and encouragement coming from this position are based on what the

natural pagan world understands, is able to perceive, and is willing to accept. They may include logic and scientific fact, but will quickly degenerate into myths, legends and bizarre speculation once the issues move beyond the physical world and enter into the unseen realm of the soul or spirit.

3. **"We believe...according to the Lord's own word"** – To accurately answer questions and provide powerful words of encouragement, we must speak from the authority of the Lord's own Word. If we do that, we can like Paul, make true doctrinal statements as he does when he says with confidence, "We believe...". And, we can then reason logically to the next level of understanding, as Paul does when he says, "...and so we believe...". These answers and words of encouragement are based on God's own Word and can be taught and understood logically and reasonably.

These same three perspectives (Ignorance, Pagan and Doctrinal) can be seen when Paul addressed the manifestation of spiritual gifts in the Corinthian church four years later:

> *Now about spiritual gifts, brothers, I do not want you to be ignorant. You know that when you were pagans, somehow or other you were influenced and led astray to mute idols. Therefore I tell you that no one who is speaking by the Spirit of God says....*   – 1 Corinthians 12:1-3

Paul follows the words "I tell you" with detailed teaching from the Word of God concerning spiritual gifts – that is, the manifestation of the Holy Spirit in the lives of believers. You can imagine the confusion that would result if Christians were left to figure out spiritual gifts from either their past experience as pagans with demonic manifestations, or as ignorant believers judging spiritual matters from the carnal human perspective. And, if you cannot imagine it, just take a look at churches today, and you will see that most are in the ditch on one side of the road or the other. Some churches fall on the pagan side with demonic chaos manifesting rampantly in the area of spiritual gifts. Many others are in the ditch of human reasoning, entrenched in the wisdom of the world (the Western world, in this case), and totally reject any form of spiritual manifestation in the modern church. Only through the Word of God will the believer find true instruction concerning the use and development of spiritual manifestations.

As we have seen, there are three basic directions a believer can go after conversion to Christianity through faith in Jesus Christ:
1. They can continue in their pagan worldview
2. They can get involved with an ignorant Christian group
3. They can learn the Word of God, preferably in a Bible-teaching church

Because every new believer has these three options, but only one will result in maximum production during the spiritual journey, it would be wise to take a closer look at each.

1. Pagan – Continue in a Pagan world view

Even after conversion, believers can remain in a pagan state of mind and continue to use their old world's system of values, morals and priorities to evaluate circumstances and discern right from wrong (1 Corinthians 12:1-3; 1 Thessalonians 4:13-14).

> *You must no longer live as the Gentiles do, in the futility of their thinking. They are darkened in their understanding and separated from the life of God because of the ignorance that is in them due to the hardening of their hearts.* – Ephesians 4:17-18

2. Ignorance – Embrace a form of "Christian" ignorance that replaces biblical truth with something else

Believers can also get involved in a Christian church or organization that is not founded on the Word of God, and instead teaches cultural values, emotions, and the remnants of a biblical heritage that has been watered down or even lost through the years (Ephesians 4:14; Colossians 2:8).

In this situation, believers may try to substitute the power of scriptural truth with one of these empty alternatives:

a. Mysticism – Adherents of this alternative believe that God mystically impresses his will on them. They desire God to speak directly to them so they can "hear" him and "know" what he wants them to understand. Because it seems to be a more real and personal form of communication, mysticism can trump the written Word of God with its visions, dreams, voices, or simple impressions from "god".

Every man's own word becomes his oracle and so you distort the words of the living God, the Lord Almighty, our God. – Jeremiah 23:36

"I did not send these prophets, yet they have run with their message; I did not speak to them, yet they have prophesied. But if they had stood in my council, they would have proclaimed my words to my people and would have turned them from their evil ways and from their evil deeds. Am I only a God nearby," declares the Lord, "and not a God far away? Can anyone hide in secret places so that I cannot see him?" declares the Lord. "Do not I fill heaven and earth?" declares the Lord. "I have heard what the prophets say who prophesy lies in my name. They say, 'I had a dream! I had a dream!' How long will this continue in the hearts of these lying prophets, who prophesy the delusions of their own minds? They think the dreams they tell one another will make my people forget my name, just as their fathers forgot my name through Baal worship. Let the prophet who has a dream tell his dream, but let the one who has my word speak if faithfully. For what has straw to do with grain?" declares the Lord. "Is not my word like fire," declares the Lord, "and like a hammer that breaks a rock in pieces? Therefore," declares the Lord, "I am against the prophets who steal from one another words supposedly from me. Yes," declares the Lord, "I am against the prophets who wag their own tongues and yet declare, 'The Lord declares.' Indeed I am against those who prophesy false dreams," declares the Lord. "They tell them and lead my people astray with their reckless lies, yet I did not send or appoint them. They do not benefit these people in the least," declares the Lord. – Jeremiah 23:21-33

b. Emotionalism – These people just do what they feel is right and respond to situations based on emotions, rather than on the truth of God's word. Emotionalism will often strive to change the written word of God or at least reinterpret it, so that it seems to be "more Christian".

How long will this continue in the hearts of these lying prophets, who prophesy the delusions of their own minds? – Jeremiah 23:26

c. Legalism – Some form of asceticism that demands religious regulations that flatter the person practicing them, and provide the sensation of being spiritual. This is godliness that denies the transforming power of the true Word of God.

Three systems for the believer to establish the Christian life
during phase two are pagan, religious ignorance or Word of God.

RELIGIOUS IGNORANCE
Replaces the Word of God and is based on:

1 **MYSTICISM** - Direct spiritual communication

2 **EMOTIONALISM** - God's will is what seems right

3 **LEGALISM** - Regulations and asceticism that flatters worshipper

4 **DISCONNECTED BIBLE REFERENCES** - Verses out of context or with personal interpretatation

5 **RELIGIOUS TRADITIONS IN POST-CHRISTIAN CULTURE** - Remains of a past Christian influence

6 **SINCERITY IN DECEPTION**

After entering salvation (phase one) the believer can chose to
establish their lives, values and world view (phase two) on one
of these systems:
- Pagan
- Religious Ignorance
- Word of God

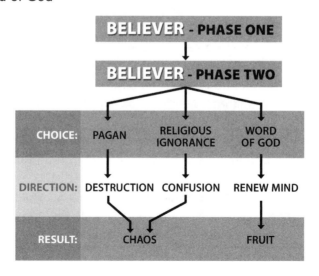

"Do not handle! Do not taste! Do not touch!" These are all destined to perish with use, because they are based on human commands and teachings. Such regulations indeed have an appearance of wisdom, with their self-imposed worship, their false humility and their harsh treatment of the body, but they lack any value in restraining sensual indulgence.   *– Colossians 2:20-23*

Having a form of godliness but denying its power. Have nothing to do with them.   *– 2 Timothy 3:5*

d. Fractured Literacy – This alternative is created by people who are limited to splintered and fractured portions of Bible truth. Their incomplete study of, or lack of desire to know, the full revelation, creates a warped worldview and an unbalanced life. This problem is manifested in very shallow Bible understanding or in Christian groups who use only a limited set of Bible verses such as "God is love" (1 John 4:8), or "Jacob I loved, but Esau I hated" (Romans 9:13), or "Repent and be baptized" (Acts 2:38), or "we know that we have what we asked" (1 John 5:14-15) as the basis of everything they believe. Any scripture that seems contrary to these "Bible-quotes-on-steroids" is twisted by false teachers to fit the desired doctrinal position. When fractured literacy combines with mysticism, the believer exists, pretty much solely, on devotional material.

Turn away from godless chatter and the opposing ideas ("contradictions") of what is falsely called knowledge, which some have professed and in so doing have wandered from the faith.
                                        – 1 Timothy 6:20

e. Evening Shadows – These are the doctrinal remains of a distant Christian influence from another time, most often based on bits and pieces of scattered traditions. Although the memory of the previous Christian age has left only shadows of the original substance, desperate people embrace the skeletons of earlier religious traditions in a post-Christian setting. Meaning and life are gone from them and have long since been replaced with human traditions.

See to it that no one takes you captive through hollow and deceptive philosophy, which depends on human tradition and the basic principles of this world rather than on Christ.   *– Colossians 2:8*

Of course, there is a third option – one that both promises and produces victory, fruit and rewards. This option is to learn the Truth of the Word of God, which is your physical and spiritual reality in both time and eternity.

3. Truth and Power – Learn the Word of God

The third option is that believers can receive the pure teaching of the apostolic revelation found in the Word of God. This will result in them growing up to maturity and being empowered to rightly evaluate the world around them with a sound biblical perspective that lines up with that of the Holy God (1 Peter 2:2; 1 Corinthians 2:6; Romans 12:2).

For you have been born again, not of perishable seed, but of imperishable, through the living and enduring word of God…. this is the word that was preached to you. Therefore, rid yourselves of all malice, and all deceit, hypocrisy, envy, and slander of every kind. Like newborn babies, crave pure spiritual milk, so that by it you may grow up in your salvation, now that you have tasted that the Lord is good.
– 1 Peter 1:23-2:3

Jesus spoke to the clergy of his day – the Sadducees, the teachers, and the scribes – concerning this very issue. The Sadducees had rejected the power and authority of much of the Scriptures and had replaced them with current popular human reasoning and philosophies. Jesus rebuked them, their views and their failure as teachers when he said:

You are in error because you do not know the Scriptures or the power of God.   – Matthew 22:29

Similarly, if churches today choose to apply the second option above to people being trained by them, they fall under the same condemnation as the Pharisees of Jesus' day. That is, if they do gain a convert to their brand of "Christianity", they will have made that person twice as distorted as they are by the time they have finished training them in their corrupt doctrine and its application to life.

You travel heaven and earth to get a convert and when you do you make them twice the child of hell that you are.   – Matthew 23:15

Before a church can do anything (good deeds, service to community, evangelism, worship, etc.), it must first teach the Word of God to its members, because that is the basis of the new birth and, according to the Apostles, the source of spiritual nutrition, growth, maturity and fruitful production. All works of service and worship of a believer spring from the word of God in the soul (mind) of a person. We must continue in the same Truth we began in.

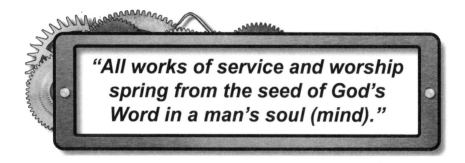

"All works of service and worship spring from the seed of God's Word in a man's soul (mind)."

Chapter Seven
Phase Two and the Word of God

Phase two of salvation is the renewing of the believer's mind to the knowledge and truth found in God's Word. This phase of the Christian life occurs during the believer's life on earth, beginning the moment they accept the Gospel, and not ending until they die. The renewing of the mind will result in personal growth into spiritual maturity and believers, in this continually developing stage of growth, will begin manifesting good works (the fruit of the Spirit) in their lives. This matured life, with its abundant fruit, will result in a blameless appearance before the Judgment Seat (bema seat) of Christ (2 Corinthians 5:10).

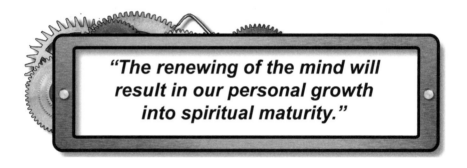

"The renewing of the mind will result in our personal growth into spiritual maturity."

… so that you will be blameless on the day of our Lord Jesus Christ.
– 1 Corinthians 1:8

This is my prayer: that your love may abound more and more in knowledge and depth of insight, so that you may be able to discern what is best and may be pure and blameless until the day of Christ, filled with the fruit of righteousness.   – Philippians 1:9-11

May he strengthen your hearts so that you will be blameless and holy in the presence of our God and Father when our Lord Jesus comes with all his holy ones.   – 1 Thessalonians 3:13

For we must all appear before the judgment seat of Christ, that each one may receive what is due him for the things done while in the body whether good or bad.   *– 2 Corinthians 5:10*

The phrase "judgment seat of Christ" in this last verse is bematos tou christou, or "the tribunal of Christ". The word bematos is the genitive singular of the Greek word bema, which referred to the stepped platform of the tribunal where official rulings and decisions were handed down. Appearing before the bema ideally resulted in a person being judged and rewarded. This future day of judgment before Jesus Christ is also described as a place of evaluation and reward for all believers in Romans 14:10:

For we will all stand before God's judgment (bema) *seat…. so then, each of us will give an account of himself to God.* – Romans 14:10, 12

The bema seat is where Christians will receive an evaluation of the production they brought forth during phase two of their lives, and this judgment will result in either being rewarded (2 Corinthians 5:10; Romans 14:10) or suffering the loss of rewards (1 Corinthians 3:15). The bema seat is not the same eschatological event as the judgment referred to in Matthew 25:31, which occurs when the King, Jesus Christ, returns to set up his kingdom on earth. Nor is it the judgment of Revelation 20:11, referred to as the Great White Throne judgment, which occurs after the heavens and the earth have disappeared.

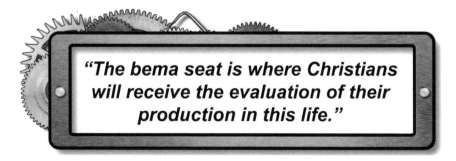

"The bema seat is where Christians will receive the evaluation of their production in this life."

The Word of God is the source of the knowledge, insight, wisdom and understanding that renews the human mind toward a perspective that can correctly analyze, discern and provide motivation to execute God's will.

A mature man of God manifests God's will and ways in his own thoughts, words and deeds. The Word of God is the seed (Matthew 13), and this seed is the source of both our salvation (phase one) and our maturity (phase two).

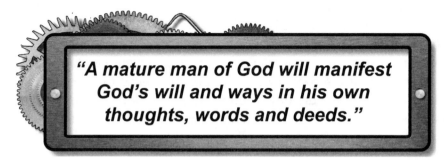

"A mature man of God will manifest God's will and ways in his own thoughts, words and deeds."

For you have been born again (phase one), *not of perishable seed, but of imperishable, through the living and enduring word of God…. Like new born babies, crave pure spiritual milk, so that by it you may grow up in your salvation* (phase two).   – 1 Peter 1:23 and 2:2

As has already been pointed out, the Word of God reveals the true means of salvation from sin and death, which is faith in Jesus Christ and his work on the cross. Understanding and belief in this truth secures eternal salvation for an individual and causes the Christian life to begin. But, if the Christian life is going to continue developing, the believer must be instructed and rooted in the exact same Word that saved them.

As for you, continue in what you have learned and have become convinced of.   – 2 Timothy 3:14

So then, just as you received Christ Jesus as Lord (phase one), *continue to live in him* (phase two), *rooted and built up in him, strengthened in the faith as you were taught.*   – Colossians 2:6, 7

You were running a good race. Who cut in on you to keep you from obeying the truth?   – Galatians 5:7

Find out what pleases the Lord.   – Ephesians 5:10

When a person is saved, or born again, they have believed a truth from the Word of God concerning salvation through Jesus Christ. They have understood and believed this truth.

> *You also were included in Christ when you heard the word of truth, the gospel of your salvation.*   – Ephesians 1:13

> *This gospel is bearing fruit and growing, just as it has been doing among you since the day you heard it and understood God's grace in all its truth. You learned it from Epaphras.*   – Colossians 1:6,7

This truth brings light and life to them. This salvation brings them out of the kingdom of darkness and transfers them into God's kingdom of light.

> For he has rescued us from the dominion of darkness and brought us into the kingdom of the Son he loves, in whom we have redemption, the forgiveness of sins.   – Colossians 1:13-14

> *If anyone is in Christ, he is a new creation; the old has gone, the new has come.*   – 2 Corinthians 5:17

But, even though it causes them to be made alive in their spirit and to become a new creature in Christ, there are two things this salvation does not do.

First, it does not change the way a person looks physically. If they have a scar on their body, the scar remains. If they are suffering from malnutrition, they remain malnourished. If they were a six foot four unsaved athlete with highly trained basketball skills, they are now a saved, six foot four athlete with those very same skills. Salvation affects the physical body in totality only at the resurrection of the dead. Until that time the power of sin and its penalty of death remain in our body:

> *What a wretched man I am! Who will rescue me from this body of death? Thanks be to God – through Jesus Christ our Lord!*
>   – Romans 7:24-25

> *We ourselves, who have the firstfruits of the Spirit* (from phase one), *groan inwardly as we wait eagerly* (during phase two) *for our adoption as sons, the redemption of our bodies* (phase three).   – Romans 8:23

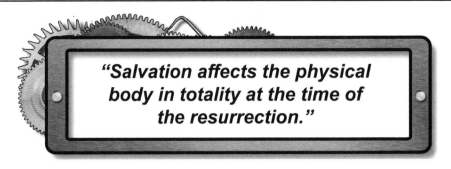

"Salvation affects the physical body in totality at the time of the resurrection."

Our citizenship is in heaven. (phase one is complete after we have accepted Jesus as Lord) *And we eagerly await* (waiting today during phase two) *a Savior from there, the Lord Jesus Christ, who, by the power that enables him to bring everything under his control, will transform our lowly bodies* (Phase Three, in the future) *so that they will be like his glorious body.*   – Philippians 3:20-21

The second thing being born again does not change is a person's knowledge or understanding of natural and spiritual things. A new believer in Christ does not miraculously know math at a new level or suddenly understand a foreign language they have never studied. A person's intellect is not altered simply because they understood and believed the Gospel message. The same principle also applies to spiritual truth and knowledge. They do not automatically know the events recorded in the book of Genesis, the prophecies of Daniel, or the miracles of Jesus. Nor do they instantly gain an understanding of God's plan as revealed in the letters of the Apostles. They do not fully know the nature of God or all that he considers to be sin. They do not completely understand that they will stand before God's judgment; nor can they list out what the basis of God's evaluation of them will be. This is why Christians must read the Word of God, study the Word of God, and be taught the Word of God.

You must teach what is in accord with sound doctrine.   – Titus 2:2

In the presence of God and of Christ Jesus, who will judge the living and the dead, and in view of his appearing and his kingdom, I give you this charge: Preach the Word; be prepared in season and out of season; correct, rebuke and encourage, – with great patience and careful instruction. For the time will come when men will not put up with sound doctrine.   – 2 Timothy 4:1-3

Until I come, devote yourself to the public reading of Scripture, to preaching and to teaching.   *– 1 Timothy 4:13*

In the church at Antioch there were prophets and teachers. – Acts 13:1

Paul and Barnabas remained in Antioch, where they and many others taught and preached the Word of the Lord.   *– Acts 15:35*

Indeed, by faith in Jesus an individual enters into the kingdom of God. But, they do not gain the full knowledge and council of God for their lives at the new birth. This knowledge is something they must begin to pursue after they have been born again, and they will continue in their pursuit of it for the rest of their time on earth. This is phase two.

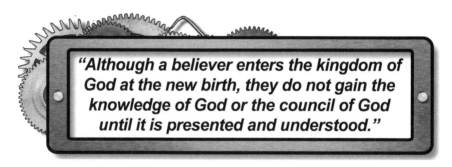

"Although a believer enters the kingdom of God at the new birth, they do not gain the knowledge of God or the council of God until it is presented and understood."

After he confirms the Ephesian believers' faith in the Word of God for their salvation (phase one), Paul continues to write in his letter to them that he is praying for their understanding of the Word of God (phase two):

You also were included in Christ when you heard the word of truth, the gospel of your salvation (phase one).... For this reason, ever since I heard about your faith in the Lord Jesus...I keep asking that the God of our Lord Jesus Christ, the glorious Father, may give you the Spirit of wisdom and revelation, so that you may know him better. I pray also that the eyes of your heart may be enlightened in order that you may know the hope to which he has called you, the riches of his glorious inheritance in the saints and his incomparably great power for us who believe.   *– Ephesians 1:13-19*

Paul prays a similar prayer for the believers in Colosse:

For this reason, since the day we heard about you (as new believers
in Jesus), *we have not stopped praying for you and asking God to
fill you with the knowledge of his will through all spiritual wisdom and
understanding. And we pray this in order that you may live a life worthy
of the Lord and may please him in every way: bearing fruit in every
good work, growing in the knowledge of God, being strengthened with
all power according to his glorious might so that you may have great
endurance and patience, joyfully giving thanks to the Father.*
                                                    – Colossians 1:9-12

And Paul writes this to the church in Rome:

*Do not conform any longer to the pattern of this world, but be
transformed by the renewing of your mind. Then you will be able to test
and approve what God's will is – his good, pleasing and perfect will.*
                                                    – Romans 12:2

The Word of God must be understood by the Christian believer in order to
mature. They first must understand the importance of the Word of God.

*We have the word of the prophets made more certain, and you will
do well to pay attention to it, as to a light shining in a dark place (soul
or mind of a believer early in phase two), until the day dawns and the
morning star rises in your hearts (maturity and fruit of righteousness
growing in the believer's life during phase two). Above all, you must
understand that no prophecy of Scripture came about by the prophet's
own interpretation. For prophecy never had its origin in the will of man,
but men spoke from God as they were carried along by the Holy Spirit.*
                                                    – 2 Peter 1:19-21

Once believers understand the necessity of the Word of God for their
spiritual growth and maturity, they must still be continually taught and
reminded of that Word.

I want to remind you of the gospel I preached to you, which you received and on which you have taken your stand (phase one). By this gospel you are saved (phase two), if you hold firmly to the word I preached to you. Otherwise, you have believed in vain (still a child of God, but with no growth, maturity or fruit). — 1 Corinthians 15:1

In fact, negligence in the study of the Word can lead to a reversal in understanding and a loss of the fruit of righteousness in our lives.

We must pay more careful attention, therefore, to what we have heard, so that we do not drift away…. Though by this time you ought to be teachers, you need someone to teach you the elementary truths of God's word all over again…. we want each of you to show this same diligence to the very end, in order to make your hope sure. We do not want you to become lazy. — Hebrews 2:1, 5:12 and 6:11-12

According to Paul, the hearing of the Word of God will produce faith:

Consequently, faith comes from hearing the message, and the

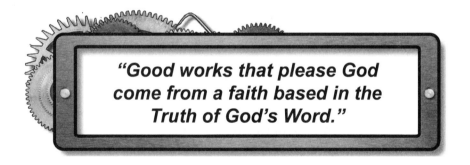

"Good works that please God come from a faith based in the Truth of God's Word."

message is heard through the word of Christ. — Romans 10:17

And, Hebrews 11:6 says that:

Without faith it is impossible to please God.

The Scripture says this for several reasons:
• If the Word of God does not renew our minds, all of our "good" thoughts, words and actions will still be based on the human viewpoint

"Productive Christian faith must believe something True."

and motivated by false teaching, hollow philosophies and deviant worldviews – which Paul says are doctrines of demons and deceiving spirits (1 Timothy 4:1).

- Good works that are pleasing to God must come from an accurate faith that is based on the Truth as revealed in his Word.
- True and productive Christian faith is not believing something that is impossible or hard to accept, but is instead believing something that is True (the Word of God).
- The power of faith does not come from the person believing, but instead comes from the Truth that is believed.
- The thing that gives a person of faith power is the Truth that is in them.
- For a person to have great faith, that person must know Great Truth.
- They must know, understand and trust that Truth for there to be any faith. An absence of the knowledge of Truth results in an absence of faith.
- Truth must be understood in order for it to be believed. No understanding equals no faith.
- Faith is confidence in something you know to be true. Faith is not hope in something you know very well is probably not going to happen. That is called a wish. Jesus didn't pop out of a bottle to give you three wishes. Jesus came and gave you his Word so you could know the Truth and believe it.
- Where there is no Word of God, there is no faith.
- Where there is no faith, there are no good works

That is why the writer of Hebrews says, *"Without faith it is impossible to please God."*

It is also for this reason that Paul, when writing to the saints in Ephesus, says he is praying for them to have "the Spirit of wisdom and revelation"

"For a person to have great faith, that person must know great Truth."

and "that the eyes of your heart may be enlightened". The "eyes of your heart" refers to "not only the emotional nature, but also to the reason and to the faculty of intelligence" according to Wuest, who comments on the Greek language of that verse (vol. 1, p. 53).

He also mentions four reasons for this prayer. He prays that the born again believers in Ephesus might:

1. **Know God** – *"may know him better"* (Ephesians 1:17) The word used is epignosis ("a full knowledge"). This is a true and accurate knowledge of God that would empower these believers to be intimately acquainted with the person of God. This knowledge would be reflected in the Ephesians' attitudes and actions because they knew they belonged to God.

2. **Know the hope** – *"know the hope to which he has called you"* (1:18 This word is elpis tes kleseos ("hope of the calling"). It is the hope of the salvation they have entered into. Paul desires that their knowledge would open up to an understanding and a confidence in the actual salvation experience they had undergone in phase one when they placed faith in Jesus Christ. A greater knowledge of their salvation would give them an ever-increasing hope in the work of God that was already accomplished in their lives when, at a time in the past, they placed faith in Jesus Christ.

3. **Know the riches** – *"know the riches of the glorious inheritance"* (1:18) The Greek phrase is ploutos tes doxes tes kleronomias ("riches of the glory of the inheritance"). Paul writes that this "inheritance" is "in the saints" which means that God has invested his riches and glory into the body of believers called the church. Paul is praying that we would understand who we, the church, are and how valuable we are to God in the working of his plan and purpose.

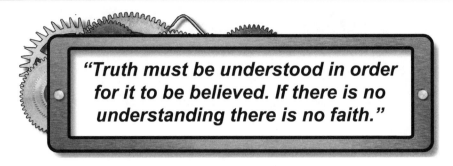

"Truth must be understood in order for it to be believed. If there is no understanding there is no faith."

4. **Know the power** – *"know the incomparably great power for us"* (1:19 Huperballon megethos tes dunameus ("excelling greatness of the power") is not something we will see someday in heaven after phase three of salvation is complete, but includes God's activity in all three phases:
   a. Phase one when we were made alive in Christ and born again as new creations in his kingdom of light
   b. Phase two as we continue to mature and produce the works of God during our lives in this dark world
   c. Phase three when that great power resurrects our physical bodies and transforms them into immortal, incorruptible, spiritual bodies like Christ's

The Greek word for "incomparably" is huperballon which is a compound word made up of huper which means "beyond" and ballon which means "a throwing" (this is where we get our English word for "ball"). Together these two words mean "a throwing beyond", giving the image of a person throwing an object way over the goal line – and by extension, "superiority, excellence, incomparability". The word for "great" is megathos, and you can see the English word "mega" in it. The word "power" is from dunamis meaning "natural ability, general and inherent ability" (Wuest, vol. 1, p. 54). The English word "dynamite" comes from dunamis. A very rough English comparison of the idea would be that God threw his mega dynamite-power way, way, way beyond the goal when he executed the three phases of our salvation.

This is what Paul prays that you would understand!

Section Two
Ten Concepts for Reaching Spiritual Maturity

Ten Concepts in the Model

Concept One: The Word is Foundational

Concept Two: The Word is a Revealed Mystery

Concept Three: The Word is Entrusted to the Church

Concept Four: The Word Must Be Heard and Known

Concept Five: The Word Must be Believed

Concept Six: The Word Contains the Gospel of Salvation

Concept Seven: The Word Renews the Mind and Matures the Believer

Concept Eight: The Mature Believer Produces Fruits of Righteousness

Concept Nine: The Production of the Believer is Rewarded in Eternity

Concept Ten: False Teaching, Doctrinal Errors, Deceit, and Ignorance Destroy any Possibility of Christian Maturity and Production

Chapter Eight:
Ten Concepts in the Model

At this point I would like to explain the important features of this process I have laid out. A thumbnail sketch of this model shows the Word of God in a state of eternal existence, and climaxes with us standing blameless before God in glory. There are ten basic concepts that are used to construct this model.

The process begins with the fact that the eternal the Word of God that was revealed to the Apostles is foundational. The Apostles were entrusted with proclaiming and teaching this Word in order for pagans to hear the plan of salvation and believe it. The process then continues with the same people who heard the word of salvation also hearing the full content of the revealed Word of God until they understand and believe it as well. This knowledge of and faith in the Word of God renews their minds and results in them being empowered to change their sinful, crooked, depraved ways and, instead, produce the fruit of good deeds which result in a rich inheritance into the eternal kingdom of God.

The model of this process is quite simple in its agenda: teach the Truth revealed by God to men, who then either receive it and grow, or reject it and perish. But not only is God's process simple – so is Satan's. That is why the model must also include a description of the spiritual attack that comes against it. The Word of God consistently warns of the enemy's counterattack strategy: Mix in with the Word of God false doctrines and the hollow philosophies of demons which are spread by deceitful and corrupt imposters within the church. These false, empty, and artificial teachings will not merely prevent growth, but will actually train and prepare "believers" to work against the plan of God and the force of his revealed Word. Thus, we have the battle lines set.

And thus we arrive at a good place to recall Jesus' parable of the sower and the seed, since in this teaching we have a situation that is exactly parallel to our model.

A farmer went out to sow his seed. As he was scattering the seed, some fell along the path, and the birds came and ate it up. Some fell on rocky places, where it did not have much soil. It sprang up quickly, because the soil was shallow. But when the sun came up, the plants were scorched, and they withered because they had no root. Other seed fell among thorns, which grew up and choked the plants. Still other seed fell on good soil, where it produced a crop – a hundred, sixty or thirty times what was sown. He who has ears, let him hear…. Listen then to what the parable of the sower means: When anyone hears the message about the kingdom and does not understand it, the evil one comes and snatches away what was sown in his heart. This is the seed sown along the path. The one who received the seed that fell on rocky places is the man who hears the word and at once receives it with joy. But since he has no root, he lasts only a short time. When trouble or persecution comes because of the word, he quickly falls away. The one who received the seed that fell among the thorns is the man who hears the word, but the worries of this life and the deceitfulness of wealth choke it, making it unfruitful. But the one who received the seed that fell on good soil is the man who hears the word and understands it. He produces a crop, yielding a hundred, sixty or thirty times what was sown.   *– Matthew 13:3-9; 18-23*

Jesus followed this parable and explanation with another like it:

The kingdom of heaven is like a man who sowed good seed in his field. But while everyone was sleeping, his enemy came and sowed weeds among the wheat, and went away. When the wheat sprouted and formed heads, then the weeds also appeared. The owners' servants came to him and said, "Sir, didn't you sow good seed in your field? Where then did the weeds come from?" "An enemy did this," he replied. The servants asked him, "Do you want us to go and pull them up?" "No," he answered, "because while you are pulling the weeds you may root up the wheat with them. Let both grow together until the harvest. At that time I will tell the harvesters: First collect the weeds and tie them in bundles to be burned; then gather the wheat and bring it into my barn." … The one who sowed the good seed is the Son of Man. The field is the world, and the good seed stands for the sons of the kingdom. The weeds are the sons of the evil one, and the enemy who sows them is the devil. The harvest is the end of the age, and the harvesters are angels. As the weeds are pulled up and burned in the fire, so it will be at the end of the age. The Son of Man will send out his

*angels, and they will weed out of his kingdom everything that causes
sin and all who do evil. They will throw them into the fiery furnace,
where there will be weeping and gnashing of teeth. Then the righteous
will shine like the sun in the kingdom of their Father. He who has ears,
let him hear.*   – Matthew 13:24-30; 13:37-43

I would like to break the model of this process down into ten concepts
that will be explored in detail in the next ten chapters. These concepts are
the important components of our model in which the Word of God is the
source of our salvation, maturity and production – all of which culminate
in our glorification and rewarding in God's eternal state.

Concept #1 – The Word is Foundational

Concept #2 – The Word is a Revealed Mystery

Concept #3 – The Word is Entrusted to the Church

Concept #4 – The Word Must be Heard and Known

Concept #5 – The Word Must be Believed

Concept #6 – The Word Contains the Gospel of Salvation

Concept #7 – The Word Renews the Mind and Matures the Believer

Concept #8 – The Mature Believer Produces Fruits of Righteousness

Concept #9 – The Production of the Believer is Rewarded in Eternity

Concept #10 – False Teaching, Doctrinal Errors, Deceit, and Ignorance
Destroy any Possibility of Christian Maturity and Production

THE TEN CONCEPTS

WORD OF GOD - Eternal foundation of reality

REVEALED - Unknown to natural man, but revealed by God

ENTRUSTED - The revealed Word is entrusted to men to proclaim and teach

KNOWLEDGE - Knowledge and wisdom are in the Word

HEARING - Hearing the Word must occur

GOSPEL - Phase One - Jesus is Savior. Understanding and accepting this brings New Life

MIND - Phase Two - The understanding of the Word renews the human mind

FRUIT - The born again man with a renewed mind will produce thoughts, words and deeds of righteousness

CROWNS - This fruit will result in eternal honors recognition and rewards

DOCTRINES OF DEMONS - Satan's primary attack is to replace the Word with false teaching that will not produce righteousness in people's lives

Chapter Nine:
Concept One – Word of God is Foundational

We know that the Word of God is eternal.

The grass withers and the flowers fall, but the word of our God stands forever.   *– Isaiah 40:8*

Your word, O Lord, is eternal; it stands firm in the heavens.
                                                   – Psalm 119:89

Until heaven and earth disappear, not the smallest letter, not the least stroke of a pen, will by any means disappear from the Law until everything is accomplished.   *– Matthew 5:18*

Heaven and earth will pass away, but my words will never pass away.
                                                   – Matthew 24:35

We understand that the Word created our reality.

By faith we understand that the universe was formed at God's command, so that what is seen was not made out of what was visible.
                                                   – Hebrews 11:3

By the word of the Lord were the heavens made.   *– Psalm 33:6*

Angels…heavenly hosts…sun…moon…stars…highest heavens… waters above the skies…Let them praise the name of the Lord, for he commanded and they were created.   *– Psalm 148:1-5*

Through him all things were made; without him nothing was made that has been made. In him was life, and that life was the light of men.
                                                   – John 1:3-4

For by him all things were created; things in heaven and on earth, visible and invisible, whether thrones or powers or rulers or authorities; all things were created by him and for him. He is before all things, and in him all things hold together.   *– Colossians 1:16-17*

They deliberately forget that long ago by God's word the heavens existed and the earth was formed out of water and by water.
— 2 Peter 3:5

We have seen that the Word is the exact expression of God.

In the beginning was the Word, and the Word was with God, and the Word was God. He was with God in the beginning.   — John 1:1-2

His name is the Word of God. The armies of heaven were following him.
— Revelation 19:13

You have exalted above all things your name and your word.
— Psalm 138:2

That which was from the beginning, which we have heard, which we have seen with our eyes, which we have looked at and our hands have touched – this we proclaim concerning the Word of life. The life appeared; we have seen it and testify to it, and we proclaim to you the eternal life, which was with the Father and has appeared to us.
— 1 John 1:1-3

We have experienced the Word's power of Truth in our lives.

I am not ashamed of the gospel, because it is the power of God for the salvation of everyone who believes.   — Romans 1:16

For the message of the cross is foolishness to those who are perishing, but to us who are being saved it is the power of God.
— 1 Corinthians 1:18

My message and my preaching were not with wise and persuasive words, but with a demonstration of the Spirit's power.
— 1 Corinthians 2:4

For he has rescued us from the dominion of darkness and brought us into the kingdom of the Son he loves.   — Colossians 1:13

We have this treasure in jars of clay to show that this all-surpassing power is from God and not from us.   – 2 Corinthians 4:7

We pray this in order that you may live a life worthy of the Lord… bearing fruit in every good work, growing in the knowledge of God, being strengthened with all power according to his glorious might so that you may have great endurance and patience.   – Colossians 1:10-11

In his great mercy he has given us new birth into a living hope through the resurrection of Jesus Christ from the dead (phase one), *and into an inheritance that can never perish, spoil of fade – kept in heaven for you, who through faith are shielded by God's power* (phase two) *until the coming of the salvation that is ready to be revealed in the last time* (phase three).   – 1 Peter 1:3-5

From the first word of the Old Testament and all the way through the New, we see the foundational position of the Word of God in the preservation and presentation of Truth that transforms, renews and produces eternal results in the life of believers.

…the Holy Scriptures, which are able to make you wise for salvation through faith in Christ Jesus. All Scripture is God-breathed and is useful for teaching, rebuking, correcting and training in righteousness, so that the servant of God may be thoroughly equipped for every good work.
     – 2 Timothy 3:15-17

First, we see that the Apostles used the Word of God, already in existence in the Old Testament, to present, defend and clarify the Word of God that they spoke:

For what I received I passed on to you as of first importance: that Christ died for our sins according to the Scriptures, that he was buried, that he was raised on the third day according to the Scriptures.
     – 1 Corinthians 15:3

So it is written: "The first man Adam became a living being."
     – 1 Corinthians 15:45

In just eight verses of a New Testament letter, Paul quoted the Old Testament six times:

So also Abraham:
"believed God, and it was credited to him as righteousness.'"
Understand, then, that those who have faith are children of Abraham.
Scripture foresaw that God would justify the Gentiles by faith, and announced the gospel in advance to Abraham:
"All nations will be blessed through you."
So those who rely on faith are blessed along with Abraham, the man of faith. For all who rely on the works of the law are under a curse, as it is written:
"Cursed is everyone who does not continue to do everything written in the Book of the Law."
Clearly no one who relies on the law is justified before God, because:
"the righteous will live by faith."
The law is not based on faith; on the contrary, it says:
"The person who does these things will live by them."
Christ redeemed us from the curse of the law by becoming a curse for us, for it is written:
"Cursed is everyone who is hung on a pole."   – Galatians 3:6-13

Second, the Apostles considered their own teachings and writings to be comparable to what had long been acknowledged to be God's Word. The words of the Old Testament prophets had been confirmed by God through the fulfillment of their prophecies and predictions, and had also stood the test of comparison with both reality and God's nature, revelation and will. Knowing these prophecies as "Scripture", the Apostles still confidently referred to their own teaching and writing as God's command, God's Word and Scripture:

Did the word of God originate with you? Or are you the only people it has reached? If anyone thinks they are a prophet or otherwise gifted by the Spirit, let them acknowledge that what I am writing to you is the Lord's command. But if anyone ignores this, they will themselves be ignored.   – 1 Corinthians 14:37

You became imitators of us and of the Lord, for you welcomed the message in the midst of severe suffering with the joy given by the Holy Spirit. And so you became a model to all the believers in Macedonia and Achaia. The Lord's message rang out from you not only in Macedonia and Achaia—your faith in God has become known everywhere.   *– 1 Thessalonians 1:6-8*

Although I am less than the least of all God's people, this grace was given me: to preach to the Gentiles the unsearchable riches of Christ, and to make plain to everyone the administration of this mystery.
– Ephesians 3:8

I have become its servant by the commission God gave me to present to you the word of God in its fullness – the mystery that has been kept hidden for ages and generations, but is now disclosed to the saints.
– Colossians 1:25

We also thank God continually because, when you received the word of God, which you heard from us, you accepted it not as a human word, but as it actually is, the word of God, which is indeed at work in you who believe.   *– 1 Thessalonians 2:13*

Just as our dear brother Paul also wrote you with the wisdom that God gave him. He writes the same way in all his letters, speaking in them of these matters. His letters contain some things that are hard to understand, which ignorant and unstable people distort, as they do the other Scriptures, to their own destruction.   *– 2 Peter 3:15-16*

Write on a scroll what you see and send it to the seven churches: to Ephesus, Smyrna, Pergamum, Thyatira, Sardis, Philadelphia and Laodicea.   *– Revelation 1:11*

Third, the writers of the New Testament continually call us back to their words so that we might remain in the Truth. They encourage us to continue in their words and their teaching, because they knew the source of their words was God, and because they had seen the power it had in transforming the lives of their listeners:

Let the message of Christ dwell among you richly as you teach and admonish one another with all wisdom through psalms, hymns, and songs from the Spirit, singing to God with gratitude in your hearts.
– Colossians 3:16

I charge you before the Lord to have this letter read to all the brothers and sisters. – 1 Thessalonians 5:27

But we ought always to thank God for you, brothers and sisters loved by the Lord, because God chose you as firstfruits to be saved through the sanctifying work of the Spirit and through belief in the truth. He called you to this through our gospel, that you might share in the glory of our Lord Jesus Christ. So then, brothers and sisters, stand firm and hold fast to the teachings we passed on to you, whether by word of mouth or by letter. – 2 Thessalonians 2:13-15

We must pay the most careful attention, therefore, to what we have heard, so that we do not drift away. -Hebrews 2:1

If the Word of God is not foundational – or worse, if what the Apostles claim is the Word of God in their letters is not actually Scripture but instead legends and pseudo-writings – then we have no hope in holding to the Christian faith. If the Scriptures are in fact not the Word of God, or are not the Truth we claim them to be, then every honest and sincere person who swears allegiance to the church should abandon their hope and resume their search for some vein of truth somewhere among men. Even Paul writes:

If Christ has not been raised, our preaching is useless and so is your faith… if Christ has not been raised, your faith is futile.
– 1 Corinthians 15:14, 17

Chapter Ten:
Concept Two – The Word is a Revealed Mystery

The Word of God contains knowledge, insight and wisdom that is not available to men any other way. The theological term for this kind of information is special revelation. The other kind of knowledge – knowledge that God has revealed about the spiritual realm which is accessible through natural means (personal experience, the creation, history, etc.) – is referred to as general revelation, or natural revelation.

General revelation can provide people with knowledge and wisdom concerning God's existence and about the kinds of things that generally considered true, good and moral. Certain details can also be inferred by the natural mind through reason and philosophy: things such as the fact that time and creation had a beginning, and thus will also eventually have an end. Also available to all is the understanding that, since God the creator exists, there will be some kind of judgment by him at the end of time. This general knowledge is available to all honest, reasonable men who live on planet earth. As Scripture says:

The heavens declare the glory of God; the skies proclaim the work of his hands. Day after day they pour forth speech; night after night they display knowledge. There is no speech or language where their voice is not heard. Their voice goes out into all the earth, their words to the ends of the world.   – Psalm 19:1-4

To demonstrate this fact, Paul credited pagan poets and philosophers (even calling them "prophets" in Titus 1:12) with having perceived and written truthfully about God, his ways, and his judgment of man:

He made from one man every nation of mankind to live on all the face of the earth, having determined allotted periods and the boundaries of their dwelling place, that they should seek god, in the hope that they might feel their way toward him and find him. Yet he is actually not far from each one of us, for "In him we live and move and have our being" (quote from Epimenides, a Pagan philosopher/poet from Crete)*; as even some of your own poets have said, "For we are indeed his offspring."* (quote from the poem "Phainomena" by the pagan poet Aratus).   – Acts 17:26-28 (ESV)

God's existence, his power, and certain aspects of his character are clearly revealed in the created world and are available to everyone, whether or not they have access to a Bible. This is why we find un-churched people who have a reverence for deity, who know the universe is created, who have a general sense about God's nature, and who possess the knowledge that he is the righteous judge.

And even more available to us is that part of God's nature that is stamped on his greatest creation, man (since man is made in the image of God). Even though mankind has fallen into sin, the image of God is still engraved in our created nature. This is why we find good people living moral lives – or at least, knowing what a moral life is – and that it is something we should be doing.

> God created man in his own image, in the image of God he created him.   – Genesis 1:27

> Whoever sheds the blood of man, by man shall his blood be shed; for in the image of God has "God made man."   – Genesis 9:6

> When Gentiles, who do not have the law (the Law of Moses revealed by special revelation), do by nature things required by the law, they are a law for themselves, even though they do not have the law, since they show that the requirements of the law are written on their hearts, their consciences also bearing witness, and their thoughts now accusing, now even defending them. This will take place on the day when God will judge men's secrets through Jesus Christ.   – Romans 2:14-16

> What may be known about God is plain to them, because God has made it plain to them. For since the creation of the world God's invisible qualities – his eternal power and divine nature – have been clearly seen, being understood from what has been made, so that men are without excuse.   – Romans 1:19-20

So we see that natural man, even without the Word of God as revealed in Scripture, can seek God and know certain things about God: God's character, God's plan and God's expectations. But, not everything is revealed by general revelation through the created world or the image of God stamped on man's inner being (his heart and conscience). Many things, including the means of eternal salvation and the knowledge necessary for spiritual maturity, are not available through the natural world. This kind of information comes to man only as the Word of God given to prophets (mainly Old Testament), apostles (New Testament) and, of course, the teaching and life of the man Jesus Christ, the Son of God who came down from heaven (John 3:13; 6:38).

In the Old Testament God revealed his Word to certain people called prophets (and a few prophetesses), who then recorded the historical accounts of God's activity among men, along with the words that God gave directly to them. Moses collected (and edited) the documents that make up parts of the book of Genesis, and some of those records were written by Gentiles such as Noah, Shem, and others. Then with the founding of God's chosen nation, Israel, God began to reveal his specific will for them through prophets. This chosen people was to serve God both as a nation and as individuals. Men like Samuel, David, Nathan, Elijah, Jonah, Isaiah, Jeremiah, Habakkuk, Nahum, Zechariah, and more received, spoke and recorded information from God.

These collections became the recorded written Word of God. It contained not simple general revelation, but what theology refers to as special revelation. Notice, though, that although this special revelation only came to Israel, in many cases it was spoken also to the pagan nations through Israel. Men like David, Isaiah, Jeremiah, Obadiah, Jonah, Nahum, etc. not only spoke to the people of Israel, but also spoke and wrote the revealed Word of God directly to pagan peoples. And, these words were not only spoken to the nations in existence in the days of the Old Testament prophets, but were often spoken and recorded for nations and people who would appear on the world stage later in history.

You kings, be wise; be warned, you rulers of the earth. Serve the Lord with fear and rejoice with trembling…..   – David (Psalm 2:10)

This is what the Lord says to his anointed, to Cyrus, whose right hand I take hold of to subdue nations before him…. – Isaiah speaking in approximately 701 BC to Persian Emperor Cyrus who would live 163 years later in 538 BC (Isaiah 44:27-45:2)

*This is the word of the Lord that came to Jeremiah the prophet
concerning the nations: Concerning Egypt… the Philistines... Moab…
Ammon… Edom… Babylon….–* Jeremiah (Jeremiah 46:1-2; 47:1; 48:1;
49:1, 7, 28, 34; 50:1)

This is what the Sovereign Lord says about Edom…. – Obadiah 1

*The word of the Lord came to Jonah, son of Amittai: "Go to the great city of
Nineveh and preach against it, because its wickedness has come up before
me." –* Jonah was sent to Nineveh of the Assyrians (Jonah 1:1-2)

An oracle concerning Nineveh…. – Nahum also spoke against
Nineveh 100 years after Jonah (Nahum 1:1)

With the coming of Jesus Christ, the Son of God, a deeper and richer
view of God was provided to men. Jesus' life, words and teaching built
onto general revelation and the special revelation of the Old Testament.
Jesus revealed God in a very clear way, yet this revelation of the Word
of God was consistent with what had been previously made known.
This particular Word of God was also recorded in what we call the four
Gospels: Matthew, Mark, Luke and John.

*The Word became flesh and made his dwelling among us. We have
seen his glory, the glory of the One and Only, who came from the
Father, full of grace and truth…. From the fullness of his grace we have
all received one blessing after another. For the law was given through
Moses; grace and truth came through Jesus Christ. No one has ever
seen God, but God the One and Only, who is at the Father's side, has
made him known.*   *– John 1:14, 16-18*

After Jesus' ministry, death, resurrection and ascension, God continued
to provide special revelation to man through the Apostles and Prophets of
the church in the first century AD:

*In the past (Old Testament) God spoke to our forefathers through the
prophets at many times and in various ways, but in these last days
(26-30 AD) he has spoken to us by his Son, whom he appointed heir of
all things…. This salvation, which was first announced by the Lord, was
confirmed to us by those who heard him (the Apostles).*
                                              – Hebrews 1:1-2; 2:3

The apostles were appointed and sent to the pagan nations (as well as to the Jews) by Jesus to proclaim and explain the final phase of the special revelation that was to be given to man. The apostles knew they were presenting the Word of God. Their teaching was recorded and preserved from the very first day the believers and the churches received their instructions and letters. These documents have been collected and preserved since the days of the apostles (30-98 AD). This portion of the Word of God comes to us in what we call the New Testament.

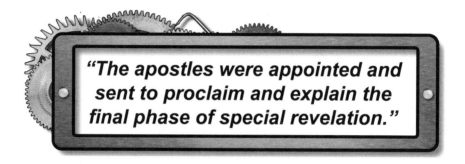

"The apostles were appointed and sent to proclaim and explain the final phase of special revelation."

Below are some verses that document the understanding that Paul, one of the writers of the New Testament had about the Word that was revealed to him. He, and others, knew they were receiving and documenting the mystery of God's Word which had not been revealed to men of previous generations, but was now being revealed by God to mankind through them.

Now to him who is able to establish you in accordance with my gospel, the message I proclaim about Jesus Christ, in keeping with the revelation of the mystery hidden for long ages past, but now revealed and made known through the prophetic writings by the command of the eternal God, so that all the Gentiles might come to the obedience that comes from faith. — Romans 16:25-26

For since in the wisdom of God the world through its wisdom did not know him, God was pleased through the foolishness of what was preached to save those who believe. — 1 Corinthians 1:21

GOD'S WORD

REVEALS

GOD'S WILL

NATURAL REVELATION	SPECIAL REVELATION
• Nature	• Prophets
• Math	• Apostles
• Science	
• Conscience	
• Self Awareness	
REVEALED TO ALL MEN	**REVEALED IN WRITTEN WORD** (SCRIPTURE)
• Gravity	• Salvation
• Morality	• Jesus, Son of God
• Marriage	• Israel
• Government	• Church
• Family	

TRUTH AND REALITY

We do, however, speak a message of wisdom among the mature, but not the wisdom of this age or of the rulers of this age, who are coming to nothing. No, we declare God's wisdom, a mystery that has been hidden and that God destined for our glory before time began. None of the rulers of this age understood it, for if they had, they would not have crucified the Lord of glory. However, as it is written:
"What no eye has seen,
what no ear has heard,
and what no human mind has conceived" —
the things God has prepared for those who love him—
these are the things God has revealed to us by his Spirit.
— 1 Corinthians 2:6-10

This, then, is how you ought to regard us: as servants of Christ and as those entrusted with the mysteries God has revealed.
— 1 Corinthians 4:1

I want you to know, brothers and sisters, that the gospel I preached is not of human origin. I did not receive it from any man, nor was I taught it; rather, I received it by revelation from Jesus Christ.
— Galatians 1:11

I went in response to a revelation and, meeting privately with those esteemed as leaders, I presented to them the gospel that I preach among the Gentiles. I wanted to be sure I was not running and had not been running my race in vain. Yet not even Titus, who was with me, was compelled to be circumcised, even though he was a Greek. This matter arose because some false believers had infiltrated our ranks to spy on the freedom we have in Christ Jesus and to make us slaves. We did not give in to them for a moment, so that the truth of the gospel might be preserved for you.   — Galatians 2:2-5

Surely you have heard about the administration of God's grace that was given to me for you, that is, the mystery made known to me by revelation, as I have already written briefly.   — Ephesians 3:2,3

In reading this, then, you will be able to understand my insight into the mystery of Christ, which was not made known to people in other generations as it has now been revealed by the Spirit to God's holy apostles and prophets. – Ephesians 3:4,5

This grace was given me: to preach to the Gentiles the boundless riches of Christ, and to make plain to everyone the administration of this mystery, which for ages past was kept hidden in God, who created all things. His intent was that now, through the church, the manifold wisdom of God should be made known to the rulers and authorities in the heavenly realms. – Ephesians 3:8-10

(Note: This mystery becomes known to believers, who then produce the fruit of righteousness in their lives. This transformation in people, who are the church, will then make known God's character, nature, glory, and word to the rulers and authorities in the heavenly realms.)

My goal is that they may be encouraged in heart and united in love, so that they may have the full riches of complete understanding, in order that they may know the mystery of God, namely, Christ, in whom are hidden all the treasures of wisdom and knowledge. I tell you this so that no one may deceive you by fine-sounding arguments. – Colossians 2-4

Chapter Eleven:
Concept Three – The Word is Entrusted to the Church

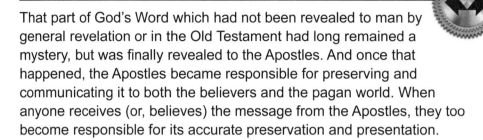

That part of God's Word which had not been revealed to man by general revelation or in the Old Testament had long remained a mystery, but was finally revealed to the Apostles. And once that happened, the Apostles became responsible for preserving and communicating it to both the believers and the pagan world. When anyone receives (or, believes) the message from the Apostles, they too become responsible for its accurate preservation and presentation.

Two key words used by the New Testament writers to describe the responsibility that they and we have after receiving the revealed Word of God are "entrusted" and "deposit".

> *This, then, is how you ought to regard us: as servants of Christ and as those entrusted with the mysteries God has revealed.*
> — 1 Corinthians 4:1

> *What you heard from me, keep as the pattern of sound teaching, with faith and love in Christ Jesus. Guard the good deposit that was entrusted to you—guard it with the help of the Holy Spirit who lives in us.*
> — 2 Timothy 1:13, 14

The word "entrusted" is the word oikonomous and can also be translated as "steward" when it refers to a manager of a household (who was often a trusted slave, similar to Joseph's situation in overseeing Potiphar's entire household in the book of Genesis). To be "entrusted" means to be placed in charge of the household and its operations. The concept here is not focused on the state of being in charge, or even on being the boss, but on the great responsibility and importance of performing diligent management activities to prove accountability. This word is used by Jesus in Luke 16:1:

> *There was a rich man whose manager* (oikonomon) *was accused of wasting his possessions. So he called him in and asked him, "What is this I hear about you? Give an account of your management, because you cannot be manager any longer."*

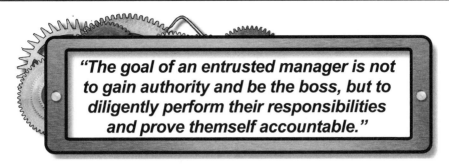

"The goal of an entrusted manager is not to gain authority and be the boss, but to diligently perform their responsibilities and prove themself accountable."

The word "deposit" is paratheken. It refers to something that belongs to a person who is giving it to another person, whom they trust, for safe keeping. It is a legal term used of someone trusting someone else to take care of their money, a family member, a harvest of grain, or a secret. The owner does not give up ownership, but requests that the person they entrust it to, guards their deposit faithfully.

Each person who accepts the message of the Word of God has entered into the responsibility of stewardship of this great deposit of the mystery of the Word of God that was placed in their lives:

I felt compelled to write and urge you to contend for the faith that was once for all entrusted to God's holy people. – Jude 3

Here are some other verses that shed light on the attitude of the New Testament writers, who understood that they, and the church, have been entrusted, and are therefore responsible for the deposit:

They recognized that I had been entrusted with the task of preaching the gospel to the Gentiles. – Galatians 2:7

We speak as those approved by God to be entrusted with the gospel. We are not trying to please people but God. – 1 Thessalonians 2:4

Timothy, guard what has been entrusted to your care. Turn away from godless chatter and the opposing ideas of what is falsely called knowledge, which some have professed and in so doing have departed from the faith. – 1 Timothy 6:20

Now it is required that those who have been given a trust must prove faithful.   *– 1 Corinthians 4:2*

If I preach voluntarily, I have a reward; if not voluntarily, I am simply discharging the trust committed to me.   *– 1 Corinthians 9:17*

That God was reconciling the world to himself in Christ, not counting people's sins against them. And he has committed to us the message of reconciliation.   *– 2 Corinthians 5:19*

In the presence of God and of Christ Jesus, who will judge the living and the dead, and in view of his appearing and his kingdom, I give you this charge: Preach the word; be prepared in season and out of season; correct, rebuke and encourage—with great patience and careful instruction.   *– 2 Timothy 4:1-2*

The hope of eternal life, which God, who does not lie, promised before the beginning of time, and which now at his appointed season he has brought to light through the preaching entrusted to me by the command of God our Savior.   *– Titus 1:2,3*

One of the primary ways we fulfill our stewardship responsibility is by communicating the revelation of God's Word. There is a wide variety of ways to accomplish this, but no matter what vehicle or method is used, it can be classified as preaching and teaching the Word of God.

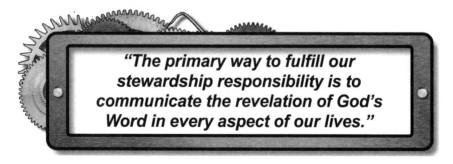

"The primary way to fulfill our stewardship responsibility is to communicate the revelation of God's Word in every aspect of our lives."

What is preaching? Preaching means "to proclaim" or "to announce". It is the clear transmission of an idea, a truth or a thought to another person in order for them to know, understand and make use of the information preached.

What is teaching? Teaching is more than standing up and filling time with talk about God. Teaching is the communication of the revelation from God to members of his church. It involves:

- Reading the text
- Explaining the background
- Explaining the context of the book
- Explaining the context of the verse and the words in the verse
- Providing exegesis of the words in the text to illuminate the fullest meaning
- Connecting all the concepts in the words, the verse and the book with the rest of Scripture
- Organizing similar concepts to develop definitions, doctrines, and a comprehensive insight

Teaching is empowering others with understandable and useful information. The primary purpose of the church is to teach, to successfully communicate the mystery of God that has been revealed through the written Scriptures – first to the pagan world for their salvation, and then to believers who came out of that pagan world to help them achieve full understanding and maturity. Teaching will bring about the maturity of believers and the church. Maturity will allow the true production of the fruits of righteousness that God desires.

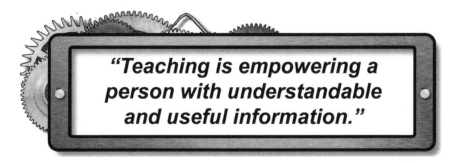

"Teaching is empowering a person with understandable and useful information."

Here are a few verses that capture the importance of teaching the Word of God:

Yet I have written you quite boldly on some points to remind you of them again, because of the grace God gave me to be a minister of Christ Jesus to the Gentiles. He gave me the priestly duty of

proclaiming the gospel of God, so that the Gentiles might become
an offering acceptable to God, sanctified by the Holy Spirit.
– Romans 15:15, 16

Therefore I glory in Christ Jesus in my service to God. I will not venture
to speak of anything except what Christ has accomplished through
me in leading the Gentiles to obey God by what I have said and done
– by the power of signs and wonders, through the power of the Spirit
of God. So from Jerusalem all the way around to Illyricum, I have fully
proclaimed the gospel of Christ. It has always been my ambition to
preach the gospel where Christ was not known, so that I would not be
building on someone else's foundation. Rather, as it is written:
  "Those who were not told about him will see,
  and those who have not heard will understand."
– Romans 15:15-21

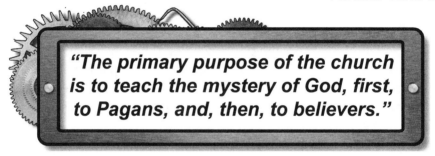

"The primary purpose of the church is to teach the mystery of God, first, to Pagans, and, then, to believers."

For Christ did not send me to baptize, but to preach the gospel—not
with wisdom and eloquence, lest the cross of Christ be emptied of
its power. – 1 Corinthians 1:17

The weapons we fight with are not the weapons of the world. On
the contrary, they have divine power to demolish strongholds. We
demolish arguments and every pretension that sets itself up against
the knowledge of God, and we take captive every thought to make
it obedient to Christ. And we will be ready to punish every act
of disobedience, once your obedience is complete.
– 2 Corinthians 10:4-6

I want you to know, brothers and sisters, that the gospel I preached is
not of human origin. I did not receive it from any man, nor was I taught
it; rather, I received it by revelation from Jesus Christ. – Galatians 1:11

Surely you have heard about the administration of God's grace that was given to me for you, that is, the mystery made known to me by revelation, as I have already written briefly.   – Ephesians 3:2, 3

In reading this, then, you will be able to understand my insight into the mystery of Christ, which was not made known to people in other generations as it has now been revealed by the Spirit to God's holy apostles and prophets.   – Ephesians 3:4, 5

This grace was given me: to preach to the Gentiles the boundless riches of Christ, and to make plain to everyone the administration of this mystery, which for ages past was kept hidden in God, who created all things. His intent was that now, through the church, the manifold wisdom of God should be made known to the rulers and authorities in the heavenly realms.   – Ephesians 3:8-10

If I am to go on living in the body, this will mean fruitful labor for me. Yet what shall I choose? I do not know! I am torn between the two: I desire to depart and be with Christ, which is better by far; but it is more necessary for you that I remain in the body. Convinced of this, I know that I will remain, and I will continue with all of you for your progress and joy in the faith.   – Philippians 1:22

You learned it from Epaphras, our dear fellow servant. – Colossians 1:7

Now I rejoice in what I am suffering for you, and I fill up in my flesh what is still lacking in regard to Christ's afflictions, for the sake of his body, which is the church. I have become its servant by the commission God gave me to present to you the word of God in its fullness— the mystery that has been kept hidden for ages and generations, but is now disclosed to the Lord's people.   – Colossians 1:24-26

Pray for us, too, that God may open a door for our message, so that we may proclaim the mystery of Christ, for which I am in chains. Pray that I may proclaim it clearly, as I should.   – Colossians 4:3, 4

Surely you remember, brothers and sisters, our toil and hardship; we worked night and day in order not to be a burden to anyone while we preached the gospel of God to you.   – 1 Thessalonians 2:9

We sent Timothy, who is our brother and co-worker in God's service in spreading the gospel of Christ, to strengthen and encourage you in your faith.   *– 1 Thessalonians 3:2*

I charge you before the Lord to have this letter read to all the brothers and sisters.   *– 1 Thessalonians 5:27*

This is good, and pleases God our Savior, who wants all people to be saved and to come to a knowledge of the truth…. And for this purpose I was appointed a herald and an apostle—I am telling the truth, I am not lying—and a true and faithful teacher of the Gentiles.
                                                    – 1 Timothy 2:3, 4, 7

How, then, can they call on the one they have not believed in? And how can they believe in the one of whom they have not heard? And how can they hear without someone preaching to them?   *– Romans 10:14*

We have different gifts, according to the grace given to each of us. If your gift is… teaching, then teach.   *– Romans 12:7*

These things happened to them as examples and were written down as warnings for us, on whom the culmination of the ages has come.
                                                    – 1 Corinthians 10:11

Now you are the body of Christ, and each one of you is a part of it. And God has placed in the church first of all apostles, second prophets, third teachers….   *– 1 Corinthians 12:27*

Now, brothers and sisters, if I come to you and speak in tongues, what good will I be to you, unless I bring you some revelation or knowledge or prophecy or word of instruction? Even in the case of lifeless things that make sounds, such as the pipe or harp, how will anyone know what tune is being played unless there is a distinction in the notes? Again, if the trumpet does not sound a clear call, who will get ready for battle? So it is with you. Unless you speak intelligible words with your tongue, how will anyone know what you are saying? You will just be speaking into the air.   *– 1 Corinthians 14:6-9*

So it is with you. Since you are eager for gifts of the Spirit, try to excel in those that build up the church.   *– 1 Corinthians 14:12*

So Christ himself gave the apostles, the prophets, the evangelists, the pastors and teachers, to equip his people for works of service, so that the body of Christ may be built up until we all reach unity in the faith and in the knowledge of the Son of God and become mature.
– Ephesians 4:11-13

That, however, is not the way of life you learned when you heard about Christ and were taught in him in accordance with the truth that is in Jesus. You were taught, with regard to your former way of life, to put off your old self, which is being corrupted by its deceitful desires; to be made new in the attitude of your minds; and to put on the new self, created to be like God in true righteousness and holiness.
– Ephesians 4:20-24

They feed and care for their body, just as Christ does the church.
– Ephesians 5:29

Stand firm then, with the belt of truth buckled around your waist.
– Ephesians 6:14

Pray also for me, that whenever I speak, words may be given me so that I will fearlessly make known the mystery of the gospel, for which I am an ambassador in chains. Pray that I may declare it fearlessly, as I should.   *– Ephesians 6:19*

… whether I am in chains or defending and confirming the gospel….
– Philippians 1:7

He is the one we proclaim, admonishing and teaching everyone with all wisdom, so that we may present everyone fully mature in Christ. To this end I strenuously contend with all the energy Christ so powerfully works in me.   *– Colossians 1:28-29*

Let your conversation be always full of grace, seasoned with salt, so that you may know how to answer everyone.   *– Colossians 4:16*

With the help of our God we dared to tell you his gospel in the face of strong opposition.   *– 1 Thessalonians 2:2*

Night and day we pray most earnestly that we may see you again and supply what is lacking in your faith.   *– 1 Thessalonians 3:10*

Don't you remember that when I was with you I used to tell you these things?   *– 2 Thessalonians 2:5*

But we ought always to thank God for you, brothers and sisters loved by the Lord, because God chose you as firstfruits to be saved through the sanctifying work of the Spirit and through belief in the truth. He called you to this through our gospel, that you might share in the glory of our Lord Jesus Christ. So then, brothers and sisters, stand firm and hold fast to the teachings we passed on to you, whether by word of mouth or by letter.   *– 2 Thessalonians 2:13-15*

Pray for us that the message of the Lord may spread rapidly and be honored, just as it was with you.   *– 2 Thessalonians 3:1*

If you point these things out to the brothers, you will be a good minister of Christ Jesus, nourished on the truths of the faith and of the good teaching that you have followed.   *– 1 Timothy 4:6*

Command and teach these things.   *– 1 Timothy 4:11*

Until I come, devote yourself to the public reading of Scripture, to preaching and to teaching. Do not neglect your gift!   *– 1 Timothy 4:13*

The elders who direct the affairs of the church well are worthy of double honor, especially those whose work is preaching and teaching.
                                                          – 1 Timothy 5:17

So that God's name and our teaching may not be slandered.
                                                          – 1 Timothy 6:1

These are the things you are to teach and insist on.   *– 1 Timothy 6:2*

I am reminded of your sincere faith…. For this reason I remind you to fan into flame the gift of God, which is in you. (Note: this was the gift of teaching)   – 2 Timothy 1:5, 6

Keep reminding God's people of these things. Warn them before God against quarreling about words; it is of no value, and only ruins those who listen. Do your best to present yourself to God as one approved, a worker who does not need to be ashamed and who correctly handles the word of truth. Avoid godless chatter.   – 2 Timothy 2:14-16

Don't have anything to do with foolish and stupid arguments, because you know they produce quarrels….The Lord's servant must not be quarrelsome but must be kind to everyone, able to teach, not resentful.
                                                           – 2 Timothy 2:23-24

He (an elder) *must hold firmly to the trustworthy message as it has been taught, so that he can encourage others by sound doctrine and refute those who oppose it.*   – Titus 1:9

You, however, must teach what is appropriate to sound doctrine. Teach the older men…. Likewise, teach the older women…. teach what is good…. In your teaching show integrity, seriousness and soundness of speech that cannot be condemned, so that those who oppose you may be ashamed because they have nothing bad to say about us. Teach slaves… so that in every way they will make the teaching about God our Savior attractive. For the grace of God has appeared that offers salvation to all people. It teaches us to say "No" to ungodliness and worldly passions, and to live self-controlled, upright and godly lives in this present age, while we wait for the blessed hope—the appearing of the glory of our great God and Savior, Jesus Christ, who gave himself for us to redeem us from all wickedness and to purify for himself a people that are his very own, eager to do what is good. These, then, are the things you should teach. Encourage and rebuke with all authority. Do not let anyone despise you.
        – Titus 2:1-15 (Note: All of Titus chapter two is about teaching.)

In fact, though by this time you ought to be teachers, you need someone to teach you the elementary truths of God's word all over again.   – Hebrews 5:11-14

Remember your leaders, who spoke the word of God to you. Consider the outcome of their way of life and imitate their faith.   – Hebrews 13:7

Not many of you should become teachers (or, presume to be teachers), my fellow believers, because you know that we who teach will be judged more strictly.   – James 3:1

Each of you should use whatever gift you have received to serve others, as faithful stewards of God's grace in its various forms. If anyone speaks, they should do so as one who speaks the very words of God.   – 1 Peter 4:10, 11

We write this to make our joy complete.   – 1 John 1:4

Chapter Twelve:
Concept Four – The Word of God Must be Heard and Known

The Word of God that came into the world through the apostles must be heard to be known – and known to be believed. So, before there can be faith, there must be knowledge. And before knowledge there must be hearing. It is just as the Apostle Paul explained:

Faith comes from hearing the message, and the message is heard through the word of Christ.   – Romans 10:17

In other words, the Word of God provides the message, and that message is presented to a person who hears it. When the person who hears the message knows the knowledge contained it, they can trust it, accept it, and believe it – or, as more simply put in Romans 10:17, have faith:

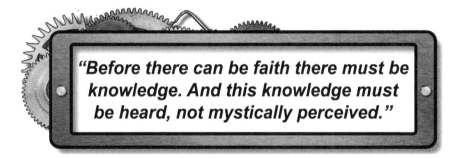

"Before there can be faith there must be knowledge. And this knowledge must be heard, not mystically perceived."

The Word → The message → The hearing → The knowing → The faith!

When a person has faith they can call on God, they can pray to God, they can receive salvation, they can seek his wisdom and they can walk in his ways. Of course, for a person to ultimately have the faith to trust God there has to be some form of messenger, communicator, preacher or teacher to transmit the Word of God to the person hearing it. That is why the Apostle Paul quotes Isaiah as he explains the process:

"Everyone who calls on the name of the Lord will be saved." – (the fruit)
How, then, can they call on the one they have not believed in? (faith)
And how can they believe in the one of whom they have not heard? (hearing)
And how can they hear without someone preaching to them? (teaching)
And how can they preach unless they are sent? (entrusted)

– Romans 10:13-15

In these verses, Paul identifies the people who have been entrusted with the mystery of the Word of God, and he identifies their mission as preaching the Word of God to others. Paul also describes the importance of that Word being heard and understood – it frees those who hear and

understand it to believe the Truth they now know. And when people believe the message they heard from teachers sent with the Word of God, they will call on the Lord, and there will be salvation.

The Word of God is the message that is taught – and when the Word is heard and believed, it produces faith. And faith unleashes the power of God's Word in a believer's life and in the world. So, teach the Word! Give God the opportunity to move through the faith produced in a person who believes the Word!

We see that Romans 10:13-15 explains the full cycle, which begins with God giving his Word and climaxes with God responding to faith in his Word with salvation.

God Reveals Word → Sent → Preached → Heard → Believed → Calls → God Saves

The concepts that Paul presents in these verses line up with the ten concepts of the model presented in this book. A comparison of Paul's terms and sequence with my model would look like this:

Paul's Model in Romans	**Galyn's Model in this Book**
God **Reveals** Word......	Word of God is Foundational and the Mystery is **Revealed**
A Man is **Sent** by God.........	Word of God is **Entrusted** to the Apostles and the Church
A Man **Preaches**...............	Word of God is **Taught** to Pagans and Believers
Message is **Heard**.............	Word of God is **Heard** and Known
Message is **Believed**.........	Accepted as Truth Resulting in **Faith** and Confidence
Belief Produces **Call** to God...	Faith Results in **Salvation (phase one); Maturity (phase two)**
God **Saves**........................	God Produces Fruit – i. **New Birth** by Holy Spirit (phase one); ii. Good Deeds, **Fruit of Spirit** by Holy Spirit (phase two)

The emphasis of this chapter is on the hearing of the Word of God that is entrusted to the church to be taught to the world. Here are some verses that comment on the hearing and knowing of the Word of God:

You also were included in Christ when you heard the message of truth, the gospel of your salvation. When you believed, you were marked in him with a seal, the promised Holy Spirit.   – Ephesians 1:13

For we do not write you anything you cannot read or understand.
      – 2 Corinthians 1:13

Faith comes from hearing the message, and the message is heard through the word of Christ.   – Romans 10:17

We also thank God continually because, when you received the word of God, which you heard from us, you accepted it not as the word of men, but as it actually is, the word of God, which is at work in you who believe.   – 1 Thessalonians 2:13

What you heard from me, keep as the pattern of sound teaching.
      – 2 Timothy 1:13

I keep asking that the God of our Lord Jesus Christ, the glorious Father, may give you the Spirit of wisdom and revelation, so that you may know him better. I pray that the eyes of your heart may be enlightened in order that you may know the hope to which he has called you, the riches of his glorious inheritance in his holy people, and his incomparably great power for us who believe. – Ephesians 1:17, 18

In reading this, then, you will be able to understand my insight into the mystery of Christ, which was not made known to people in other generations as it has now been revealed by the Spirit to God's holy apostles and prophets.   – Ephesians 3:4, 5

For this reason, since the day we heard about you, we have not stopped praying for you. We continually ask God to fill you with the knowledge of his will through all the wisdom and understanding that the Spirit gives, so that you may live a life worthy of the Lord and please him in every way: bearing fruit in every good work, growing in the knowledge of God, being strengthened with all power according to his glorious might so that you may have great endurance and patience, and giving joyful thanks to the Father, who has qualified you to share in the inheritance of his holy people in the kingdom of light.
                                                – Colossians 1:9-12

I myself am convinced, my brothers and sisters, that you yourselves are full of goodness, filled with knowledge and competent to instruct one another.   – Romans 15:14

Paul, a servant of God and an apostle of Jesus Christ to further the faith of God's elect and their knowledge of the truth that leads to godliness.   – Titus 1:1

Grace and peace be yours in abundance through the knowledge of God and of Jesus our Lord.   – 2 Peter 1:2

WORD
Eternal Truth

MESSAGE
Proclaimed amoung men

HEARD
Heard by men who understand and decide

KNOWN
Information is now known by men

FAITH
Men logically reason with the Truth they possess and believe

Chapter Thirteen:
Concept Five – The Word Must be Believed

Hearing the Word of God is important, but the process does
not continue to a productive end unless that Word is also accepted.
We know that the Word of God itself has the ability to produce faith,
which means that Truth has the authority to convince the hearer of its
reality, which in turn produces confidence in the new understanding.
However, the hearer is still responsible to accept both the Word and the
confidence it brings. So, while faith comes from hearing the message, the
message must also be accepted and believed. The message that brings
faith can be rejected by the hearer, stopping the process, and producing
no further development toward salvation (phase one) or maturity (phase
two). As Jesus said:

*Though seeing, they do not see; though hearing, they do not hear
or understand.*   – Matthew 13:13

**"Truth has the authority to
convince the hearer of its reality."**

*"You will be ever hearing but never understanding;
You will be ever seeing but never perceiving.
For this people's heart has become calloused;
They hardly hear with their ears,
And they have closed their eyes.
Otherwise they might see with their eyes,
Hear with their ears,
Understand with their hearts
And turn, and I would heal them."*
                               – Matthew 13:14-15 (Isaiah 6:9-10)

Notice how the last three lines of Matthew 13:14-15 capture several of the ten concepts of this process:

Teach→Hear→Know (Believe)→Turn (Repent, Renew)→Be Healed (Salvation, Maturity)

Jesus and Isaiah are saying that if the people would hear and believe the Word of God, they would understand it and faith would produce God's work of healing. Healing, as the word is used here, refers to the healing of both the spirit (being born again) and the soul (maturity) with salvation.

The writer of Hebrews explains how the message could be spoken but not heard – and why the Truth could end up being unproductive in the lives of some:

> *For we also have had the gospel preached to us, just as they did; but the message they heard was of no value to them, because those who heard did not combine it with faith. Now we who have believed enter that rest.*   *– Hebrews 4:2-3*

The writer of Hebrews is speaking to his generation in 68 AD and using the Exodus generation (of 1400 BC) as an example to warn his readers about the importance of accepting (believing) the Word of God as Truth, so that it can produce maturity in their lives. Here he quotes from David's Psalm 95 which was written around 1000 BC addressing his own generation:

> *"Today, if you hear his voice, do not harden your hearts as you did in the rebellion…that is why I was angry with that generation, and I said, 'Their hearts are always going astray, and they have not known my ways.'" …. See to it, brothers, that none of you has a sinful, unbelieving heart that turns away from the living God… So we see that they were not able to enter, because of their unbelief.*   *– Hebrews 3:7-10, 12, 19*

We learn that the Word of God is powerful enough to create and sustain the universe (Hebrews 1:3; 11:3), but is powerless in the soul of man unless it is combined with faith (acceptance, trust, belief) (Hebrews 3:7-4:11; esp. 4:2). The fact is that even upon a man's rejection of the Word of God, that same Word remains absolute and will serve as that man's judge

(Hebrews 4:12-13). We will have to give an account to the Word whether we accept it or reject it.

For the word of God is living and active. Sharper than any double-edged sword, it penetrates even to dividing soul and spirit, joints and marrow; it judges the thoughts and attitudes of the heart. Nothing in all creation is hidden from God's sight. Everything is uncovered and laid bare before the eyes of him to whom we must give account.
                                                    – Hebrews 4:12-13

Here are some verses which explain that faith in the Word of God must exist in the heart of a man before the Word's power of salvation, maturity and deliverance can be implemented in the spirit and soul of a man:

The one who received the seed that fell on good soil is the man who hears the word and understands it. He produces a crop, yielding a hundred, sixty or thirty times what was sown. – Matthew 13:23

I am not ashamed of the gospel, because it is the power of God for the salvation of everyone who believes. – Romans 1:16

Note: The Word of God – the gospel – is the "power of God," but only for the man who "believes". The powerful, life-changing Word of God can come to a man who remains completely unchanged because he rejected the Words of salvation, deliverance and maturity.

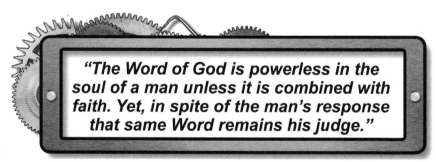

"The Word of God is powerless in the soul of a man unless it is combined with faith. Yet, in spite of the man's response that same Word remains his judge."

He came to that which was his own, but his own did not receive him. Yet to all who received him, to those who believed in his name, he gave the right to become children of God. – John 1:11-12

You foolish Galatians! Who has bewitched you? Before your very eyes Jesus Christ was clearly portrayed as crucified. I would like to learn just one thing from you: Did you receive the Spirit by the works of the law, or by believing what you heard? Are you so foolish? After beginning by means of the Spirit, are you now trying to finish by means of the flesh? Have you experienced so much in vain—if it really was in vain? So again I ask, does God give you his Spirit and work miracles among you by the works of the law, or by your believing what you heard?
– Galatians 3:1-5

So also Abraham "believed God, and it was credited to him as righteousness"… Understand, then, that those who have faith are children of Abraham. *– Galatians 3:6*

And you also were included in Christ when you heard the message of truth, the gospel of your salvation. When you believed, you were marked in him with a seal, the promised Holy Spirit.
– Ephesians 1:13

We also thank God continually because, when you received the word of God, which you heard from us, you accepted it not as the word of men, but as it actually is, the word of God, which is at work in you who believe. *– 1 Thessalonians 2:13*

Pray for us that the message of the Lord may spread rapidly and be honored, just as it was with you. *– 2 Thessalonians 3:1*

Now the Bereans were of more noble character than the Thessalonians, for they received the message with great eagerness and examined the Scriptures every day to see if what Paul said was true. Many of the Jews believed, as did also a number of prominent Greek women and many Greek men. *– Acts 17:11-12*

Chapter Fourteen:
Concept Six – The Word Contains the Gospel of Salvation

In the Word of God is the Gospel of our salvation.

The word "gospel" is the Greek word euaggelion and means "good message". The Word of God presents the good message of how a man can be delivered from sin, death, destruction and damnation. This is a very, very good message. This good message comes to man as does the rest of God's special revelation. First, it was the eternal Word of God that existed as a mystery beyond man's natural understanding. Later, it became part of the general revelation. Although the way of salvation was still a mystery, natural man could perceive from the natural world around him – and his own personal nature – that he was struggling with sin, death and destruction in his daily life. A fear of death, and a fear of what proceeds death, also testify in the heart of natural man:

He too (Jesus) shared in their humanity so that by his death he might destroy him who holds the power of death – that is, the devil – and free those who all their lives were held in slavery by their fear of death.
– Hebrews 2:14-15

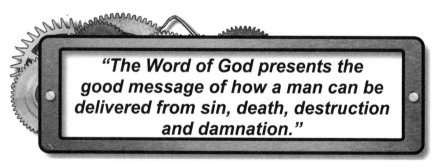

"The Word of God presents the good message of how a man can be delivered from sin, death, destruction and damnation."

Even without realizing it, natural man was looking for a "good message" concerning bondage to sin, death and damnation. This gospel was revealed to apostles and prophets who were entrusted with the deposit. The good message was then proclaimed and explained to all who would listen. And we are charged with continuing to preach and teach it until the end of time. Those who hear and believe the gospel message will have the power of the message released into their own lives. They will be born again, re-created, made alive, delivered from the kingdom of darkness into the kingdom of light, given the right to be sons of God, and death will have no power over them. They will live again!

I am not ashamed of the gospel, because it is the power of God for the salvation of everyone who believes.   – Romans 1:16

To all who received him, to those who believed in his name he gave the right to become children of God – children born not of natural descent, nor of human decision or a husband's will, but born of God.
     – John 1:12-13

For God so loved the world that he gave his one and only son, that whoever believes in him shall not perish but have eternal life. For God did not send his Son into the world to condemn the world, but to save the world through him. Whoever believes in him is not condemned, but whoever does not believe stands condemned already because he has not believed in the name of God's one and only son.   – John 3:16-18

I tell you the truth, no one can see the kingdom of god unless he is born again.   – John 3:3

He (Jesus) was delivered over to death for our sins and was raised to life for our justification. Therefore, since we have been justified through faith, we have peace with God through our Lord Jesus Christ, through whom we have gained access by faith into this grace in which we now stand. And we rejoice in the hope of the glory of God.
     – Romans 4:24-5:2

If anyone is in Christ, he is a new creation; the old has gone, the new has come.   – 2 Corinthians 5:17

God raised us up with Christ and seated us with him in the heavenly realms in Christ Jesus.   – Ephesians 2:6

Our citizenship is in heaven.   – Philippians 3:20

He has rescued us from the dominion of darkness and brought us into the kingdom of the Son he loves, in whom we have redemption, the forgiveness of sins.   – Colossians 1:13-14

You have been born again.   – 1 Peter 1:23

How great is the love the Father has lavished on us, that we should be called children of God! (phase one) *And that is what we are! ... Dear friends, now we are children of God* (phase two), *and what we will be has not yet been made known. But we know that when he appears, we shall be like him, for we shall see him as he is.* (phase three) *Everyone who has this hope in him purifies himself* (today during phase two), *just as he is pure.*   – 1 John 3:1-3

A tremendous power is released to transform a man from an object of wrath, existing in a state of judgment before God, into an object of God's love, who has been born into an eternal state of grace and is being prepared for everlasting glory. This power is the Gospel that is revealed in the Word of God.

The reception of the Gospel is the first of three phases of the salvation process that will eventually deliver a man from sin, death and destruction in his spirit, soul (mind) and body. A man's faith in the Gospel will save him spiritually, causing him to be born again and re-created into a child of God. He becomes a new man spiritually since has been raised with Christ, seated in heavenly places and made a citizen of heaven. At this point, this man is saved. It is a completed work. The transfer from the kingdom of darkness into the kingdom of light is finished and final. It will not – it cannot – be undone. Phase one of this man's salvation is complete.

But, it is exactly at this point that the battle for that man's soul and mind begins. The renewing of his mind (Rom. 12:2) and the clothing of himself with Christ daily (Rom. 13:4; Col. 3:10; Eph. 4:22-24) will be an ongoing process for the rest of his life on earth. He will continue to "press on to take hold of that for which Christ Jesus took hold of" him (Philippians 3:12). He will continually say with the Apostle Paul, "Not that I have already obtained all this, or have already been made perfect" (Philippians 3:12-13). This phase, phase two, will be discussed next. But, concerning the Gospel, the Good Message, of phase one this man has been eternally delivered out of spiritual sin, death and destruction. Having believed the Word of God the man is a new creature in Christ. He is born again! He is saved! He is eternally in the family of God as a son of God! Phase one, the salvation of the spirit, has been completed because of faith in the Word of God, the Gospel.

For since in the wisdom of God the world through its wisdom did not know him, God was pleased through the foolishness of what was preached to save those who believe.   – 1 Corinthians 1:21

I want to remind you of the gospel I preached to you, which you received and on which you have taken your stand. By this gospel you are saved, if you hold firmly to the word I preached to you. Otherwise, you have believed in vain.   – 1 Corinthians 15:1-2

Note that this verse has three parts:
   a) The Gospel was preached, received, believed – and the hearer took a stand
   b) The hearer was saved and entered phase two to "hold firmly to the word"
   c) If the hearer does not hold firmly, he has believed "in vain"

This verse is also about Paul saying "I want to remind you":

Just like Peter did in 2 Peter 1:13:
   I think it is right to refresh your memory as long as I live in the tent of this body…. I will make every effort to see that after my departure you will always be able to remember these things.

And in 2 Peter 3:1:
   This is now my second letter to you. I have written both of them as reminders to stimulate you to wholesome thinking. I want you to recall the words spoken in the past by the holy prophets and the command given by our Lord and Savior through your apostles.

Like Jude did in Jude 5:
   Though you already know all this, I want to remind you.

John did in 1 John 5:13:
   I write these things to you who believe in the name of the Son of God so that you may know that you have eternal life.

The writer of Hebrews, in Hebrews 2:1, says the same thing:

*We must pay more careful attention, therefore, to what we have heard,
so that we do not drift away.*

*I went in response to a revelation and, meeting privately with those
esteemed as leaders, I presented to them the gospel that I preach
among the Gentiles. I wanted to be sure I was not running and had not
been running my race in vain. Yet not even Titus, who was with me,
was compelled to be circumcised, even though he was a Greek. This
matter arose because some false believers had infiltrated our ranks to
spy on the freedom we have in Christ Jesus and to make us slaves.
We did not give in to them for a moment, so that the truth of the gospel
might be preserved for you.*   – Galatians 2:2-5

*And you also were included in Christ when you heard the message
of truth, the gospel of your salvation. When you believed, you were
marked in him with a seal, the promised Holy Spirit.* – Ephesians 1:13

*Take the helmet of salvation and the sword of the Spirit, which is the
word of God.*   – Ephesians 6:17

Note:

Phase one – helmet of salvation
Phase two – sword of the spirit, the word of God

*... the faith and love that spring from the hope stored up for you in
heaven and about which you have already heard in the true message
of the gospel that has come to you. In the same way, the gospel is
bearing fruit and growing throughout the whole world—just as it has
been doing among you since the day you heard it and truly understood
God's grace. You learned it from Epaphras, our dear fellow servant,
who is a faithful minister of Christ on our behalf, and who also told us of
your love in the Spirit.*   – Colossians 1:5-8

But now he has reconciled you by Christ's physical body through death to present you holy in his sight, without blemish and free from accusation—if you continue in your faith, established and firm, and do not move from the hope held out in the gospel. This is the gospel that you heard and that has been proclaimed to every creature under heaven, and of which I, Paul, have become a servant.

– Colossians 1:22-23

Note:

> Phase one – "reconciled you by Christ's physical body"
> Phase Two – "if you continue in your faith, established and firm, and do not move from the hope held out in the gospel"
> Phase Three – "to present you holy in his sight, without blemish and free from accusation"

They displease God and are hostile to everyone in their effort to keep us from speaking to the Gentiles so that they may be saved.

– 1 Thessalonians 2:15-16

This is good, and pleases God our Savior, who wants all people to be saved and to come to a knowledge of the truth.   – 1 Timothy 2:3-4

Note:

> Phase one – "wants all men to be saved"
> Phase two – "come to a knowledge of the truth"

Which God created to be received with thanksgiving by those who believe and who know the truth.   – 1 Timothy 4:3

Note:

> Phase one – "those who believe"
> Phase two – "know the truth"

Remember Jesus Christ, raised from the dead, descended from David. This is my gospel, for which I am suffering even to the point of being chained like a criminal. But God's word is not chained. – 2 Timothy 2:8-9

Paul, a servant of God and an apostle of Jesus Christ to further the faith of God's elect and their knowledge of the truth that leads to godliness.   -Titus 1:1

Note:

Phase one – "faith of God's elect"
Phase two – "knowledge of the truth that leads to godliness"

He chose to give us birth through the word of truth, that we might be a kind of firstfruits of all he created.   – James 1:18

As for you, see that what you have heard from the beginning remains in you. If it does, you also will remain in the Son and in the Father. And this is what he promised us—eternal life.   – 1 John 2:24-25

Chapter Fifteen:
Concept Seven –
The Word Renews the Mind and Matures the Believer

If the natural man, even the natural man who has been born again, is going to walk in God's ways he will need to know God's Word, because it is not natural for him to think, reason or discern as God does. Yet, that is exactly what man needs to do in order to please God. David wrote on this topic around 990 BC:

> *Who may ascend the hill of the Lord?*
> *Who may stand in his holy place?*
> *He who has clean hands and a pure heart,*
> *Who does not lift up his soul to an idol or swear by what is false.*
> *He will receive blessing from the Lord and vindication from God his Savior.*
> *Such is the generation of those who seek him, who seek your face, O God of Jacob.*   — Psalm 24:3-6

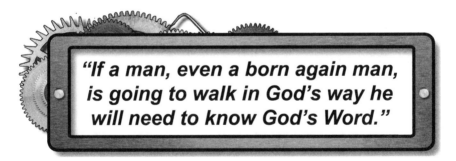

"If a man, even a born again man, is going to walk in God's way he will need to know God's Word."

David answers the question "Who may ascend?" and "Who may stand?" by listing four conditions:

1. Clean hands
2. Pure heart
3. Refusal to offer the soul (mind) to be trained in worship of an idol or false god. (An idol is simply the physical object that represents false ideologies, false philosophies and false realities)
4. Refusal to commit to follow a false world view

While David's questions and answers provide us important information, I would like to look at the issue from a slightly different angle. The question I will ask is not "Who" but "How?" I would ask:
1. How can a man have clean hands?
2. How can a man have a pure heart?
3. How does a man avoid offering his soul (mind) to an idol?
4. How does a man avoid swearing allegiance to something false that leads him to misplace his priorities and misidentify evil because he has embraced a false reality?

David answered "Who?" by describing a condition. I would answer "How?" by stating this: That person must know Truth. For David's man to have clean hands and a pure heart, he must know the Word of God In fact, Psalm 119 answers the "how" question the same way:

How can a young man keep his way pure? By living according to your word... I have hidden your word in my heart that I might not sin against you.   – Psalm 119:9, 11

Jesus also agreed when he prayed this prayer concerning his believing disciples:

Sanctify them by the truth; your word is truth.   – John 17:17

The word "sanctify" is the Greek word hagiason which is the aorist imperative active of hagiazo. The meaning of hagiazo is "to make holy" so that a thing or person can be set apart for God. The opposite of hagiazo is koinos which means "common".

To "sanctify" or hagiazo something means to set it apart for God and to separate it from the common. The thing or person who is sanctified is holy (set apart); the thing or person who is not sanctified is secular (worldly, temporal). In this prayer, Jesus was asking God to set the believers apart (to make them holy, to sanctify them) by the Truth, which is the Word of God. The aorist imperative could mean that the action of sanctifying began with Jesus' prayer, or more likely, the aorist imperative is saying that Jesus' prayer to sanctify men by the Word of God is a timeless principle in the Kingdom of God.

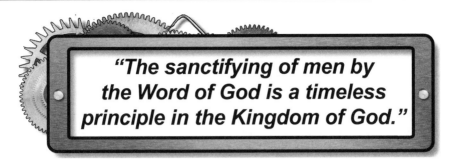

"The sanctifying of men by the Word of God is a timeless principle in the Kingdom of God."

To help David's man ascend the hill of the Lord and stand in the Lord's holy place, we need to determine how he can have clean hands, a pure heart, avoid committing to idols or swearing by what is false. If David's answer were laid out in a sequence of events, the process would look something like this:

1. Do not commit to a false reality;
2. Do not let your mind (soul) accept the principles of a false reality;
3. Purify your inner being by replacing the false principles in your inner being with Truth and reality (the Word of God) – and thus have a pure heart;
4. Once you know the Truth (the Word of God) in your inner being then you can think it, speak it, and do it in your life – and thus have clean hands;

David's man needs to reject false reality and get rid of false teaching in his inner being by replacing it with the Word of God. The Word of God must be in his soul (mind) before he can live a life with clean hands (thoughts, words, deeds). In other words, David's man needs to be sanctified by the Truth, which is the Word of God. This is true even if David's man is "saved" and seeking God. The saved man who is seeking God still needs to be sanctified by the Truth, just like the disciples of Jesus who were sitting around him the night he prayed for them and said, "Sanctify them by your truth; your word is truth." We must know the Truth before we can be free. Being sanctified (as in John 17:17) or being qualified to ascend the Lord's hill and stand in his holy place (Psalm 24:3-6) involves more than just accepting Jesus as savior and being born again (phase one). It requires the continuation of sanctification which is the renewing of the mind (phase two).

If you hold to my teaching, you are really my disciples. Then you will know the truth, and the truth will set you free.   – John 8:31-32

And so we see the pattern for the believer who wants to prepare himself for an effective life as a born-again child of God. Knowledge of the Word of God will produce the character of God. The seed that produced the crop in Jesus' parable in Matthew 13:1-24 was the Word of God sown into the hearts of men. The production that is called thirty, sixty and one hundred times what was sown is the godlike qualities that appear in a believer's life. The production from the Word of God is godliness. The crop is called the fruit of the Spirit (Gal. 5:22-23) and the fruit of righteousness (Phil. 1:11).

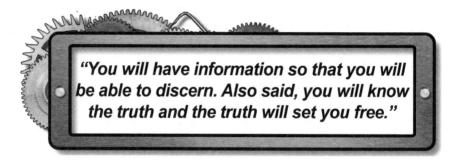

"You will have information so that you will be able to discern. Also said, you will know the truth and the truth will set you free."

Success in phase two involves a serious commitment to replacing the false views of the soul with the Truth of the Word of God. The false views that need to be replaced are captured in this verse:

You must no longer live as the Gentiles do, in the futility of their thinking. They are darkened in their understanding and separated from the life of God because of the ignorance that is in them due to the hardening of their hearts. Having lost all sensitivity, they have given themselves over to sensuality so as to indulge in every kind of impurity, and they are full of greed.   – Ephesians 4:17

The mind needs to receive the Word of God in phase two so that its thoughts can be renewed to conform with God's eternal Truth and reality:

Therefore, I urge you, brothers, in view of God's mercy, to offer your bodies as living sacrifices, holy and pleasing to God—this is your spiritual act of worship. Do not conform any longer to the pattern of this world, but be transformed by the renewing of your mind. Then you will be able to test and approve what God's will is—his good, pleasing and perfect will.   – Romans 12:1-2

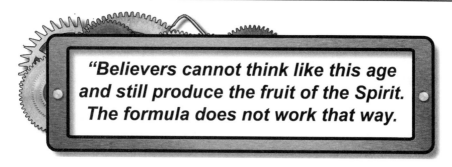

"Believers cannot think like this age and still produce the fruit of the Spirit. The formula does not work that way.

Notice in this passage how following the "pattern of this world" is forbidden, and in its place renewing the mind is commanded. The renewed mind will result in thoughts, words and deeds being transformed. And, what is more, from this renewed position, the believer will be able to "test and approve" what God's will is.

Notice also that these verses do not tell us we will know God's will by receiving a vision, experiencing a feeling, or perceiving a sense of peace (these would be considered mysticism and called false by the Apostles when compared with the written revelation of the Word of God). No. Romans 12:1-2 says that when your mind is renewed, then you will be able to test and approve what God's will is. You will know so that you can judge. You will have information so that you can discern. You will know the truth and the truth will set you free.

The beginning of Romans 12:2 in the Greek says:

me	*suschematizesthe*	*to*	*aioni*	*touto*	*alla*
not	conform		age	to this	but

metamorphousthe	*te*	*anakainosei*	*tou*	*voos*
you be transformed	by the	renewing	of the	mind

The word "conform" is the present imperative passive of suschematizo and means "to form or mold" after a model. It means to conform your mind and your expression to a pattern that is not yours. This word is made up of su– and schematizo. The word schematizo refers to a man assuming an expression or position that does not represent his changed inner being. The prefix su– adds to schematizo the meaning that the pattern being imitated is some definite image or mold outside the man who is assuming that expression or position. It refers to imitating a pose or accepting a mode of conduct. The word right before suschematizo is the Greek word me which is the negative or the "not" of the sentence. This means that Paul is forbidding the continuation of the "conforming to a pattern outside the believer which is contrary to what is inside the believer." Paul says, "Stop imitating the model you see outside yourself," or "Stop bending to a pattern that is not your pattern."

The next word aioni tells us where the wrong pattern is coming from. The pattern or mold causing the problem comes from the aion which simply means "age". And the age is then identified by the next Greek word, touto, which informs us that it is "this" age. The word aion indicates a period of indefinite duration but related to a sequence of unbroken time marked by specific characteristics. Thus, "this age" (aioni touto) refers to this age in which we live as born-again believers in a world that is dominated by sin, Satan and fallen men. We are to have a different pattern than the world around us.

Richard C. Trench in his book, Synonyms of the New Testament published in 1880, describes the biblical concept of aion when he says:

> "We speak of 'the times,' attaching to the word an ethical signification; or, still more to the point, 'the age,' 'the spirit or genius of the age,'… All that floating mass of thoughts, opinions, maxims, speculations, hopes, impulses, aims, aspirations, at any time current in the world, which it may be impossible to seize and accurately define, but which constitute a most real and effective power, being the moral, or immoral, atmosphere which at every moment of our lives we inhale, again inevitably to exhale – all this is included in the aion, which is, as Bengel has expressed it, the subtle informing spirit of the kosmos, or world of men who are living alienated and apart from God." (p. 217-218)

This "floating mass of thoughts, opinions, maxims, speculations, hopes, impulses, aims, aspirations, at any time current in the world" are the erroneous concepts that form the basis of what the New Testament writers call false doctrines, hollow philosophies, traditions of men and doctrines of demons. This floating mass of thoughts, etc. are what we are commanded to remove from our minds and replace with the Word of God. If a believer continues to allow himself to be formed to the pattern of this age (aion), he will never be able to mature and produce the work of God in his life. It cannot be done. In the realm of spiritual arithmetic, it is simply impossible. Believers cannot think like the aion and, at the same time, produce the fruit of the Spirit. The formula just does not work that way. It is illogical and incorrect to think we can be productive Christians and not know the Truth of God's Word. The numbers just do not add up. Just as you must be born again to see the kingdom of God, so also, your mind must be renewed in order to mature and function as a child of God in this age.

At this point we need to pause momentarily to make a distinction between being legalistic (ascetic) and "not conforming to the pattern of this age". Far from representing spiritual growth, legalism is actually one way believers conform to the pattern of this age. The believer must be very careful not to fall into this trap. Remember that the world was created by God, and everything God created is good. Paul's command to not conform to the world refers to something much more complicated and evil than normal cultural standards such as clothing fashions, musical tastes, cultural festivities, communication styles, family tradition, political views, educational systems, etc. Likewise, renewing your mind to the Word of God is more than serving a self-enforced stint in a self-created monastery where you act out some pseudo spirituality by avoiding "the world". The problem with the Monastery Model is that even though you cut yourself off from the world, you have still not renewed your mind to the Truth. The Monastery Model incorrectly assumes that victory lies in eliminating any contact with the world; however, this false religious experience is itself one of the doctrines of demons that Paul identifies in 1 Timothy:

Some will abandon the faith (the body of Truth in the Word of God)
And follow deceiving spirits and things taught by demons.
...They forbid people to marry (marriage is instituted by God and
    called "good")
And order them to abstain from certain foods
    (God created the need for food and he created food itself; Jesus ate;
    food and eating are also good)
which God created to be received with thanksgiving (we honor God by
    enjoying his goodness in the world)
by those who believe (who accept the message of the Word of God
    as true)

and who know the truth. (Thus we see the problem with legalism and asceticism – they do not know the truth. They have replaced the discipline of renewing their minds with fake spirituality which cuts them off from the good things in the world. In this verse, we see a classic case of calling good evil and evil good.)

For everything God created is good, and nothing is to be rejected if it is received with thanksgiving, because it is consecrated by the word of God and prayer. (The mature do not need to reject the good things of life and society such as marriage, food, etc., because, the mature man knows God, knows God's word and express gratitude for God's goodness.)   – 1 Timothy 4:1-5

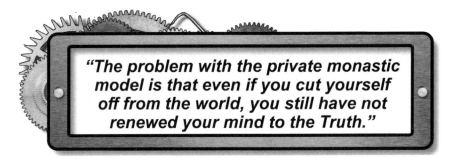

"The problem with the private monastic model is that even if you cut yourself off from the world, you still have not renewed your mind to the Truth."

The corrupt pattern of this aion not only molds people to live wickedly immoral lives, but it also invites the extreme opposite position, which rejects things that are good and decent in an attempt to live an ascetic life. The inability to discern the difference is the result of not having a renewed mind. Paul writes in Romans 12:2:

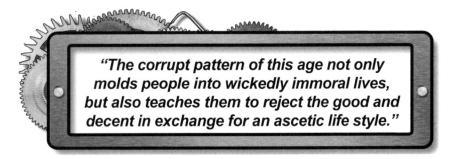

"The corrupt pattern of this age not only molds people into wickedly immoral lives, but also teaches them to reject the good and decent in exchange for an ascetic life style."

Be transformed by the renewing of your mind. Then you will be able to test and approve what God's will is – his good, pleasing and perfect will.

The phrase "test and approve" comes from one Greek word, dokimazo, in the active voice. The word dokimazo means "to prove by testing" and then "to accept as approved after testing" (Linguistic, p.339). These two basic meanings work together as a single process, and this is why the NIV uses two words to translate the one Greek word.

To truly dokimazo takes two steps. First, a person must test a thing; and then, second, they must have the ability to analyze the results of that test to make a judgment, a decision, or a correction. The mature man who has a mind renewed by the Word of God will be able to test his life and his surroundings, analyze them by comparing them to God's Word, and then with discernment make judgments concerning how they line up with God's will. Wuest writes that "test and approve" translated from dokimazo means,

> ... to put to the test for the purpose of approving, and finding that the thing tested meets the specifications laid down, to put one's approval upon it. As a result of the Spirit's control of the mental processes of the saint, the latter is enabled to put his life to the test for the purpose of approving it, the specifications being that it conform to the Word of God, and thus, experiencing what obedience is to the Word, and finding out what it feels like to have the Word saturated and control the life, he sees that it really is the Word of God and puts his approval upon it. (Wuest, Vol. 1, p. 208)

The writer of Hebrews makes this same point very clear for the immature believers reading his letter:

> *Anyone who lives on milk, being still an infant, is not acquainted with the teaching about righteousness. But solid food is for the mature, who by constant use have trained themselves to distinguish good from evil.*
> *– Hebrews 5:13-14*

The mature believer can "distinguish" good from evil and make the choices necessary for a righteous life. But the immature believer is "not acquainted with the teaching about righteousness" so must substitute legalism and rules to supplant their deficient ability to discern right from wrong. Again, this immature Christian life of legalism is in itself conforming to the wicked pattern of this aion.

"The mature believer can distinguish good from evil and make the choices necessary to live a righteous life."

The inability of the immature believer to discern the difference is what Paul addresses in 1 Corinthians 8 in regard to food sacrificed to idols. The weak, immature believer cannot eat the food coming from an idol's temple because "their conscience is weak" (or, their mind is not renewed) as a result of not knowing the Truth (1 Corinthians 8:7). They are called "the weak brother" (8:11), and the mature believer ("you who have this knowledge" – 8:10) is advised by Paul to temper their "knowledge" with love and also refrain from eating the food. The knowledge of the Truth, when fully understood, will produce love toward others (including the ignorant Christian).

The problem in this example was not the food, but the ignorance of the immature believers. The mature believers had to avoid some food so as to not accidently encourage the immature to do something they perceived in their un-renewed conscience to be "sinful". The real problem was that the immature believers needed to attend Bible class and be delivered from their ascetic and ignorant legalistic lifestyle. But, until then, if the mature and immature went to a restaurant in Corinth, the mature believer needed to temper his knowledge with love and order salad instead of steak. (Which is very sad!) And then when the meal was over, the mature believer needed to get his immature friend to some Bible classes in order to renew his mind with the Word of God so they could both order and enjoy steak the next time they ate out.

We know that "We all possess knowledge." But knowledge puffs up while love builds up. Those who think they know something do not yet know as they ought to know… So this weak brother or sister, for whom Christ died, is destroyed by your knowledge. When you sin against them in this way and wound their weak conscience, you sin against Christ. Therefore, if what I eat causes my brother or sister to fall into sin, I will never eat meat again, so that I will not cause them to fall.
– 1 Corinthians 8:1, 11

Romans 12:2 uses the following phrase to describe the process of maturing in phase two:

metamorphousthe	te	anakainosei	tou	voos
you be transformed	by the	renewing	of the	mind

We are "transformed" into maturity by "renewing" our "mind". The word "transformed" comes from the Greek word metamorphousthe which is the present imperative passive tense of metamorphoo. The passive voice indicates that we are not doing the transforming to ouselves, but someone or something else is the force behind the change. This, of course, is the seed of the Word of God growing, maturing and producing in our lives. The passive tense here agrees with the other images and illustrations presented in the Word of God concerning our spiritual growth and production during phase two: "produce thirty, sixty and one hundred fold," "fruit of the spirit," "fruit of righteousness," "new born babies," etc. Our job is to hear, read, study, and believe the Word of God with our minds. The Word of God then renews our minds by creating a new pattern to imitate, and we are transformed. The word metamorphoo is the same word used by Matthew when he describes Jesus' transfiguration:

There he was transfigured (metamorphothe) *before them. His face shone like the sun, and his clothes became as white as the light.*
                                                        – Matthew 17:2

Just as Jesus' outward appearance was changed to that of light, so the believer's appearance will also change to that of the character of God – in the form of good deeds, gifts of the spirit, righteous attitudes and edifying words. We will no longer be like the aion, but will become instead like sons of God. What is on the inside will appear on the outside.

The present tense of metamorphoo in Romans 12:2 indicates that this process of being transformed is a continuing thing. We are never fully transformed during phase two, which agrees with Paul's attitude described in Philippians 3, where he writes:

Not that I have already obtained all this, or have already been made perfect…I do not consider myself yet to have taken hold of it… I press on toward the goal to win the prize.   – Philippians 3:12-14

Our outward transformation is a continuing process that involves renewing our minds with the Word of God – and the Word of God transforming our lives. We inhale the Word of God into our minds (soul) and it is exhaled into our lives as attitudes, words and deeds. The imperative mood of metamorphoo in Romans 12:2 is the mood of command. This word in the imperative mood combined with the passive voice and the present tense indicates an ongoing command – that we are to allow the Word of God to transform our lives continually.

The English word "metamorphosis" comes from this Greek word metamorphoo. The English word describes a complete change in appearance and character, such as those that take place from one stage to the next as a caterpillar turns into a pupa and then emerges as a butterfly.

Transformation like this comes by "the renewing of our minds". The emphasis placed on the mind in this verse and throughout the New Testament tells us that the Christian experience is not a mindless, ecstatic experience that bases daily decisions and the priorities of life on mystical or emotional sensations. Instead, the scriptural approach to the Christian life is intelligent and intellectual, giving the believer the power to discern and evaluate. The Christian life is ultimately an experience that includes the power to be moral, to know God's will, and to choose what is good and right.

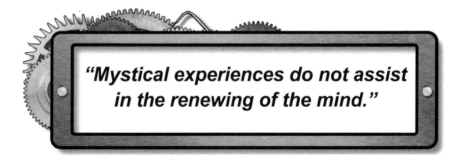

"Mystical experiences do not assist in the renewing of the mind."

Peter makes a simple statement concerning how to correctly live the Christian life in phase two:

Therefore, prepare your minds for action.   – 1 Peter 1:13

We have been born again in phase one, just as Paul says: "If anyone is in Christ, he is a new creation; the old has gone, the new has come" (Romans 5:17). Yet, in phase two we need to add to this new nature a renewed mind, which will empower us to manifest that new nature on the outside in our actions, as Paul says in Ephesians 4:22-24:

> *You were taught...to be made new in the attitude of your minds;*
> *and to put on the new self, created to be like God in true righteousness*
> *and holiness.*   *– Ephesians 4:22-24*

The word translated "be made new" is ananeousthai, which is the present passive infinitive of ananeow, which means "to make new again, to renew". The present tense means that "being made new again" is a continuing action. Clearly, this is not talking about continuing to be born again, or saved again. Rather, it refers to the continuing work of renewing our minds to the Word of God in phase two. The passive form means it is being done to the subject by another force, which in this case, is the teaching referred to in verse 22.

Here is a similar verse telling the Roman believers to put on or "clothe" themselves with the new nature, which is the image of Jesus Christ, and to stop thinking in line with the old nature:

Clothe yourselves with the Lord Jesus Christ, and do not think about how to gratify the desires of the sinful nature.   *– Romans 13:14*

In phase one the believer is born again in the image of God with the life of God. In phase two believers renew themselves with the knowledge of the Word of God, which places that same image of God onto their souls. From this point, the image of God in the born-again spirit and the renewed soul can put on that image of God (i.e., manifest it) as the new self in the attitudes, words and deeds.

> *Put on the new self, which is being renewed in knowledge in the image*
> *of its Creator.*   *– Colossians 3:10*

Paul wrote a letter to his fellow minister, Titus, who was organizing the churches and their leadership on the isle of Crete. The letter opens with a verse that identifies Paul's purpose in ministry: To further the faith of people who have passed through phase one by advancing their knowledge of God's Word (as in Romans 10:17), with the result being that they will be godly in their words and actions. Like other places in the scriptures, this verse confirms that growth in knowledge will lead to the production of the spiritual fruit of godliness:

> *Paul, a servant of God and an apostle of Jesus Christ to further the faith of God's elect and their knowledge of the truth that leads to godliness.*   – Titus 1:1

Note:
> • Phase one – "faith of God's elect"
> • Phase two – "knowledge of the truth that leads to godliness"

It is a constant exercise for the believer to focus on the Truth and reality expressed in the Word of God so that they may avoid thinking the futile thoughts of the world, while at the same time maintaining and advancing the renewal of their mind to line up with God's will:

> *Since, then, you have been raised with Christ, set your hearts on things above, where Christ is, seated at the right hand of God. Set your minds on things above, not on earthly things.*   – Colossians 3:1-2

> *Therefore, holy brothers and sisters, who share in the heavenly calling, fix your thoughts on Jesus.*   – Hebrews 3:1

It is interesting to note in this next verse that mystical experiences do not help in the renewing of the mind:

> *For if I pray in a tongue, my spirit prays, but my mind is unfruitful.*[6]
>   – 1 Corinthians 14:14

As we have seen, when a man believes on Jesus Christ for his salvation he is saved (John 3:18). At the very moment of belief, this salvation has recreated him (Titus 3:5; Romans 8:16; 1 Corinthians 2:14), placed

---

[6] Please note, however, that in this same chapter – and in other New Testament verses as well – it is clear that spiritual value and spiritual power are gained through appropriate spiritual manifestations.

him into the body of Christ (John 15:5; Ephesians 1:4), seated him in heavenly places (Ephesians 2:19; Philippians 3:20), removed the penalty of sin (Romans 3:25; 1 John 4:10; 2:2; Hebrews 2:17) and secured him a place in the eternal kingdom of God (1 Peter 1:4; Colossians 3:24; Hebrews 9:15). In fact, it can be shown from scripture that forty different things happen to a person when faith is placed in Jesus Christ. (See "Framework for Christian Faith," by Wiemers, p. 479-483) This list represents phase one and is correctly referred to as being "saved" or "born again".

Yet, in scripture there are references to us being in the process of salvation even today. These references can be confusing and cause some believers to think they could lose the salvation that they have already received by faith in phase one – verses like "work out your salvation with fear and trembling" (Philippians 2:12) and "by this gospel you are saved, if you hold firmly to the word I preached" (1 Corinthians 15:2). By understanding the process of phase two of salvation, though, this confusion will be resolved. Once you understand that, while Phase one is done, phase two is an ongoing process, everything becomes clear.

Phase one is also called positional sanctification, while phase two is commonly known as progressive sanctification (also, experiential, practical or temporal sanctification). In phase one the man's spirit is saved and the penalty of sin is removed. So in this regard, salvation can be said to be final, complete and secure. But, in phase two, the believer is straining toward spiritual maturity, which will manifest the fruit of righteousness in his daily life and impede the power of sin. Indeed, the penalty of sin is removed in phase one, yet is there any person who, after having been born again, does not continue daily to struggle against the power of sin? No. Sin is real. And, there is a difference between the penalty of sin and the power of sin. In phase one the penalty of sin is removed, but we are left in here on earth to struggle against the power of sin.

Luckily, we are not left to struggle alone, for when we were born again, we were also given the Holy Spirit of God and presented with the Word of God which promises to renew our minds if we let it. This process of attaining maturity in order to overcome the power of sin is part of salvation and is often referred to in scripture in the present tense as "being saved". So, we have been saved (past tense) from the penalty of sin, but we are being saved (present tense) from the power of sin.

Below are some verses that use the word "saved" in the present tense in reference to phase two of the salvation process. In these examples, the people referred to are already "saved", but are now striving for "salvation," or maturity.

> *For the message of the cross is foolishness to those who are perishing* (those who rejected the gospel of phase one), *but to us who are being saved it is the power of God.* — 1 Corinthians 1:18

James tells his believing readers to accept the Word of God into their souls because it can save them. Notice the mention of the power of sin called "moral filth and the evil". This verse is not about being saved from the punishment of sin because, if it were, its message would be that it is necessary for a man to stop sinning and to clean his life up before he can accept Jesus Christ as Savior. But, of course, if he can stop sinning and clean up his life without Christ, why would he need Christ? Why would he need the Word of God? Instead, we must read this verse to say that a man needs Jesus for salvation in phase one – and that same man needs the Word of God for salvation in phase two.

> *Therefore, get rid of all moral filth and the evil that is so prevalent and humbly accept the word planted in you, which can save you.*
> — James 1:21

In this next verse it is clear that Peter is also addressing people who are already believers, since they already have faith. Their faith is active and remains so, and as they hear and accept the Word of God they will continue to grow in the renewing of their minds, which Peter describes as "the salvation of your souls".

> *For you are receiving the end result of your faith, the salvation of your souls.* — 1 Peter 1:9

In another passage, Paul tells Timothy, who is the pastor of a church filled with believing members, to be "diligent" concerning the Word of God. Pastor Timothy, and those listening to him teach, were clearly already saved; yet Paul tells Timothy that if he perseveres in healthy doctrine and in living a godly life both he and his church members will be saved. What does Paul mean? How can Timothy "save" them and himself if they are all already saved? And, if Jesus is the savior why is Timothy told to save them? Timothy, the teacher of the church in Ephesus, is told by Paul to be diligent and watch his lifestyle and the doctrine that he teaches "so that everyone may see". Timothy is the teacher, and as a teacher, he is responsible for leading others in learning the Word of God which can renew their minds, as well as his own.

The only logical conclusion is that Paul is referring to Timothy saving the souls (minds) of the believers in who are in phase two. Timothy and the members of the Ephesian church were already saved from the penalty of sin (phase one), but Paul is encouraging Timothy to press on to bring about maturity, spiritual fruit, and power over sin.

> *Be diligent in these matters; give yourself wholly to them, so that everyone may see your progress. Watch your life and doctrine closely. Persevere in them, because if you do, you will save both yourself and your hearers.*   – 1 Timothy 4:15

Below are more portions of scripture (italic) with comments or notes (not italic) which help explain these concepts.

> *Those who live* (in phase two)
> *according to the flesh have their minds set on what the flesh desires*
>   (they are saved but they have not learned the Word of God which
>   will renew their minds);
> *but those who live* (during phase two)
> *in accordance with the Spirit have their minds set on what the Spirit
> desires* (having learned Word of God which has renewed their mind).
> *The mind governed by the flesh is death* (still existing in emptiness and
>   sin even though born again),
> *but the mind governed by the Spirit is life and peace* (thinking and
>   living in agreement with the Truth of the Word in phase two).
> *The mind governed by the flesh is hostile to God* (even the un-renewed
>   mind of a believer is against God);
> *it does not submit to God's law, nor can it do so* (since it has not been
>   changed, even though the man's spirit is saved).

Those who are in the realm of the flesh cannot please God (they are
 still in the kingdom of darkness under the power of Satan and have
 not been saved in phase one).
You, however, are not in the realm of the flesh but are in the realm of
the Spirit (transferred into the kingdom of light and seated with Christ in
 heavenly places because they were saved in phase one),
if indeed the Spirit of God lives in you (from phase one).
And if anyone does not have the Spirit of Christ, they do not belong to
Christ (not saved in phase one).   – Romans 8:5-9

I want to remind you of the gospel (Word of God)
I preached to you, which you received (believed, had faith in Jesus,
 phase one)
and on which you have taken your stand (to live your life on earth,
 phase two).
By this gospel you are saved (renewed mind, maturity),
if you hold firmly to the word I preached to you (continue in the Word
 of God).
Otherwise, you have believed in vain (your mind will not be renewed
 and you will continue to live like a pagan during phase two, even
 though you have accepted Jesus as savior in phase one).
                                              – 1 Corinthians 15:1-2

Grace, mercy and peace from God the Father and from Jesus Christ,
the Father's Son, will be with us in truth and love.   – 2 John 3

Note:
 - "Truth" = Mind
 - "Love" = Fruit
 - In phase two, "truth" in the soul produces "love" in thought, speech
   and deed
 - In maturity we will experience the grace, mercy and peace that God
   has freely given us already, but which we do not understand until we
   mature in knowledge and understanding

What we have received is not the spirit of the world (Eph. 2:2, "the spirit
 who is now at work in those who are disobedient"),
but the Spirit who is from God (the Holy Spirit at the new birth),
so that we may understand what God has freely given us (the Spirit

of God will help us understand the Word of God that explains our
  salvation and our place in Christ).
This is what we speak, not in words taught us by human wisdom
  (religion, philosophy, etc.)
but in words taught by the Spirit (the Word of God revealed to
  natural man),
explaining spiritual realities with Spirit-taught words (the mysteries
  revealed in written form in the New Testament letters).
The person without the Spirit (not born again in phase one)
does not accept the things that come from the Spirit of God (teaching
  and insight from the Word of God)
but considers them foolishness, and cannot understand them because
they are discerned only through the Spirit (discerned only by a man
  born again by the Holy Spirit who understands the mystery revealed
  in the Word of God through the Holy Spirit).
The person with the Spirit (the mature Christian)
makes judgments about all things, but such a person is not subject to
merely human judgments (i.e., natural man's limited understanding of
  God and spiritual matters),
for, "Who has known the mind of the Lord so as to instruct him?"
  (the answer: no one – especially no natural man who has rejected
  God's revelation, because he cannot even perceive it)
But we have the mind of Christ (that is, people like us, who have
  been born of the Spirit, who have God's Spirit to empower us to
  understand the revealed Word of God; mature, believing men have
  the mind of Christ).   – 1 Corinthians 2:12-16

Not only is the mind used by God to produce maturity and the spiritual
fruit of righteousness, the Bible also records Satan using the mind to
plant the seeds of his thoughts – ones that produce the fruit
of wickedness.

I am afraid that just as Eve was deceived by the serpent's cunning,
your minds may somehow be led astray from your sincere and pure
devotion to Christ.   – 2 Corinthians 11:3

Note:

- Minds are either renewed to Christ's Word or they will be deceived by the Serpent
- "Sincere and pure devotion" are hearts devoted to Christ; but this devotion to Christ needs minds renewed to the truth, to avoid being led astray
- Sincerity and devotion are noble attitudes, but they will follow the direction of the intellect. If there is no truth in the soul, sincerity and devotion can be misled and the person will be spiritually abused

For such people are not serving our Lord Christ, but their own appetites. By smooth talk and flattery they deceive the minds of naive people.   *– Romans 16:18*

You were running a good race. Who cut in on you to keep you from obeying the truth? That kind of persuasion does not come from the one who calls you. "A little yeast works through the whole batch of dough" (yeast refers to false teaching). *I am confident in the Lord that you will take no other view. The one who is throwing you into confusion, whoever that may be, will have to pay the penalty.*   *– Galatians 5:7-10*

The difference between a saved man and an unsaved man is simply this: One has received the light of God's Word into his soul, and the other continues to reject it:

In the beginning was the Word, and the Word was with God, and the Word was God… Through him all things were made… In him was life, and that life was the light of men. The light shines in the darkness, but the darkness has not understood it.   *– John 1:1-4*

The reality that some men will perish in time – and in eternity – is determined by the simple fact that they refused to allow the light of the Word of God to permeate their dark, sinful being:

Just as they did not think it worthwhile to retain the knowledge of God, so God gave them over to a depraved mind, so that they do what ought not to be done. They have become filled with every kind of wickedness, evil, greed and depravity. They are full of envy, murder, strife, deceit and malice.   *– Romans 1:28*

You also were included in Christ when you heard the word of truth, the gospel of your salvation…. For this reason, ever since I heard about your faith in the Lord Jesus…I keep asking that the God of our Lord Jesus Christ, the glorious Father, may give you the Spirit of wisdom and revelation, so that you may know him better. I pray also that the eyes of your heart may be enlightened in order that you may know the hope to which he has called you, the riches of his glorious inheritance in the saints and his incomparably great power for us who believe.

– Ephesians 1:13-19

God provided Jesus to deliver you from the penalty of sin, just like God has provided his Word to deliver you from the power of sin. It is time to stop being spiritually foolish, but, instead, seek out and understand what the Lord's will is. It is not too difficult to understand. But, even if you think it is, you need to know that there will never be any other alternative.

Be very careful, then, how you live—not as unwise but as wise, making the most of every opportunity, because the days are evil. Therefore do not be foolish, but understand what the Lord's will is.

– Ephesians 5:15-17

… find out what pleases the Lord.   *– Ephesians 5:10*

For we do not write you anything you cannot read or understand.

– 2 Corinthians 1:13

The truth, which lives in us and will be with us forever…   *– 2 John 1:2*

Chapter Sixteen:
Concept Eight
The Mature Believer Produces Fruits of Righteousness

Paul knew that if the believers could hear the Word of God, the seed of Truth would grow in their souls causing them to mature. They would naturally produce the fruit of righteousness in their lives. Much of Paul's apostolic ministry was spent advancing the knowledge of the Word of God through whatever means he could find. Paul communicated the Word of God through travel, speaking, correspondence with letters, training teachers in local churches, and sending trained representatives out with the Word. Paul knew that the Word of God would produce faith for salvation in phase one and knowledge for spiritual maturity in phase two. Paul trusted that the Spirit of God would manifest the fruit of the mature believer's life just as surely as a mature crop produces fruit in the harvest season.

So I say, live by the Spirit, and you will not gratify the desires of the sinful nature….the fruit of the Spirit is love, joy, peace, patience, kindness, goodness, faithfulness, gentleness and self-control…. Since we live by the Spirit, let us keep in step with the Spirit.
– Galatians 5:16, 22, 23, 25

Paul knew his message was not merely man's opinion or human philosophy, but the actual Word of God, so it had the power to transform people. Paul knew he was but a messenger who presented God's Word to people who were then transformed by the power of the Holy Spirit.

I will not venture to speak of anything except what Christ has accomplished through me in leading the Gentiles to obey God by what I have said and done.   *– Romans 15:18*

As for other matters, brothers and sisters, we instructed you how to live in order to please God, as in fact you are living. Now we ask you and urge you in the Lord Jesus to do this more and more. For you know what instructions we gave you by the authority of the Lord Jesus…. Therefore, anyone who rejects this instruction does not reject a human being but God, the very God who gives you his Holy Spirit.
– 1 Thessalonians 4:1-2, 8

I am writing you these instructions so that, if I am delayed, you will know how people ought to conduct themselves in God's household, which is the church of the living God, the pillar and foundation of the truth.   — 1 Timothy 3:14-15

… the faith and love that spring from the hope stored up for you in heaven and about which you have already heard in the true message of the gospel that has come to you. In the same way, the gospel is bearing fruit and growing throughout the whole world—just as it has been doing among you since the day you heard it and truly understood God's grace. You learned it from Epaphras, our dear fellow servant, who is a faithful minister of Christ on our behalf, and who also told us of your love in the Spirit.   — Colossians 1:5-8

Paul knew that if he could just present the Word of God to people, especially believers already living in phase two, there would be production of the fruit of the Spirit and a harvest of righteous deeds among those who heard and received his message.

I planned many times to come to you (but have been prevented from doing so until now) in order that I might have a harvest among you, just as I have had among the other Gentiles.   -Romans 1:13

The mystery of the eternal Word of God becomes known to believers, and that knowledge produces the fruit of righteousness in their lives. This transformation in people, who are the church, make God's character, nature and glory known – not just to other men, but even to the rulers and authorities in heavenly realms. It is not just other people who see the change and witness the fruit of righteousness that spring from the Word of God, but spiritual forces and angelic hosts observe and understand the manifold wisdom of God as it is revealed in man's dramatic transformation.

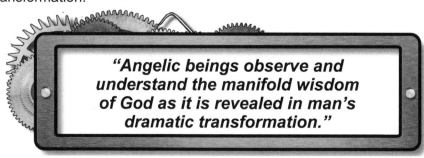

"Angelic beings observe and understand the manifold wisdom of God as it is revealed in man's dramatic transformation."

This grace was given me: to preach to the Gentiles the boundless riches of Christ, and to make plain to everyone the administration of this mystery, which for ages past was kept hidden in God, who created all things. His intent was that now, through the church, the manifold wisdom of God should be made known to the rulers and authorities in the heavenly realms.   – Ephesians 3:8-10

The transforming power of the Word of God in a believer in phase two is not a human work, but the power of God's Spirit. In fact, the message itself isn't powerful because of how prettily it is packaged or how convincingly it is presented, but its power is in itself. The power of the Word is in the message, not in the presentation. The mystery is revealed by the Spirit, not by an articulate orator. Likewise, the proof of the truth of the message is its innate ability to transform a man's soul and produce the fruit of godliness. This transforming power of God is what man needs. It is the power that man should seek from God:

My message and my preaching were not with wise and persuasive words, but with a demonstration of the Spirit's power, so that your faith might not rest on human wisdom, but on God's power.
                                            – 1 Corinthians 2:4-5

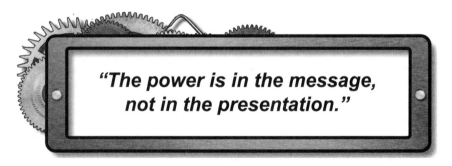

"The power is in the message, not in the presentation."

For the kingdom of God is not a matter of talk but of power.
                                            – 1 Corinthians 4:20

I keep asking that the God of our Lord Jesus Christ, the glorious Father, may give you the Spirit of wisdom and revelation, so that you may know him better. I pray that the eyes of your heart may be enlightened in order that you may know the hope to which he has called you, the riches of his glorious inheritance in his holy people, and his incomparably great power for us who believe. – Ephesians 1:17, 18

"The mystery is revealed by the Spirit, not by an articulate orator."

It is clear that when the Word of God is rejected by man or is replaced in the church with a false message such as legalism, mysticism, philosophy, entertainment or ritualism, the transforming power of the message is lost. It is an obvious blunder for a man to harden his heart against the Word of God. Likewise, it is shortsighted idolatry for a church to follow the cowardly spirit of this age and neglect the teaching of the Truth. Men, even believing Christian men, either remain in or return to worldly views and fleshly behavior when they are scripturally illiterate and malnourished from lacking the bread of life.

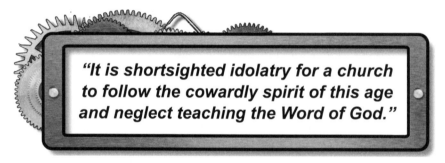

"It is shortsighted idolatry for a church to follow the cowardly spirit of this age and neglect teaching the Word of God."

Brothers and sisters, I could not address you as people who live by the Spirit but as people who are still worldly—mere infants in Christ. I gave you milk, not solid food, for you were not yet ready for it. Indeed, you are still not ready. — 1 Corinthians 3:1-2

The Corinthian church had replaced Paul's teaching with philosophical orations presented by skilled rhetoricians who actively mocked Paul's message and his speaking ability. The result was a church adrift in sin and chaos, and suffering with demonic activity.

You are still worldly. For since there is jealousy and quarreling among you, are you not worldly? Are you not acting like mere men?
                                                          – 1 Corinthians 3:3

When I came to you, brothers, I did not come with eloquence or superior wisdom as I proclaimed to you the testimony about God. For I resolved to know nothing while I was with you except Jesus Christ and him crucified.   *– 1 Corinthians 2:1-2*

For if someone comes to you and preaches a Jesus other than the Jesus we preached, or if you receive a different spirit from the one you received, or a different gospel from the one you accepted, you put up with it easily enough. But I do not think I am in the least inferior to those "super-apostles". I may not be a trained speaker, but I do have knowledge. We have made this perfectly clear to you in every way…. And I will keep on doing what I am doing in order to cut the ground from under those who want an opportunity to be considered equal with us in the things they boast about. For such men are false apostles, deceitful workmen, masquerading as apostles of Christ. And no wonder, for Satan himself masquerades as an angel of light. It is not surprising, then, if his servants masquerade as servants of righteousness. Their end will be what their actions deserve.   *– 2 Corinthians 11:4-6; 12-15*

Realizing that a false Jesus, a false spirit, a false gospel or anything that replaces the Word of God will not only result in the lack of a harvest of righteousness, but will also breed sinful behavior, Paul continued to teach the Word of God and call lost believers back to the Truth. In this next verse, Paul calls the bad teaching "bad company", and refers to the fruit of the Spirit in the transformed man as "good character". Paul says:

Do not be misled: "Bad company corrupts good character."
                                                          – 1 Corinthians 15:33

Simply said, "bad doctrine corrupts the righteous transformation of a man," and "bad teaching produces bad fruit".

The Apostle John contrasts the man who is born again but remains ignorant of God's Word with the man who is born again and knowledgeable of the Word.

Whoever says, "I know him," but does not do what he commands is a liar, and the truth is not in that person. But if anyone obeys his word, love for God is truly made complete in them. This is how we know we are in him: Whoever claims to live in him must live as Jesus did.
                                                            – 1 John 2:2-6

In this verse, the man who is saying "I know him" is born again, but he does not know the Word of God. Since he does not know the Word, he does not do what God's word commands. He is lying because he thinks he knows God, but his actions prove otherwise. Since he is living in ignorance and sin during phase two, he proves he has not continued in the Word of God that saved him in phase one. John writes here that we need to know and obey the Word of God in phase two, so that our salvation from phase one will continue on and ultimately lead to our salvation being made complete in phase three – which is the resurrection of the physical body into an eternal state.

Paul uses the phrase "in him" to refer to our positional righteousness in Christ (as in Ephesians 1:4, 7, 11; Colossians 2:11). John uses it to refer to our hearing, knowing, believing and living the Word in our lives – that is, in reference to our temporal righteousness (phase two). Consider how John uses "in him" in John 17:20-23 and John 15:1-17 in reference to a believer continuing in the Word of God during phase two in order to produce the fruit of righteousness in his life:

My prayer is not for them alone. I pray also for those who will believe in me through their message (phase one)*, that all of them may be one, Father, just as you are in me and I am in you. May they also be in us* (phase two) *so that the world may believe that you have sent me. I have given them the glory that you gave me, that they may be one as we are one— I in them and you in me—so that they may be brought to complete unity* (see also Ephesians 4:12-14)*. Then the world will know that you sent me and have loved them even as you have loved me.*
                                                            – John 17:20-23

I am the true vine, and my Father is the gardener. He cuts off every branch in me that bears no fruit, while every branch that does bear fruit he prunes so that it will be even more fruitful. You are already clean because of the word I have spoken to you (phase one). *Remain in me, as I also remain in you* (phase two). *No branch* (a born-again person) *can bear fruit by itself; it must remain in the vine* (the Word of God). *Neither can you bear fruit unless you remain in me. I am the vine; you are the branches. If you remain in me and I in you, you will bear much fruit* (in phase two); *apart from me* (ignorance of the Word) *you can do nothing. If you do not remain in me* (do not continue in the Word), *you are like a branch that is thrown away and withers; such branches are picked up, thrown into the fire and burned* (not referring to eternal damnation in the Lake of Fire, but to the Bema Seat as in 1 Corinthians 3:11-15). *If you remain in me and my words remain in you, ask whatever you wish, and it will be done for you* (accomplishing God's will in history). *This is to my Father's glory* (cf Ephesians 3:8-11), *that you bear much fruit, showing yourselves to be my disciples. As the Father has loved me, so have I loved you. Now remain in my love. If you keep my commands, you will remain in my love, just as I have kept my Father's commands and remain in his love. I have told you this so that my joy may be in you and that your joy may be complete* (phase three; see Philippians 4:1; 1 Thessalonians 2:19). *My command is this: Love each other as I have loved you* (this is one kind of fruit in phase two). *Greater love has no one than this: to lay down one's life for one's friends. You are my friends if you do what I command. I no longer call you servants, because a servant does not know his master's business. Instead, I have called you friends, for everything that I learned from my Father I have made known to you. You did not choose me, but I chose you and appointed you so that you might go and bear fruit—fruit that will last—and so that whatever you ask in my name the Father will give you. This is my command: Love each other.*   – John 15:1-17

The one who keeps God's commands lives in him, and he in them.
    – 1 John 3:24

The fruit of the mature believer who has continued in the Word of God after his salvation is the righteousness manifested in his life. The New Testament continually connects this spiritual fruit to the spiritual maturity attained by knowing, believing and understanding the Word of God.

Paul, a servant of God and an apostle of Jesus Christ to further the faith of God's elect and their knowledge of the truth that leads to godliness.   – Titus 1:1

The nature of the eternal God and the Truth and
Reality that exist because of Him have established
absolute good, right, moral. To live in agreement with
them is holiness, while deviation is sin. Holiness will
produce fruit, but sin will result in chaos.

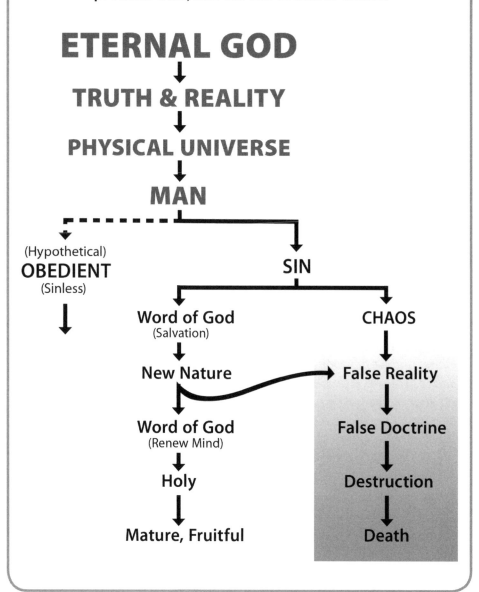

Paul tells Titus in this verse that the born-again believers – referred to as "God's elect", who already had faith – will produce a "godliness" that comes from their "knowledge of the truth". Godliness is the fruit that comes from the seed of the knowledge of God's Word.

Peter tells his readers that "grace and peace" from God are accessible through knowledge. But, not only that, Peter continues by saying that "everything we need for a godly life" has been given to us and is available "through our knowledge" of God. We were given all of this at the moment of salvation (phase one), but it is accessed when we understand (phase two):

Grace and peace be yours in abundance through the knowledge of God and of Jesus our Lord. His divine power has given us everything we need for a godly life through our knowledge of him who called us by his own glory and goodness.   *– 2 Peter 1:2, 3*

Our new nature is the result of being born again and transformed into the image of God. Now is when we renew our minds to understand this great spiritual reality and begin manifesting the new nature in our thoughts, words and deeds. Paul refers to this process as "putting on the new self":

Put on the new self, which is being renewed in knowledge in the image of its Creator.   *– Colossians 3:10*

That, however, is not the way of life you learned when you heard about Christ and were taught in him in accordance with the truth that is in Jesus. You were taught, with regard to your former way of life, to put off your old self, which is being corrupted by its deceitful desires; to be made new in the attitude of your minds; and to put on the new self, created to be like God in true righteousness and holiness.
– Ephesians 4:20-24

Only those who have believed on Jesus Christ in phase one and then learned the Word of God in phase two can really enjoy the good things God has created:

Which God created to be received with thanksgiving by those who believe and who know the truth.   *– 1 Timothy 4:3*

In the verse above, "those who believe" represent phase one; those who "know the truth" represent phase two. Mature believers can truly enjoy life and discern between fun times and immoral activity. Immature believers, who lack knowledge, will impose ascetic standards (i.e., legalistic expectations) on themselves and others in an attempt to prove or attain spiritual maturity, as is documented in 1 Corinthians chapter 8.

Legalism is not a testimony to the world; legalism is bondage to the world. The true testimony is the fruit of the mature believer. This is the testimony that will win the world.

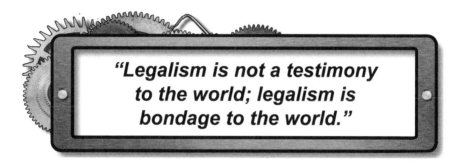

"Legalism is not a testimony to the world; legalism is bondage to the world."

If any of them do not believe the word, they may be won over without words by the behavior of their wives. — 1 Peter 3:1

The Word of God equips the man of God for the production of good works:

...the Holy Scriptures, which are able to make you wise for salvation through faith in Christ Jesus. All Scripture is God-breathed and is useful for teaching, rebuking, correcting and training in righteousness, so that the servant of God may be thoroughly equipped for every good work. — 2 Timothy 3:15-17

As we continue to hear and understand the Word of Life, our outer lives will continue to be transformed, and we will produce the fruit of righteousness.

Continue to work out your salvation (phase two, not one) *with fear and trembling, for it is God who works in you to will and to act according to his good purpose. Do everything without complaining or arguing, so that you may become blameless and pure, children of God without fault in a warped and crooked generation. Then you will shine among them like stars in the sky as you hold firmly to the word of life. And then I will be able to boast on the day of Christ* (phase three) *that I did not run or labor in vain.* – Philippians 2:15-16

The goal of a Bible teacher is to communicate the Word of God to others, just as the job of the farmer in the spring is to plant his fields with the seed of the crop he hopes to harvest in the fall. The wise farmer does not labor at harvesting in the spring, for he realizes that the fruit of the crop comes from the seed that must first be planted. Likewise, the Bible teacher first sows the Word of God into the hearts of his listeners and does not try to harvest where no seeds have been sown. Legalism does this. Legalism demands production based merely on the need for a harvest. The foolish Bible teacher is just like the foolish farmer who searches for a crop he never planted.

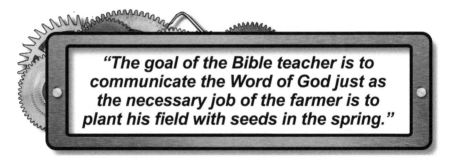

"The goal of the Bible teacher is to communicate the Word of God just as the necessary job of the farmer is to plant his field with seeds in the spring."

Like the wise farmer plants seeds in the spring, the wise Bible teacher also sows seed – and they are both filled with joy when the crop appears bearing its fruit. This is the joy that the Apostle John and the other New Testament writers speak of. It is the joy of a harvest of righteousness in the lives of those who heard the teaching of the Truth:

It has given me great joy to find some of your children walking in the truth, just as the Father commanded us. – 2 John 4

The "walking" above is the fruit of righteousness, and the "truth" is the seed in the mind of the believer. It was a great day in the fall of John's life when he heard that his teaching was producing fruit.

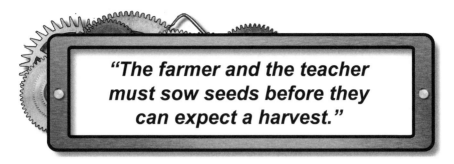

"The farmer and the teacher must sow seeds before they can expect a harvest."

It gave me great joy when some believers came and testified about your faithfulness to the truth, telling how you continue to walk in it. I have no greater joy than to hear that my children are walking in the truth.   — 3 John 3-4

We are made righteous in Christ and delivered from the penalty of sin in phase one. We are delivered from the power of sin in phase two when we dwell in the Truth of God's Word.

You have purified yourselves by obeying the truth.   — 1 Peter 1:22

Chapter Seventeen:
Concept Nine
The Production of the Believer is Rewarded in Eternity

Believers will be rewarded in eternity.

This fact has been made more than clear in scripture. It should also be clear that our rewards in heaven will not be based on what happens in phase one, since salvation is a gift and the gift is in itself the reward. An illustration of this point could be made by imagining someone receiving a birthday present, and then being awarded a trophy for having received a gift. This would make no sense. The gift is by nature greater in meaning than any reward that could be given for having received it. And certainly the idea of getting a reward for having done nothing but receive a gift is illogical in itself.

The point here is that the receiving of salvation in phase one is not worthy of being rewarded. Salvation is offered equally to all, and it is equally powerful to all who receive it. One person cannot be saved to a higher position in heaven, or with a more intense level of "salvation energy" than another person. Nor can someone work harder and believe extra earnestly in order to receive a special upgraded salvation package. There is one Savior and one salvation offered to all. So we can see that there are no rewards for receiving the gift of salvation – other than the gift itself, which is the indescribable grace that recreates us into children of God who will abide with him forever in eternity.

It is only in phase two that different levels of understanding, obedience, accomplishments and rewards are achieved. Salvation is not maintained or destroyed in phase two, nor is it earned or lost. Instead, what ideally happens in phase two is that:
- Our minds are renewed to the truth of the Word of God
- We grow in our salvation
- We employ the powers of our salvation to produce the good works, service, ministry, and fruit appropriate to eternal salvation in our temporal lives as mature believers

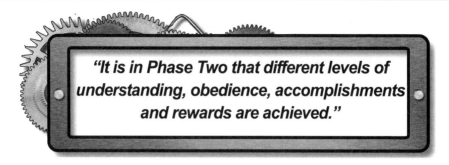

"It is in Phase Two that different levels of understanding, obedience, accomplishments and rewards are achieved."

Or, of course, we could fail to progress in our knowledge of salvation, which would result in a less than desirable level of spiritual maturity, incapable of producing the fruits of righteousness. In the end, the assessment of our production in phase two could be compared to an evaluation based on a scale of one through ten. For illustration purposes, imagine standing before the Bema Seat of Christ and being judged on a scale of one to ten with one being no spiritual growth and ten being maximum spiritual growth, with the corresponding production. Two through nine on this scale would fall somewhere between zero growth with zero production and a completely mature life filled with fruitful service.

Growth and maturity in phase two begin with a mind renewed to the Word of God. The mature soul will naturally produce the fruit desired by God. This fruit will manifest in a mature believer's life in a variety of ways, some of which are described in the Bible as:
1. Fruit of the Spirit (Galatians 5:22-23)
2. Fruit of Righteousness (Philippians 1:11)
3. Identification and development of spiritual gifts (1 Peter 4:10-11)
4. Ministry service (1 Corinthians 3:6-9)
5. Good deeds (2 Corinthians 5:9-10)

This entire process is captured in these words written by Paul to the Philippians in 61 AD:

This is my prayer: that your love may abound more and more in knowledge and depth of insight, so that you may be able to discern what is best and may be pure and blameless until the day of Christ, filled with the fruit of righteousness that comes through Jesus Christ – to the glory and praise of God.   – Philippians 1:9-11

Paul explains that during phase two, insight into God's Word will empower the believers' minds to discern the correct course of action in their daily lives and ministries. As these believers live their lives in the light of this insight, they will live blameless lives and produce the fruit of righteousness until they stand before Jesus Christ on the day he evaluates his saints.

The day of this judgment is a day in the future which occurs after the resurrection from the dead (phase three, the salvation of our bodies). It is at this time that our salvation will be complete, and we will be evaluated and rewarded for our production during phase two:

You will be repaid at the resurrection of the righteous (phase three).
— Luke 14:14

Now there is in store for me the crown of righteousness, which the Lord, the righteous Judge, will award to me on that day – and not only to me, but also to all who have longed for his appearing.
— 2 Timothy 4:8

For the Son of Man is going to come in his Father's glory with his angels, and then he will reward each person according to what he has done.   — Matthew 16:27

Paul considers himself to be on this same performance-based reward system. In his letter to the Corinthians, he describes himself in partnership with another Bible teacher, Apollos. Both Paul and Apollos have assignments from God, and each will be rewarded for their labor in assisting God in the growth of the seed – which is the Word of God sown in the souls of believers:

I have planted the seed, Apollos watered it, but God made it grow. So neither he who plants nor he who waters is anything, but only God, who makes things grow. The man who plants and the man who waters have one purpose, and each will be rewarded according to his own labor. For we are all God's fellow workers; you are God's field, God's building.
— 1 Corinthians 3:6-9

Therefore I do not run like someone running aimlessly; I do not fight like a boxer beating the air. No, I strike a blow to my body and make it my slave so that after I have preached to others, I myself will not be disqualified for the prize.   *– 1 Corinthians 9:26-27*

In fact, he states that his ministry will only be proven effective if he fulfills his assigned duties, which means seeing the fruit of righteousness in the lives of his listeners:

For what is our hope, our joy, or the crown in which we will glory in the presence of our Lord Jesus when he comes? Is it not you? Indeed, you are our glory and joy.   *– 1 Thessalonians 2:19-20*

Paul thinks of his life as an opportunity to continue to labor and produce the fruit of righteousness:

If I am to go on living in the body, this will mean fruitful labor for me.
                                                                  – Philippians 1:22

He tells his listeners clearly that his motivation is to please the Lord, since he will be judged in the future by the Lord at the bema seat:

So we make it our goal to please him, whether we are at home in the body or away from it. For we must all appear before the judgment seat (bema) of Christ, that each one may receive what is due him for the things done while in the body, whether good or bad.
                                                             – 2 Corinthians 5:9-10

The goal of Paul's ministry was to sow Truth into the hearts of believers and help lead them to maturity. Paul knew that the Word of God was the power of God, and that it would empower people to be saved (in phase one) and then mature to fruitfulness (in phase two) so that they could stand blameless and praiseworthy before Jesus Christ at the bema seat (in phase three):

So that you may become blameless and pure, children of God without fault in a warped and crooked generation. Then you will shine among them like stars in the sky as you hold firmly to the word of life. And then I will be able to boast on the day of Christ (bema) that I did not run or labor in vain.   *– Philippians 2:15-16*

He is the one we proclaim, admonishing and teaching everyone with all wisdom, so that we may present everyone fully mature in Christ. To this end I strenuously contend with all the energy Christ so powerfully works in me.   *– Colossians 1:28-29*

Paul warns the Bible teachers and those who hear the teaching of the Word of God to be careful how they build in the souls of people. If the Bible teacher is diligent to present the Word faithfully, it will produce the desired results in the lives of the people. And on the day of judgment at the bema seat of Christ, there will be rewards for the faithful Bible teacher who has planted the Truth in people's souls and built his teaching on the Word of God. The building materials of his ministry are noble and eternal because they are Truth and reality.

But, Paul then goes on to explain that some men are imposters, teaching things that are not truth, are not reality, and are not based on the eternal Word of God. These men are teaching mere human philosophies, religious rituals or legalistic standards. The fruit from this teaching is worthless, since the fields of people's souls have been sown with lies – and the building, which represents their lives and was supposed to be built upon the foundation of Jesus Christ, is instead built with worthless and worldly things called wood, hay and straw. These buildings and this work will be consumed in the fire of evaluation, and the foolish Bible teachers and their students will lose everything they thought they had accomplished during phase two. It must be understood that they will be saved from eternal damnation, since they had understood and believed the truth of salvation in Jesus. But in phase two they soon left the Truth and did not continue in the Word. They will suffer loss. They will suffer a lifetime of loss.

By the grace God has given me (he was called to be an apostle), I laid a foundation as an expert builder (Paul taught the Corinthians salvation through Jesus, phase one),
and someone else is building on it (other Christian leaders are teaching the Corinthians, phase two).
But each one (each of the teachers)
should be careful how he builds. For no one can lay any foundation other than the one already laid, which is Jesus Christ (the true Bible teacher must build his doctrine upon the common doctrine that Jesus Christ is the means of salvation).

If any man builds (phase two)
on this foundation (salvation from phase one)
using gold, silver, costly stones (Truth and reality from the Word
    of God),
wood, hay or straw, (philosophy, tradition, asceticism in imitation of
    God's Word)
his work will be shown for what it is (good or worthless),
because the Day (bema seat of Christ)
will bring it to light (motive and doctrine of teacher revealed to all).
It will be revealed with fire (the judgment of Christ),
and the fire will test the quality of each man's work (teaching, doctrine).
If what he has built survives (as true and good),
he will receive his reward. If it is burned up (as empty and worthless),
he will suffer loss (loss of rewards potentially achieved in phase two;
    but not of salvation received in phase one);
he himself will be saved (eternal life),
but only as one escaping through the flames (a torched life; failure in
    phase two).   – 1 Corinthians 3:10-15

Not only will the building materials of Bible teachers be evaluated, but so will the attitude of their hearts that motivated them to build and inspired them to sow. Paul encourages believers to wait and see how God will evaluate the ministers of the Word. The motive of some men of God who are remembered as great men in history will be revealed as just that – greatness in the eyes of the world. Other unknown teachers, who were faithful to the Word and productive in their lives, will be called out of the masses on that day to receive praise and honor from the Lord for their service during phase two. Of course, we will also see those who were highly regarded on earth among those who are greatly rewarded by God (see Luke 2:52). We will not know which is which until the Lord reveals them at the bema seat:

> *...wait till the Lord comes. He will bring to light what is hidden in darkness and will expose the motives of men's hearts. At that time (phase three) each will receive his praise from God.* – 1 Corinthians 4:5

Jesus told the story of a man who would be judged worthless by the master (at the bema seat) because he did not perform the task of servanthood that had been entrusted to him (Luke 19:12-27). Jesus called him wicked and lazy. Jesus also warns the readers of Revelation to be sure no one steals their eternal rewards or crowns (crown is the word stephanos, which is not a royal crown, but the crown that goes to the victor). Jesus tells them to hold on to what they have, but he is not talking about holding on to salvation from phase one – rather, about continuing to live in obedience to the Word in phase two. Without the Word they will not attain or keep their eternal crowns of victory:

> *Hold on to what you have, so that no one will take your crown. The one who is victorious I will make a pillar in the temple of my God.*
> — Revelation 3:11

Twenty years after Peter and Paul died, the Apostle John wrote from Ephesus to the second generation of Christian believers about the importance of staying in the revealed, written Word of God and allowing the Holy Spirit to manifest the fruit of righteousness in their lives. John warned that there were false teachers who thought they could provide additions to the Word of God, but that this new teaching was false and not in line with the Apostles' doctrine. He further warned that they could lose their fruit and rewards if they accepted this false teaching and followed it:

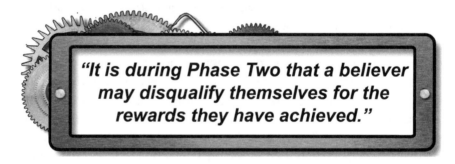

"It is during Phase Two that a believer may disqualify themselves for the rewards they have achieved."

I am writing these things to you about those who are trying to lead you astray. As for you, the anointing (the Holy Spirit) *you received from him* (in phase one) *remains in you* (during phase two), *and you do not need anyone to teach you* (anything new). *But as his anointing teaches you about all things* (concerning the Truth that has been revealed in the written Word of God; there is no new revelation for these false teachers to teach you) *and as that anointing is real, not counterfeit* (a new spirit that says it has new or additional information)—*just as it* (the Holy

Spirit and the Word) *has taught you, remain in him* (in Jesus' Word, the Holy Spirit, and the Apostolic teaching – do not follow the new, strange doctrine of false teachers). *And now, dear children, continue in him* (continue in the Word until you mature and produce fruit), *so that when he appears we may be confident and unashamed before him at his coming* (at the bema seat). *If you know that he is righteous, you know that everyone who does what is right has been born of him* (what you know becomes what you will do).   – 1 John 2:26-29

I say this because many deceivers, who do not acknowledge Jesus Christ as coming in the flesh, have gone out into the world. Any such person is the deceiver and the antichrist. Watch out that you do not lose what we have worked for (in phase two), *but that you may be rewarded fully* (at the bema seat). *Anyone who runs ahead* (into new revelation and false teaching) *and does not continue in the teaching of Christ does not have God* (in their teaching or in their minds); *whoever continues in the teaching has both the Father and the Son* (in their teaching and producing in their souls). *If anyone comes to you and does not bring this teaching, do not take them into your house or welcome them. Anyone who welcomes them shares in their wicked work* (which is destroying the maturity, production and rewards of believers).   – 2 John 7-11

In the final chapter of the last book of the Bible Jesus is recorded as speaking to the church through the Apostle John:

Behold, I am coming soon! My reward is with me, and I will give to everyone according to what he has done.   – Revelation 22:12

Chapter Eighteen:
Concept Ten
False Teaching, Doctrinal Errors, Deceit, and Ignorance
Destroy any Possibility of Christian Maturity and Production

While apostles Paul, Peter, James, John, and Jude continued to teach the truth and remind their listeners to continue in that truth, they were also active in refuting and exposing false teaching and philosophies that could interrupt the believer's spiritual growth. We should keep in mind this promise (a warning, really) given to us by Peter:

> *There were also false prophets among the people, just as there will be false teachers among you. They will secretly introduce destructive heresies.* — 2 Peter 2:1

Some false teachers in Corinth challenged Paul, claiming that his teaching was not as important as their teaching, or even as necessary as their customs. Some of the early teachers were more interested in doing what they considered to be religious activity than in teaching the Word of God. One significant reason for this neglect of teaching seems to be that focusing on other topics made it easier to attract and impress even a Christian crowd. These imposters would skip the teaching and go right to some kind of application or philosophy. In addition to this, they would mock Paul's teaching and belittle his barrage of letters as insufficient when compared to their wisdom, tolerance, legalistic code and strict ritualism. Paul responded to this pseudo-Christian approach to disciple-training in 2 Corinthians when he said:

> *You are looking only on the surface of things. If anyone is confident that he belongs to Christ, he should consider again that we belong to Christ just as much as he. For even if I boast somewhat freely about the authority the Lord gave us for building you up* (teaching the Word of God) *rather than pulling you down, I will not be ashamed of it. I do not want to seem to be trying to frighten you with my letters. For some say, "His letters are weighty and forceful, but in person he is unimpressive and his speaking amounts to nothing." Such people should realize that what we are in our letters when we are absent, we will be in our actions when we are present. We do not dare to classify or compare ourselves*

with some who commend themselves. When they measure themselves by themselves and compare themselves with themselves (instead with of the Word of God), *they are not wise.*   – 2 Corinthians 10:7-12

This first century situation is very similar to the modern church's defense for its own neglect of Bible teaching. Today many churches talk and behave in a way that says, "Preaching application is more important than teaching truth." Paul's words to the imposters of 56 AD in Corinth echo through the centuries into many modern churches that continually excuse their lack of teaching by claiming to be busy ministering to the people and taking care of "real" needs. Of course, this is exactly what the false teachers in Corinth claimed to be doing when they taught the wisdom of the philosopher and called the preaching of the cross foolish.

For the message of the cross is foolishness to those who are perishing…. For it is written: "I will destroy the wisdom of the wise; the intelligence of the intelligent I will frustrate"…. Jews demand miraculous signs and Greeks look for wisdom, but we preach Christ crucified: a stumbling block to Jews and foolishness to Gentiles, but to those whom God has called, both Jews and Greeks, Christ the power of God and the wisdom of God. For the foolishness of God is wiser than man's wisdom, and the weakness of God is stronger than man's strength.
                                                        – 1 Corinthians 1:18-25

To those today who say application is more important than pure teaching, the Word of God through Paul simply responds by saying, "We are what we write" and "We do what we teach":

Such people should realize that what we are in our letters when we are absent, we will be in our actions when we are present.
                                                        – 1 Corinthians 10:11

This question must be asked to counter those who glorify application while they neglect the teaching of the Word: If you do not teach and you do not know, what exactly are you applying? If application is not preceded by teaching, and action does not follow after knowledge, then the application is false and the action is void of spiritual value. This is exactly what the apostles warned believers to flee.

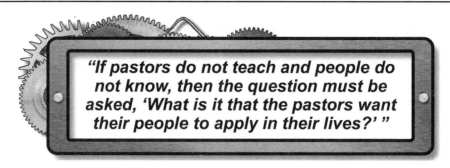

"If pastors do not teach and people do not know, then the question must be asked, 'What is it that the pastors want their people to apply in their lives?'"

In 1 Corinthians 4:1 Paul tells the Corinthians that Apollos and he are simply continuing to teach the Word of God that was entrusted to them by God:

So then, men ought to regard us as servants of Christ and as those entrusted with the secret things of God. — 1 Corinthians 4:1

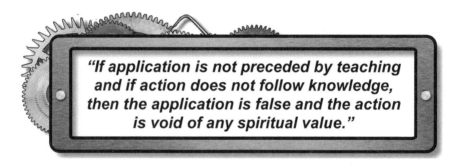

"If application is not preceded by teaching and if action does not follow knowledge, then the application is false and the action is void of any spiritual value."

Paul then goes on to tell them that he is using himself and Apollos as examples in order to demonstrate a principal. Paul and Apollos are servants of the Word of God and will be judged by the Word of God. It is important to stay within the limits of Scripture to determine what should be taught, what should be done, and how men should be evaluated. Paul then asks the Corinthians why they think they are any different from him, Apollos, and other churches:

I have applied these things to myself and Apollos for your benefit, so that you may learn from us the meaning of the saying, "Do not go beyond what is written (gegraptai)" .... For who makes you different from anyone else? What do you have that you did not receive? And if you did receive it, why do you boast as though you did not? — 1 Corinthians 4:6-7

When Paul says, "Do not go beyond what is written," he uses the perfect indicative passive tense of grapho which means "to write". This word is always used by Paul when he refers to or introduces the Old Testament scriptures. It is a word that identifies writings of an authoritative nature. Interestingly, grapho is also used by Peter in reference to Paul's writings (2 Pt. 3:16).

Paul then asks three rhetorical questions to expose the Corinthians' error of abandoning the authority of Scripture in searching for truth and defending their heretical positions. Paul's three questions make these three statements:
1. Everyone has Scripture and everyone else follows Scripture!
2. Any Scripture you Corinthians possess has come to you from God through an apostle. None of it came from your own mystical experience, ability, philosophical wisdom or insight.
3. If you have received the Truth from God (through his apostles), why are you so full of pride concerning your own philosophies. Why do you act as if you have something or know something that is not common to all of us through God's Word?

The Corinthian church was in trouble because they were moving outside of the word of God concerning:
1. What they taught
2. What they believed to be the truth
3. How they judged leaders and teachers
4. What they considered appropriate behavior
5. How they lived their lives

Because of these things, the assessment of Scripture is that the Christians in Corinth were void of spiritual fruit because of bad doctrine, their preference for imposters in the pulpits, and the neglect of teaching the Word of God by church leadership. The Corinthians' "application" of Christianity was a complete fiasco because they operated based on the wisdom of the world instead of the wisdom from God's Word. The "wisdom" of the false teachers was not producing the fruit of the Spirit, but instead, the works of the flesh (see Galatians 5:19-21). The only ones benefiting from this false doctrine were the false teachers. These imposters enjoyed the power inherent in their positions and used it to gain a financial subsidy. This, however, was only a temporary gain when compared to the eternal rewards they were forfeiting.

I urge you, brothers and sisters, to watch out for those who cause divisions (works of the flesh) *and put obstacles* (false doctrines) *in your way that are contrary to the teaching you have learned* (apostolic revelation recorded in scripture). *Keep away from them* (false teachers). *For such people are not serving our Lord Christ, but their own appetites* (power and money). *By smooth talk and flattery they deceive the minds of naive people* (those with no knowledge of the Word of God).   – Romans 16:17-18

And here is the end of the matter: False teaching destroys any possibility of spiritual maturity and its fruit. Paul says it this way:

Do not be misled: "Bad company corrupts good character."
                                                      – 1 Corinthians 15:33

Not surprisingly, when Paul talks about "Bad Company", he is not referring to the rock and roll band from the 1970's. Rather, he means the bad teaching that corrupts the production of righteousness in the life of a believer. Good teaching produces good behavior. Bad doctrine corrupts good character. Bad teaching produces bad fruit.

The mind needs Truth in order to mature and produce righteousness. Sincerity and devotion to a cause are a good starting point, but are like the fuel and engine of a locomotive. Fuel burning in a train engine set at full throttle is only successful and productive if the entire train – from engine to caboose – is on the tracks. If any car is off the tracks – or, if there are no tracks at all – that fuel becomes potentially explosive, and the whole situation is dangerous and not likely to end well. In the same way, devotion is the fuel for the engine of sincerity, but our metaphorical train must be running on the tracks of Truth. A sincere and serious Christian, even one devoted to Christ, has to get on track with the Word of God.

To better get the picture, imagine a sincere and devoted Christian without Bible teaching. Now, in your head, hear Ozzy Osbourne singing: "Life's a bitter shame, I'm going off the rails on a crazy train." And there you have it. Life without Bible doctrine is "a bitter shame" because you are "going off the rails on a crazy train". The Word of God will produce righteousness in the life of a devoted believer, but false doctrine will cause sincerity and devotion to crash on the rocks of reality. Only Truth will lead you through reality. Paul credits the Corinthians (like Eve, by the way) with having sincerity and devotion. But Paul is also having trouble getting them to live righteous lives, because their minds have been led astray.

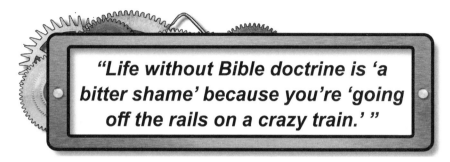

> *"Life without Bible doctrine is 'a bitter shame' because you're 'going off the rails on a crazy train.'"*

But I am afraid that just as Eve was deceived by the serpent's cunning, your minds may somehow be led astray from your sincere and pure devotion to Christ.   *– 2 Corinthians 11:3*

Minds must be renewed to Christ's Word. Otherwise, they will be deceived by the Serpent. "Sincere and pure devotion to Christ" requires minds renewed to the Word of Christ in order to avoid being led astray. This battle for the mind is the most serious battle a person can engage in. Even if a man does not know, understand, or want to engage the enemy in this war, his mind will still be the battlefield where the rebel forces of a pseudo-reality rise up to meet the forces of Truth. Given this, it would just make sense if the Christian were given some assistance by his church in the hearing, interpreting and understanding the Word of God.

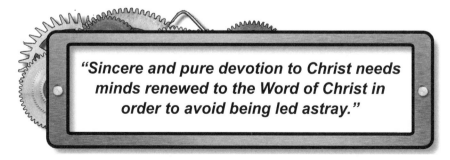

> *"Sincere and pure devotion to Christ needs minds renewed to the Word of Christ in order to avoid being led astray."*

There is no middle ground for a church: it is either actively teaching the Word of God, or it is not. To not teach the Word is to teach deception. It is really that simple. And, it is that serious. If a church is opening its doors to people, then that church is "teaching" something, even if that something is nothing more than allowing people to continue in their own personal views of God. If a church tries to stay neutral, non-combative and tolerant – perhaps passively refraining from speaking against the Bible, or actively refusing to embrace the scriptures by reading or teaching directly from them – that church is an imposter promoting false doctrine.

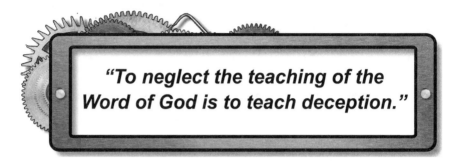

"To neglect the teaching of the Word of God is to teach deception."

Paul describes the supernatural power that the Word of God has in this battle. The Truth of the Word of God can expose and rip apart the rebel forces that try to take ground in a believer's mind. This fact is captured in a very clear military metaphor that Paul used to express to the rebel Corinthians the purpose, activity and goal of his ministry:

The weapons we fight with are not the weapons of the world. On the contrary, they have divine power to demolish strongholds. We demolish arguments and every pretension that sets itself up against the knowledge of God, and we take captive every thought to make it obedient to Christ.   – 2 Corinthians 10:4-6

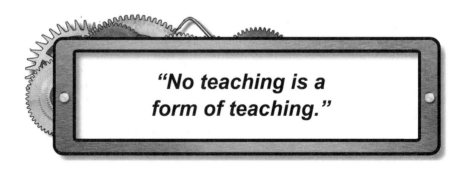

"No teaching is a form of teaching."

The Greek of 2 Corinthians 10:4-6 looks like this:

ta gar	hopla	tes	strateias	hemon	ou	sarkika	alla
for the	weapons	of the	warfare	of us are	not	fleshly	but

dunata	to	theo	pros	kathairesin	ochuromaton	logismous
powerful	to	God	to	overthrow	of strongholds	reasonings

kathairountes	kai	pan	hupsoma	epairomenon	kata	tes
overthrowing	and	every	high thing	rising up	against	the

gnoseos	tou	theou	kai	aichmalotizovtes	pan	noema	eis
knowledge	of	God	and	taking captive	every	design	to

ten	hupakoen	tou	christou
the	obedience	of	Christ

Hopla is translated "weapons" and refers to instruments of warfare. It describes either a defensive weapon such as a shield, or an offensive weapon such as a sword. In this context, the word "weapons" is a metaphor for the Truth of the Word of God. We know that the Word is supernatural seed that produces the fruit of righteousness, but here it is described as the supernatural sword that destroys the stronghold of false teaching in the minds of men. No other weapon other than the Word of God can possibly possess this supernatural power of exposing and defeating false teaching – any other will come from the same source as the false teaching, worldly philosophies and human reasoning that it attempts to banish. Only the Word of God originates with God, and so, only the Word of God can defeat wicked teachings that come from fallen men and evil spirits. The spiritual battle is an either/or battle. Everything in it is either the Truth or it is a lie. Only the Truth can crush the lie. A lesser lie cannot expose a greater lie – it can only add to the deception, which makes the wall of the evil fortress stronger and higher.

Strateias is translated "warfare" and is from the word stratos meaning an "expedition, a campaign, or warfare", and is the origin of the English word "strategy". The word involves both the style of warfare and the plan of attack. Satan and the forces of evil have a war plan (Ephesians 6:10), but here in this verse, stratos is talking about our warfare (style, strategy and plan). Our warfare involves using the weapon of the Word of God in our thinking to tear down the towering thoughts of false doctrines and hollow philosophies. Without the weapon of the Word of God we have no warfare. Without the Word of God we have no stratos. Without the Word of God we have no weapons – offensive or defensive – to save our souls in phase two. It is time the church armed their people and gave them a strategy, instead of giving them points of application and distracting them with activities. Why does teaching application instead of the Word of God – and providing distractions instead of Bible studies – sound more like Satan's stratos than Paul's vision for the church?

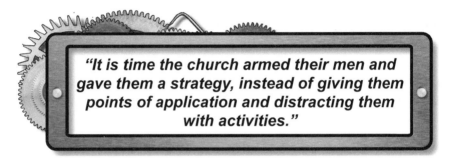

"It is time the church armed their men and gave them a strategy, instead of giving them points of application and distracting them with activities."

Kathairesin is translated "overthrow". It is from the Greek word kathairesis meaning "demolition, tearing down, pulling down, and destroying" and is also figuratively used of extinction. In 2 Corinthians 10:8 and 13:10 Paul says his ministry is not to tear down the Corinthians, but to build them up. In other words, Paul sees his ministry as one that tears down false teaching and then builds up believers by giving them the True teaching.

> *… the authority the Lord gave us for building you up rather than pulling you down* (kaithairesis).   – 2 Corinthians 10:8

> *This is why I write these things when I am absent, that when I come I may not have to be harsh in my use of authority – the authority the Lord gave me for building you up, not for tearing you down* (kaithairesis).
>   – 2 Corinthians 13:10

Ochuromaton is translated "of strongholds" and is from the Greek word ochuroma, which describes "a fortress, a castle, or a citadel" with strong rock walls built high to defend a city or community. Most often a fortress or castle would be built on an important high hill or even a mountain in a strategically valuable position. Likewise, the most important areas of a man's thinking are the first places corrupt doctrines attack with their false teaching in order to build rock walls and towers of deceptive thoughts and vain speculations. These walls are designed to keep the basic tenants of God's Word out of the human mind and forbidden in man's logic: e.g., the existence of God, the depravity of man, the grace of God, eternal judgment, natural institutions such as marriage and family, the absolute reality of truth, etc.

Logismous is translated "reasonings" and is from the Greek word logismos. The English word "logic" comes from logismos. Logic and reasonable thinking is included in God's Truth and reality as revealed in general revelation given to all men, and in special revelation revealed in Scripture. Logic is clearly referred to in the book of Proverbs, but man's ability to reason and use logic must submit itself to the fullness of God's revelation, both general and special. Man can misuse his reasoning abilities to draw seemingly logically conclusions, create philosophies and present ideologies that are actually contrary to the Word of God. Man must use natural logic, but he must also be very careful to keep his reasoning in line with God's Word. If man deviates from the Truth and the reality of God's Word, he will find himself participating in the ancient rebellion against God.

The only way to recapture the fortress of a man's soul (mind) from the rebel forces of false teaching is to tear down the towers and ramparts of empty philosophy that defend the lies, by hearing, understanding and trusting the knowledge of the Word of God. The Word of God provides an arsenal of offensive and defensive weapons necessary to capture and occupy the logic and reasoning of man. This is what Paul means when he says, "we take captive every thought". Our thoughts are like rebels under the control of Satan. We will never take Satan captive, but we can apprehend our thoughts, minds and souls. We can then make our rebel thoughts obedient to the Word of God. In this way we can think and live in God's Truth and reality instead of in Satan's emptiness and rebellion.

Kathairountes is translated "overthrowing" and comes from the world kathaireo which means simply, "to lower". But when this lowering is done with violence, it also means "to demolish". It is a compound word made up of kata ("down") and haireo ("take, cast down, demolish"). Every illogical thought and unreasonable or false teaching can be demolished with the

Word of God. The sword of the Word of God is violently throwing down the hollow philosophies and empty speculation that impersonate wisdom and authenticity. In the Old Testament, these empty philosophies and deceptive doctrines manifested as idol worship, and the images of stone, wood and metal that were created to represent these false worldviews were often "demolished" and "cast down" into rubble in an attempt to deliver the people from their bondage.

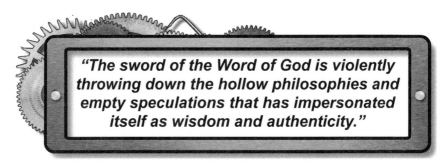

"The sword of the Word of God is violently throwing down the hollow philosophies and empty speculations that has impersonated itself as wisdom and authenticity."

Hupsoma is translated as "high thing", but could also be described as "that which is lifted up, high, and exalted". It refers to man exalting himself. It is the pride and conceit so often described as sinful in Scripture. It is not only pride in relation to other people, but here (as in Romans 1:18-23 and 28) it is pride toward God. It can be a religious attitude that suppresses the Truth of God's Word and does not consider the knowledge of God worthy of being retained when compared to the imaginations and plans of man's depraved mind. This word hupsoma represents the arrogance of man that manifests as self-sufficient in logic, reasoning and wisdom, and so rejects and despises any attempt by God to shine the light of his Truth into the soul. The ultimate result of this attitude is man's hatred, persecution and exclusion of the Word of God.

The wrath of God is being revealed from heaven against all the godlessness and wickedness of men who suppress the truth by their wickedness…. For although they knew God, they neither glorified him as God nor gave thanks to him, but their thinking became futile and their foolish hearts were darkened. Although they claimed to be wise, they became fools and exchanged the glory of the immortal God for images made to look like mortal man…. Since they did not think it worthwhile to retain the knowledge of God, he gave them over to a depraved mind, to do what ought not to be done.
– Romans 1:18, 21-22, 28

Epairomenon is translated "rising up". This word is the present middle participle of epairo which means to "lift up", but in the middle voice its meaning shifts to "to lift yourself up" or "to exalt oneself". The word is used here as an illustration of walls and towers standing defiantly against an approaching army. In this case the approaching army is the Truth of God's Word marching against the self-exalted false teaching that has taken the church captive.

Kata tes gnoseos tou theou is very important to identify accurately. It is in these words that this verse clearly pinpoints why the forces of the opposition are building walls, towers, fortresses and citadels. Paul writes that they "are against the knowledge of God". The rebel troops are bracing themselves for an assault from the Word of God. They are hoping that their elaborate system of walls will prevent escape by anyone held captive to false knowledge and deceived thoughts.

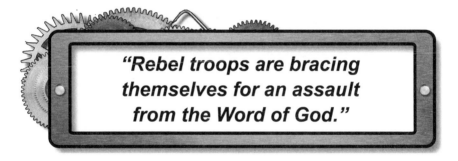

"Rebel troops are bracing themselves for an assault from the Word of God."

Aichmalotizovtes is translated "taking captive" and comes from the word aichmalotizo which means "to make captive" to "lead away captive" or "to bring into captivity". It contains the idea of subjugating and bringing something under control. Paul is saying in 2 Corinthians 10:4-6 that the hearing and understanding of the Word of God will capture disobedient minds and subjugate rebel thoughts. Through the Word, these thoughts will be trained and made obedient to the rule of Christ. It is interesting to note that in 2 Timothy 3:6 the same word is used to describe what false teachers do to the minds of people. That verse warns that imposters will be active in the church and that their deviant teaching will put simple, weak-willed people under their control. But, here in 2 Corinthians 10, the attack is coming from the Word of God, which takes people captive to do the will of God.

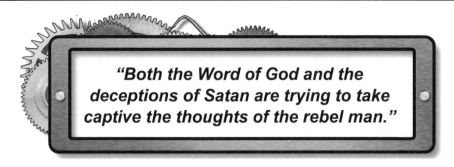

"Both the Word of God and the deceptions of Satan are trying to take captive the thoughts of the rebel man."

Eis is translated "to" which tells us that the thoughts which are taken captive are taken somewhere – to a different location or sphere. The place these thoughts are taken captive to is "to the obedience of Christ". Daniel was taken captive to Babylon where he was trained in all the wisdom, language and literature of the Babylonians. Likewise, our thoughts are taken captive by the Word of God to be trained "to the obedience of Christ". Once this "obedience of Christ" has been accomplished in our thoughts, we will be ready to serve the God of righteousness as we produce the fruit righteousness, just as Daniel was made ready over a period of three years of training to serve Nebuchadnezzar, the king of Babylon, as a Babylonian.

Noema is translated "design" and also means "thought or purpose". The word is used to capture the craftiness of human scheming, which satisfies itself by existing in the fortress of false teaching where the True God is neither needed nor desired. Instead, philosophies that exclude God and manufacture religions with false gods – which mirror the image of their human inventors – are devised.

Weust translates 2 Corinthians 10:4-6 like this:

> The weapons of our warfare are not human but mighty in God's sight, resulting in the demolition of fortresses, demolishing reasonings and every haughty mental elevation which lifts itself up against the experiential knowledge [which we believers have] of God, and leading captive every thought into the obedience to the Christ.

The spiritual weapons used to attack, conqueror, occupy and administer the thoughts of the human soul are teachings from the Word of God. Carnal weapons such as human tradition, man's philosophy, religious ritual or congregational entertainment will not penetrate the fortress of false reality that Satan uses to barricade the human soul. The walls of Satan's citadel not only prevent the infiltration of Truth, but also imprison the human soul. False teaching keeps the mind behind ever-rising prison walls, preventing the captives from even perceiving beyond the deception. In this way, Satan has blinded the minds of men with the dark looming shadows of human thoughts, logic, and reason devoid of God's word.

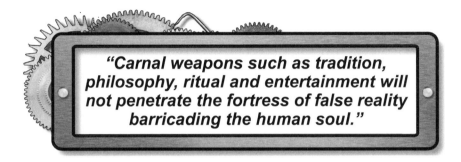

"Carnal weapons such as tradition, philosophy, ritual and entertainment will not penetrate the fortress of false reality barricading the human soul."

The god of this age has blinded the minds of unbelievers so that they cannot see the light of the gospel of the glory of Christ, who is the image of God… For God, who said, "Let light shine out of darkness," made his light shine in our hearts to give us the light of the knowledge of the glory of God in the face of Christ." – 2 Corinthians 4:4, 6

It is from behind these cold, damp stone walls of unreality and vanity that imposters create rituals and legalistic expectations in an attempt give man religion and some (other) kind of god. These ramparts will not be breached with mere human philosophy, religion, or contemporary entertainment inside a church building – even one with a non-profit status. Only the Word of God can dismantle these fortifications and eradicate the rebel forces of falsehood from the human soul.

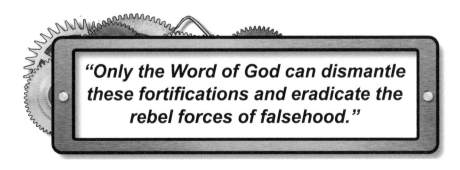

"Only the Word of God can dismantle these fortifications and eradicate the rebel forces of falsehood."

Then you will know the truth, and the truth will set you free.
– Jesus, in John 8:32

Jesus resisted Satan's three early attacks by not only quoting the Word of God, but understanding and believing that Word. Jesus told Satan:

It is written: "Man does not live on bread alone, but on every word that comes from the mouth of God."
– Matthew 4:4 quoting Deuteronomy 8:3

It is also written: "Do not put the Lord your God to the test."
– Matthew 4:7 quoting Deuteronomy 6:16

Away from me, Satan! For it is written: "Worship the Lord your God, and serve him only."
– Matthew 4:10 quoting Deuteronomy 6:13

Ironically, even Satan himself quoted the Word of God. But predictably, he twisted it in order to squeeze out of God's words his own will and desired interpretation (Matthew 4:6; Psalm 91:11, 12). Jesus, however, using scripture to interpret scripture, refuted Satan's deceit with Truth. But sadly, in the Garden, it did not happen that way. There, in the beginning, Satan twisted God's Words to deceive Eve, who did not counter with Truth but was deceived and acted in rebellion against God (Genesis 3:1-6). Satan's first recorded words in Scripture are directed against God's spoken Word revealed to man:

Did God really say, "You must not eat from any tree in the garden?"

Satan then followed up with a statement that is all too typical of the false doctrines and empty philosophies that we read about in Scripture and hear proclaimed today. The second time Satan spoke in Scripture (Genesis 3:4-5) he proclaimed five false doctrines in one statement:

"You will not surely die," the serpent said to the woman. "For God knows that when you eat of it your eyes will be opened, and you will be like God, knowing good and evil."

1. Satan denied the reality of the penalty of death that results from disobeying God's Word
2. Satan claimed to have knowledge about God that was previously unknown to man and revealed this secret knowledge
3. Satan promised benefits and advantages to man if this new philosophy is embraced and followed
4. Satan declared, falsely, that man can become like God
5. Satan predicted that if his plan is observed, the result will be the advancement of mankind from the limited, inhibited condition instigated by God to a place of higher knowledge and performance

Eve's mind was deceived by Satan's intense, tangled mess of lies, deceit, erroneous conclusions and empty philosophy. She disobeyed the Word of God, and her husband, Adam, followed her into a state of rebellion. In 56 AD Paul was rightfully concerned that the same thing was happening in his day among believers in his churches. Paul feared that, just like Satan twisted God's original Words to man, so the Gospel would be twisted by false teachers in order to mislead people.

False teaching includes proclaiming a different gospel than the one that saved us. In contrast, with God and true teaching, you begin in his Word for salvation and you continue in his Word for maturity. If a pastor's teaching leads a saved man away from the teaching of Scripture, then that man is listening to false teaching and a corrupt pastor.

Evidently some people are throwing you into confusion and are trying to pervert the gospel of Christ. Even if we or an angel from heaven should preach a gospel other than the one we preached to you, let them be under God's curse!   – Galatians 1:7, 8

Teaching is either truth from Scripture or it is not. There is no middle ground. There may certainly be some issues and doctrines that are not as precise or clear as others (for example, salvation by faith in Jesus Christ is a very clear doctrine in scripture; in comparison, details concerning optimal church size, style of church government, or how many elders should be appointed in a local church are not as precise). But the gospel cannot be altered without destroying the Truth. If the "good news" is twisted or changed, it is no longer "good news". It is no longer accurate. It can no longer save. It has become a deception after the pattern of Satan's model of deception in the Garden of Eden.

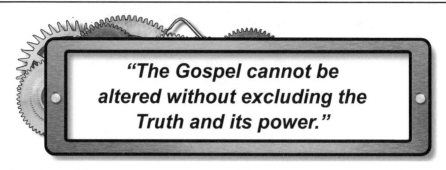

"The Gospel cannot be altered without excluding the Truth and its power."

I am astonished that you are so quickly deserting the one who called you to live in the grace of Christ and are turning to a different gospel—which is really no gospel at all.   – Galatians 1:6-7

False teachers who present twisted and altered forms of the Word of God are not to be praised, nor should they be tolerated. Of course, we should be sensitive to people who are still learning and maturing in their understanding, just as we should recognize that all of us are still progressing and developing in any number of areas of theology and Bible interpretation. Just as Satan speaks in opposition to God's Word, the false Bible teacher speaks against the believer's growth. There is no association between the Truth and the lie, just as there is no equality between a teacher of the Word of God and a teacher of deception. The false teachers must be identified and quarantined as if they carried a deadly virus.

In 2 Corinthians Paul tells the church that he will "cut the ground" (ekkopso ten aphormen) from the false apostles. The word aphormen means "a starting point", referring to a base of operations for military forces that would give them "an opportunity" to work their strategy and achieve their goal. The word ekkopso means "to cut down" and refers to Paul depriving the false teachers an opportunity to prove they were equal to him, or that their teaching was as important as Paul's.

I will keep on doing what I am doing in order to cut the ground from under those who want an opportunity to be considered equal with us in the things they boast about.   – 2 Corinthians 11:12

What Paul refers to as "the things they boast about" was the false teachers' claim that they were apostles just like Paul – but even greater apostles because they were professionals who got paid for their ministry. They belittled Paul as an untrained layman since he was not compensated for his teaching, and then claimed that fact proved their superiority. Paul, however, responded that the opposite was true, since the matter of charging proved both his sincerity and their corruption. These false apostles considered their teaching, world view, and opinions to be "equal with" the revelation Paul had from God. Paul aggressively argued the fallacy of their teaching and ministry in order to preserve the growth, maturity and production of the Corinthian believers.

The New Testament writers constantly warned churches and church leaders to avoid teaching that had been corrupted, and to have nothing to do with the false teachers of this useless information:

As I urged you when I went into Macedonia, stay there in Ephesus so that you may command certain people not to teach false doctrines any longer or to devote themselves to myths and endless genealogies. Such things promote controversial speculations rather than advancing God's work—which is by faith.   – 1 Timothy 1:3

But avoid foolish controversies and genealogies and arguments and quarrels about the law, because these are unprofitable and useless. Warn a divisive person once, and then warn them a second time. After that, have nothing to do with them. You may be sure that such people are warped and sinful; they are self-condemned.   – Titus 3:9-11

Dear friends, do not believe every spirit, but test the spirits to see whether they are from God, because many false prophets have gone out into the world.... They are from the world and therefore speak from the viewpoint of the world, and the world listens to them. – 1 John 4:1, 5

Take special note of anyone who does not obey our instruction in this letter. Do not associate with them, in order that they may feel ashamed. Yet do not regard them as an enemy, but warn them as you would a fellow believer.   – 2 Thessalonians 3:14

He must hold firmly to the trustworthy message as it has been taught, so that he can encourage others by sound doctrine and refute those who oppose it. For there are many rebellious people, full of meaningless talk and deception, especially those of the circumcision group. They must be silenced, because they are disrupting whole households by teaching things they ought not to teach—and that for the sake of dishonest gain…. Therefore rebuke them sharply, so that they will be sound in the faith and will pay no attention to Jewish myths or to the merely human commands of those who reject the truth. To the pure, all things are pure, but to those who are corrupted and do not believe, nothing is pure. In fact, both their minds and consciences are corrupted. They claim to know God, but by their actions they deny him. They are detestable, disobedient and unfit for doing anything good.

— Titus 1:9-11, 13-16

These are the things you are to teach and insist on. If anyone teaches otherwise and does not agree to the sound instruction of our Lord Jesus Christ and to godly teaching, they are conceited and understand nothing. They have an unhealthy interest in controversies and quarrels about words that result in envy, strife, malicious talk, evil suspicions and constant friction between people of corrupt mind, who have been robbed of the truth and who think that godliness is a means to financial gain. But godliness with contentment is great gain…. But you, man of God, flee from all this, and pursue righteousness, godliness, faith, love, endurance and gentleness. Fight the good fight of the faith.

— 1 Timothy 6:2-6, 11

The style and character of false teachers are clearly described in the New Testament, as are details about their teaching and deviant doctrines.

Paul says they are deceitful workers who masquerade as apostles:

For such men are false apostles, deceitful workers, masquerading as apostles of Christ.   *— 2 Corinthians 11:13*

Paul refers to the false teachers in the verse above as "such men". They are those who preach a different Jesus, a different spirit, a different gospel; they boast of and teach things they consider equal to the Word of God (2 Corinthians 11:13, 11:4). Paul goes on to sarcastically ridicule the Corinthians for tolerating these false teachers in their churches:

In fact, you even put up with anyone who enslaves you or exploits you or takes advantage of you or puts on airs or slaps you in the face. To my shame I admit that we were too weak for that!
                                                                  – 2 Corinthians 11:20-24

As we see above, a false teacher and his doctrine:
- Enslave
- Exploit
- Take advantage
- Push himself/itself forward as of the greatest priority and prominence
- And finally, "slaps you in the face" if you resist, question or rebuke in response

Paul says sarcastically that he is "too weak" to let false teachers abuse him, but certainly recalls a time when he himself forcefully promoted a false doctrine and was motivated by the same forces that influence false teachers today. His personal account of his own character and behavior at that time is revealing:

For you have heard of my previous way of life in Judaism, how intensely I persecuted the church of God and tried to destroy it. I was advancing in Judaism beyond many of my own age among my people and was extremely zealous for the traditions of my fathers.
                                                                  – Galatians 1:13, 14

Paul "persecuted the church of God" and he did so "intensely", as a method of advancing his own human views. He describes his false doctrine as "the traditions of my fathers" which he identifies as "traditions of men" in Colossians 2:8. Jesus described these same traditions as working in opposition to the Word of God:

You nullify the word of God by your tradition that you have handed down. And you do many things like that.   *– Mark 7:13*

False teachers will lead their followers (i.e., false believers) as spies to infiltrate a congregation of saints. They will attempt to alter the Truth in that church, just as Satan did in the Garden.

This matter arose because some false believers had infiltrated our ranks to spy on the freedom we have in Christ Jesus and to make us

slaves. We did not give in to them for a moment, so that the truth of the
gospel might be preserved for you.   – Galatians 2:2-5

When a group of false teachers and believers set up a serious base of
operations in a church, it can very easily get caught in the web of false
doctrine. Somehow, their false teaching becomes very attractive, even
to those in the church who are mature and in leadership positions. This
happened to Peter and Barnabas when the Antioch church was infiltrated
by Judaizers from Jerusalem:

The other Jews joined him (Peter) in his hypocrisy, so that by their
hypocrisy even Barnabas was led astray.   – Galatians 2:13

Paul had followers, including members of his ministry team, who became
deceived and deserted him toward the end of his life:

You know that everyone in the province of Asia has deserted me,
including Phygelus and Hermogenes.   – 2 Timothy 1:15

Demas, because he loved this world, has deserted me and has gone
to Thessalonica.   – 2 Timothy 4:10

In the same way, Jude also warned of imposters infiltrating churches in
order to secretly bring false teaching before an open audience:

I felt compelled to write and urge you to contend for the faith that was
once for all entrusted to God's holy people. For certain individuals
whose condemnation was written about long ago have secretly slipped
in among you. They are ungodly people, who pervert the grace of
our God into a license for immorality and deny Jesus Christ our only
Sovereign and Lord. Though you already know all this, I want to remind
you that the Lord....   – Jude 3-5

Knowing the Truth does not completely insulate a believer from hearing
or being attracted to deception. A believer must be consciously aware of
what is True and alert to the false teachers that Peter promised would
always be in our midst. Even if a person has accepted the Truth and is
living in the Truth it is possible for false teaching to "cut in" on them to
lead them off course.

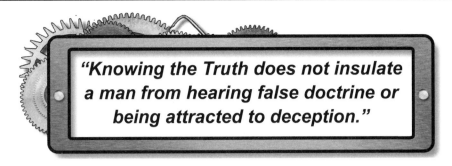

"Knowing the Truth does not insulate a man from hearing false doctrine or being attracted to deception."

You were running a good race. Who cut in on you to keep you from obeying the truth? That kind of persuasion does not come from the one who calls you. "A little yeast works through the whole batch of dough." I am confident in the Lord that you will take no other view. The one who is throwing you into confusion, whoever that may be, will have to pay the penalty.   *– Galatians 5:7-10*

In the verse above, the Galatian believers are described as "running a good race" until someone "cut in on you to keep you from obeying the truth". The phrase "cut in" is the aorist, indicative, active of the Greek word egkopto which means "to cut in or hinder". The tense, voice, and mood of this verb indicate that at a point of time in the past when the Galatians were living in the Word of God, another person decided to bring them some other teaching which resulted in them running away from the truth to follow the deception. Rogers and Rogers Linguistic and Exegetical Key says this:

> The word suggests a breaking into or obstruction of the Galatian Christians in their course of following the truth. The picture is that of the runner who has allowed his progress to be blocked or who is still running, but on the wrong course.

Here, Paul reveals another dangerous principle of false doctrine: "A little yeast works through the whole batch of dough." This statement makes the cancerous effect of a false doctrine very clear. Since the Word of God is a body of Truth and its doctrines work together in continuity, it is possible for a single area of corrupt teaching to eventually work its way through the entire body of Truth like yeast spreading through a lump of dough. The cancer of false teaching will spread through the body of Truth eating away at the subtlety of the Word of God, leaving behind a riddled, frail, broken frame of faith. Paul says exactly this to Timothy:

Avoid godless chatter, because those who indulge in it will become more and more ungodly. Their teaching will spread like gangrene (gangraina). Among them are Hymenaeus and Philetus, who have wandered away from the truth. They say that the resurrection has already taken place, and they destroy the faith of some.

– 2 Timothy 2:16-18

The word Paul uses to describe the sickness of false teaching in the soul of a believer is the Greek word gangraina, which refers to gangrene, cancer or a spreading ulcer. Rogers says in his Linguistic Key (503):

It is a disease by which any part of the body suffering from inflammation becomes so corrupted that unless a remedy be seasonably applied the evil continually spreads, attacks other parts, and at last eats away at the bones. The metaphor illustrates insidiousness. Nothing could more suitably describe the manner of advancement of most false teachings, whether ancient or modern.

One more point before we move on – notice that the point of entrance of this false teaching was through the theological door of eschatology. This particular false teaching was centered on a point of doctrine that concerned the resurrection of the dead – phase three of salvation. In order to support this error, other doctrinal points had to be adjusted by some deranged theological chiropractor posing as a Bible teacher. Bible verses had to be continually tweaked and twisted to align them with this warped eschatological view. This malignant alignment continued to work through some people's doctrinal system until their faith was completely tweaked away. The theological gangrene most likely involved an explanation of the resurrection that was laced with allegory, spiritualization, or a sacramental interpretation of the Word of God which denied Christ's physical resurrection and his bodily return. The doctrinal result would have been a depreciated view of the human body, which would have eventually manifested as extreme asceticism to control the body or even the opposite, antinomianism.

As Paul's ministry took him further and further into gentile territory he encountered additional forms of false teaching held sacred among the pagans. Besides continuing to deal with the traditions of men and various religious rituals, Paul also encountered worldly philosophies and the doctrines of demons:

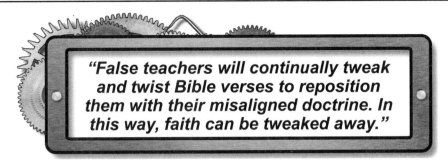

"False teachers will continually tweak and twist Bible verses to reposition them with their misaligned doctrine. In this way, faith can be tweaked away."

My goal is that they may be encouraged in heart and united in love, so that they may have the full riches of complete understanding, in order that they may know the mystery of God, namely, Christ, in whom are hidden all the treasures of wisdom and knowledge. I tell you this so that no one may deceive you by fine-sounding arguments.

– Colossians 2:2-4

If anyone teaches false doctrines and does not agree to the sound instruction of our Lord Jesus Christ and to godly teaching, he is conceited and understands nothing. He has an unhealthy interest in controversies and quarrels about words that result in envy, strife, malicious talk, evil suspicions and constant friction between men of corrupt mind, who have been robbed of the truth and who think that godliness is a means to financial gain.   *– 1 Timothy 6:3-5*

Just as the Jews manipulated their Law with traditions in order to secure wealth and power for themselves, the Gentiles used shrewd presentations and finely-tuned rhetorical skills to lure people into orbit around an array of intellectual speculation, mythical interpretation, exegetical debates and mystical experiences:

See to it that no one takes you captive through hollow and deceptive philosophy, which depends on human tradition and the elemental spiritual forces of this world rather than on Christ.   *– Colossians 2:8*

Paul recognized that teaching was necessary to mature the whole body of Christian believers, and he looked forward to the day when the church would stabilize as a result of having attained maturity. Paul explained that this goal would be reached when believers attained unity in the knowledge of the Son of God, who is the Word.

...prepare God's people for works of service so that the body of Christ may be built up until we all reach unity in the faith and in the knowledge of the Son of God and become mature, attaining to the whole measure of the fullness of Christ.
                                                                    – Ephesians 4:13

Paul identifies the false philosophies, deviant methodologies and teaching errors that would no longer be effective in disrupting the tranquil unity among believers at that time:

Then we will no longer be infants, tossed back and forth by the waves, and blown here and there by every wind of teaching and by the cunning and craftiness of men in their deceitful scheming.
                                                                    – Ephesians 4:14-15

These words speak of the individual infants who are individually tossed and blown by false doctrines. The description is intended as a contrast to the one singular unified man described in the previous verse, which introduces the unity of mature individuals as the andra teleion – the "complete man" – the unified the body of Christ, the church. At this time, the individual children tossed about in the sea of deception will be turned into a single unified man, complete and powerful.

Until the unification in doctrine and knowledge foreseen in verse 13 occurs historically, we will be plagued in the church with infants who stand divided and alone, buffeted by false teaching. They will be tossed back and forth, and pushed away from each other by the rolling waves of doctrine. The image that Paul creates here is of individual children struggling to come to grips with their understanding of the knowledge of the Word of God, while they seek direction from men teaching false doctrine and intentionally twisting information.

Here is a breakdown of five things that make it impossible for the church to find unity in the knowledge of Jesus Christ that has been revealed in his written revelation:

1. **Waves** – Waves are a symbol of instability with constantly changing position, form and appearance. The children are pictured riding these waves with no solid foundation with which to direct their course. They are trying to make progress to a destination, but the

waves, as ever-developing doctrinal positions upon which they try to proceed, make it difficult, if not impossible.

2. **Wind of Teaching** – Waves generally roll in the same direction, but winds can suddenly change. The children are driven by the teachings that first blow them one way with the waves and then turn and blow them back another direction. It is easy for the winds to toss children back and forth since they are riding on unstable waves.

3. **Cunning** – Cunning is the word kubeia, which, in addition to cunning, means "dice playing" and refers to wicked dice play with intentional fraud. In the Greek the phrase is, didaskalias en te kubeia ton anthropon or, literally, "teaching in the dice playing of men" – that is, "the teaching of men who have loaded the doctrinal dice".

This portion of the verse then captures the image of the wind and the waves more literally. The believers are being doctrinally tossed back and forth by the teaching of men who have loaded the doctrinal dice to roll the numbers they want. These men teach what they want and use the Word of God (or philosophy, or religious tradition, or whatever it takes) to prove their world view true and thus manipulate the children to believe their twisted doctrines.

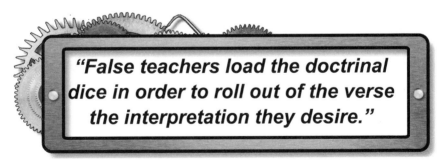

"False teachers load the doctrinal dice in order to roll out of the verse the interpretation they desire."

4. **Craftiness** – Craftiness is the word panourgia, meaning cleverness or trickery, and it describes how and why the false teachers have loaded the doctrinal dice. They load the dice to trick you with their teaching. The real problem is that the children on the waves are trying to make progress by allowing the wind to move them through the sea, but the whole time, men are manipulating that wind. The false teaching keeps the children where the false teachers want them, and it prevents them from making progress toward God's goal of unity and maturity in the body of Christ.

The children's only hope is to get on solid ground (i.e., the written Word of God) and allow the truth to move them consistently in the direction of their destination. But, if the believers then allow themselves to again leave the solid ground of the Word and get out into the waters of philosophy, tradition, doctrinal preferences, etc., they will be influenced by teachers who have loaded their dice with their human viewpoint. At that point, they will once again be captive to the false doctrinal winds.

5. **Deceitful scheming** – "Deceitful" is the word methodeian and "scheming" is planes. Methodeian has the meaning of "following after, deceit, scheming". The word planes, which is translated as "scheming" in Ephesians 4:14, means "wandering or roaming". It is "used figuratively of wandering from the path of truth" (Linguistic Key, p. 440) and is always used of mental straying, wrong opinion, and error in morals or religion. (Strongs Greek Dictionary, p. 1315)[7]. In this sense plane is a descriptive word for error, delusion, deceit. Together, as they are in the Greek (methodeian tes planes), the two words mean "deceitful deceit", "scheming error", "deceitful delusion" or, as the NIV translates it, "deceitful scheming".

It is interesting to note that the same word methodeian is used to identify Satan's warfare in his battle against believers, who are supposed to wear the armor of God which includes the shield of faith, the belt of Truth and the sword of the Word of God. It should be clear to everyone that Satan is still aggressively scheming to pollute the Word of God as he did in the Garden, in tempting Jesus, and in the Parable of the Sower and the Weeds.

Put on the full armor of God so that you can take your stand against the devil's schemes (methodeias). For our struggle is not against flesh and blood, but against the rulers, against the authorities, against the powers of this dark world and against the spiritual forces of evil in the heavenly realms.   – Ephesians 6:11-12

There are clearly great forces at work to keep the children of God tossing on the waves, lost in doctrinal error, and at odds with each other through

---

[7] See also Second Thessalonians 2:11 (where it is translated as "delusion") James 5:20, 2 Peter 3:17, 1 John 4:6, Romans 1:27, 2 Peter 2:18 and Jude 11.

intentional and deceitful loading of the dice. Although men are the ones that ultimately present the twisted, deceptive and contradictory doctrines, Paul also says that our battle is not against men ("flesh and blood") but against Satan himself – the one who originally twisted God's word in eternity past and in the Garden of Eden, to mislead God's creation.

The Spirit clearly says that in later times some will abandon the faith and follow deceiving spirits and things taught by demons. Such teachings come through hypocritical liars, whose consciences have been seared as with a hot iron. They forbid people to marry and order them to abstain from certain foods, which God created to be received with thanksgiving by those who believe and who know the truth.
                                                              – 1 Timothy 4:1-3

These are the demonic doctrines of asceticism.

Watch out for those dogs, those men who do evil, those mutilators of the flesh.   – Philippians 3:2

The mutilators of the flesh were those who enforced circumcision, which in this case, was a doctrinal error of sacramentalism (dependence on religious ritual).

The false teaching of ritualism is identified again in the passage below, but is here listed with a wide range of doctrinal errors common among both Gentiles and Jews. The powerless practices and meaningless doctrines that are identified in Colossians 2:16-23 include:

1. Dietary Laws
2. Religious Festivals
3. New Moon Celebrations
4. Sabbath Days
5. Contact with and worship of angels
6. Visions
7. Mysticism
8. Demonism
9. Legalism
10. Human Commands
11. Human Teachings

12. Worship of Self (man-made religion)
13. Asceticism
14. Mistreatment of the Body

Therefore do not let anyone judge you by what you eat or drink, or with regard to a religious festival, a New Moon celebration or a Sabbath day. These are a shadow of the things that were to come; the reality, however, is found in Christ. Do not let anyone who delights in false humility and the worship of angels disqualify you for the prize. Such a person goes into great detail about what he has seen, and his unspiritual mind puffs him up with idle notions. He has lost connection with the Head, from whom the whole body, supported and held together by its ligaments and sinews, grows as God causes it to grow. Since you died with Christ to the basic principles of this world, why, as though you still belonged to it, do you submit to its rules: "Do not handle! Do not taste! Do not touch!"? These are all destined to perish with use, because they are based on human commands and teachings. Such regulations indeed have an appearance of wisdom, with their self-imposed worship, their false humility and their harsh treatment of the body, but they lack any value in restraining sensual indulgence.

The worthless rituals, doctrines and practices listed here are said to "lack any value in restraining sensual indulgence" because they do not renew the mind with the Truth. These ascetic behaviors uselessly restrict the body of a man, but none of them renews the soul with the Word of God. The same concept is captured in this verse:

Having a form of godliness but denying its power. Have nothing to do with such people… always learning but never able to come to a knowledge of the truth.   *– 2 Timothy 3:5, 7*

Galatians 4:8-9 also identifies some of the same false practices and false doctrines:

Formerly, when you did not know God, you were slaves to those who by nature are not gods. But now that you know God—or rather are known by God—how is it that you are turning back to those weak and miserable forces? Do you wish to be enslaved by them all over again? You are observing special days and months and seasons and years! I fear for you, that somehow I have wasted my efforts on you.

The writer of the book of Hebrews warned his readers to avoid strange teachings that included dietary laws and rituals. He said the teachings provided no benefit and warned them to not be "carried away" by the false doctrines and practices:

> *Do not be carried away by all kinds of strange teachings. It is good for our hearts to be strengthened by grace, not by eating ceremonial foods, which is of no benefit to those who do so.*   – Hebrews 13:9

In 1 Timothy 6:20, Paul warns Timothy of:

1. Godless chatter
2. Opposing Ideas
3. False Knowledge

> *Timothy, guard what has been entrusted to your care. Turn away from godless chatter and the opposing ideas of what is falsely called knowledge, which some have professed and in so doing have departed from the faith.*

Men hear this talk and the paradoxes that contradict the Truth, and if they embrace them as Truth, they have left the path of the Word of God. Paul's use of the phrase "the faith" in the verse above refers to the body of doctrinal truths found in the Word of God; it is not used in the sense of believing or accepting something. In this usage, "the faith" refers to what is believed or the doctrines that are accepted.

Paul advises Timothy to "train yourself to be godly", which in context means, "nourish yourself with the truth".

> *Have nothing to do with godless myths and old wives' tales; rather, train yourself to be godly.*   – 1 Timothy 4:7

One of the struggles of the church has been that sinful man is more attracted to false teaching and religious ritual than to the renewing Truth of the Word of God. The tendency of men in the church has been to surround themselves with other men posing as Bible teachers, but who simply teach what sinful man already accepts or what carnal man finds entertaining.

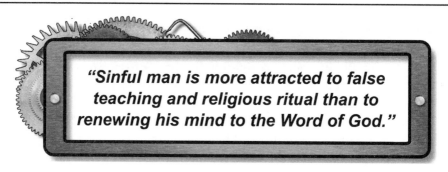

"Sinful man is more attracted to false teaching and religious ritual than to renewing his mind to the Word of God."

For the time will come when people will not put up with sound doctrine. Instead, to suit their own desires, they will gather around them a great number of teachers to say what their itching ears want to hear. They will turn their ears away from the truth and turn aside to myths. But you, keep your head in all situations.   – 2 Timothy 4:3-4

Peter's promise that "there will be false teachers among you" is confirmed by Paul, Jude, John and others. Paul calls the false teachers "impostors" and says it is only going to get worse as they continue to deceive people intentionally and, ironically, become deceived themselves by their own false doctrine and corrupt practices:

Impostors will go from bad to worse, deceiving and being deceived.
– 2 Timothy 3:13

The Apostle John also weighs in several times on the false teacher vs. true teacher conflict. The first thing John says is that some of the false teachers were trained and sent out from his own church/school/training program. But the fact that these teachers drifted away from the Truth of the apostolic revelation proves they never really were true teachers. One of the signs of a true Bible teacher is the ability to stand on his own, hold to the Truth, and continue to accurately proclaim the revelation of the Word of God, even without denominational or seminary affiliation, ministry ordination, financial support – or any other force – making him do so. John says some of the men that he sent out didn't make that cut:

They went out from us, but they did not really belong to us. For if they had belonged to us, they would have remained with us; but their going showed that none of them belonged to us.   – 1 John 2:19

Writing in his second letter, John again warns that many deceivers have gone out into the world to proclaim deceptive doctrines. One of their doctrines was to deny that Jesus Christ, the eternal God, had appeared in history in a physical body. The loss of this basic doctrine so drastically altars the Christian faith, that it renders it no longer Christian. Notice how John warns his people that this particular false doctrine could derail their entire Christian life and its production in phase two. This is such a dangerous and destructive teaching error that John, who is in his 80's when he writes this, commands the Christian community to not even allow these traveling teachers to stay in their homes when they arrived in their towns to teach. There was a no tolerance policy: do not feed them, do not house them, do not assist their ministry in any way.[8]

> *I say this because many deceivers, who do not acknowledge Jesus Christ as coming in the flesh, have gone out into the world. Any such person is the deceiver and the antichrist. Watch out that you do not lose what we have worked for (rewards gained during phase two), but that you may be rewarded fully. Anyone who runs ahead and does not continue in the teaching of Christ does not have God; whoever continues in the teaching has both the Father and the Son. If anyone comes to you and does not bring this teaching, do not take them into your house or welcome them. Anyone who welcomes them shares in their wicked work.* — 2 John 7-11

---

[8] I interpret John's words in this verse to refer to a refusal to assist the false teacher in any way concerning his ministry efforts. I assume that if the false teacher needed some type of protection from bandits or had been injured by a runaway chariot, John would have provided some humanitarian assistance. I am thinking here of the parable of the Good Samaritan. But, then again, don't forget that John was the disciple who wanted to call fire out of heaven to consume the Samaritans (Luke 9:54). So, you can decide for yourself if John would have helped a false teacher who was stranded along the interstate with a dead battery or an empty gas tank. Either way, I am sure he would not have supported their ministry with a monthly offering, nor would he have sat respectfully quiet in a Sunday evening service while a false teacher rambled about some mystical experience or a philosophical position which denied that God, the eternal Word, had really been born, lived, died and rose again for our salvation. I have to believe John would have lit some type of fireworks in the church that night!

Note that John also identifies two additional false doctrines in these verses:

1. Denial of Jesus as Messiah
2. Denial of the Father and the Son

The false teacher who preaches these things is called "the liar" and "the antichrist". False doctrine is accurately called a lie by John. What did Satan do in the Garden? He lied to Eve. What did Jesus call Satan? "He is a liar and the father of lies" (John 8:44). The antichrist is described as having two main doctrines of denial and deceit:

1. Jesus is not the Messiah
2. There is no Trinity

Who is the liar? It is whoever denies that Jesus is the Christ. Such a person is the antichrist—denying the Father and the Son. No one who denies the Son has the Father; whoever acknowledges the Son has the Father also. As for you, see that what you have heard from the beginning (the apostolic teaching from Jesus, Peter, Paul, John, etc.) *remains in you* (in phase two). *If it does, you also will remain in the Son* (productive in phase two) *and in the Father. And this is what he promised us—eternal life. I am writing these things to you about those who are trying to lead you astray.*   – 1 John 2:22-26

In John's third letter we get an unbelievable look at a man in the church who completely disrespected the Apostle John and disregarded John's teaching. Who would think such an attitude was even possible? What kind of arrogance and denial of historical information would it take to ridicule John and his teaching in one of John's own churches? How did this happen? Were there church people who actually gave this man any respect or followed his authority? Sadly, it appears there were:

I wrote to the church, but Diotrephes, who loves to be first, will have nothing to do with us. So if I come, I will call attention to what he is doing, gossiping maliciously about us. Not satisfied with that, he even refuses to welcome the brothers (John's disciples). *He also stops those who want to do so and puts them out of the church.*   – 3 John 9-10

Diotrephes was a leader, elder, or pastor who had taken over one of John's churches. This would have been around 85 AD, about 55 years after the resurrection and 13 years before John died. John had actually written letters to Diotrephes asking for an opportunity for either himself or one of his disciples (such as Papias, Polycarp, Ignatius, etc) to visit and teach in his church. Diotrephes had said, "No," and then spoke maliciously against John, spreading slander about his ministry team and his disciples. Amazingly, Diotrephes' church seems to have followed him in his arrogance and error. If anyone in the church still had an interest in hearing John, one of the disciples of Jesus, teach he was threatened by Diotrephes. And if anyone had asked John to visit his private home to teach a small group of believers, Diotrephes would have excommunicated him from the church. I would like to have been there when the old man John began to "call attention" to what Diotrephes was doing!

About ten years later John, now well into his 90's, was exiled to the isle of Patmos off the coast of Ephesus. At that time, Jesus appeared to him and dictated seven letters for him to send to seven local churches. One of them could have been Diotrephes' former church (I highly doubt that Diotrphes was any longer in operation after John finished "calling attention" to him!) In two of these letters, false teachers and false doctrine are mentioned by Jesus. To the third of the seven churches, Pergamum, Jesus had John write:

> *I have a few things against you: There are some among you who hold to the teaching of Balaam, who taught Balak to entice the Israelites to sin so that they ate food sacrificed to idols and committed sexual immorality. Likewise, you also have those who hold to the teaching of the Nicolaitans. Repent therefore! Otherwise, I will soon come to you and will fight against them with the sword of my mouth.*
> *– Revelation 2:14-16*

Another false teacher named Nicolus had appeared on the scene. He must have claimed to be a prophet with special insight and new teaching. His followers associated themselves with him, calling themselves "Nicolaitans" instead of "Christians". The Nicolaitans' false teaching in Pergamum resulted in sinful living, which is typical, since Galatians 5 tells us that the fruit of the Spirit comes from the Word of God and the works of the flesh are the product of false teaching.

The mention of idols would include the hollow philosophies and human religion that manifested in their lives as immorality. Jesus promises to unleash on them the "sword of my mouth", which is nothing other than the reality and Truth of the Word of God overwhelming them in their empty and vain conceit. The result would be the tearing down of the strongholds of this false teaching as Paul wrote in 2 Corinthians 10. Nic and his "Bible study" may not have survived this reality check.

To the fourth of seven churches, Thyatira, Jesus had John write:

> *I have this against you: You tolerate that woman Jezebel, who calls herself a prophet. By her teaching she misleads my servants into sexual immorality and the eating of food sacrificed to idols. I have given her time to repent of her immorality, but she is unwilling. So I will cast her on a bed of suffering, and I will make those who commit adultery with her suffer intensely, unless they repent of her ways. I will strike her children dead. Then all the churches will know that I am he who searches hearts and minds (note that the Word of God is said to do the same in Hebrews 4:12-13), and I will repay each of you according to your deeds. Now I say to the rest of you in Thyatira, to you who do not hold to her teaching and have not learned Satan's so-called deep secrets, "I will not impose any other burden on you, except to hold on to what you have until I come."*
>
> *– Revelation 2:20-25*

A mystic had become a leader in the church of Thyatira by 96 AD. This person had supposedly gained access to additional teachings that were "deep secrets" which supposedly had not been revealed to the church through apostolic revelation. It was newer information that went deeper than the surface meaning of the Word of God. The mystic, Jezebel, was being used by Satan to do here the same thing he did in the Garden with Eve, which was provide additional but fallacious insight into the character and plan of God.

To counter this, Jesus tells the church again that there will be no additional teaching provided other than the already-revealed Word of God. He says, "I will not impose any other burden on you, except to hold on to what you have until I come." The phrase "any other burden" refers to further revelation, prophecy and insight. In the Old Testament the word for a prophecy received by a prophet was the Hebrew word massa which means both "oracle" and "burden". The Christians in Thyatira were being told by Jesus that he will not give them any additional revelation of his Word. They were then told that they should hold on to the Word they already had. This is indeed the challenge of the Church today. We do not need any mystics or prophets telling us the deep secrets of God, because we are not even reading, teaching, hearing or understanding the "burden" he has already laid upon us. We would do well to shut up the mystics with their prophecies and instead study and live the Word of God we have been given. Is this not what Jesus and his apostles told us to do when they commanded us to "remain in him" and "continue in the truth", etc?

The Hebrew word massa is translated as "burden" in the King James translation and "oracle" in the NIV, NAS and ESV. But, even then, it is often footnoted as "burden". This word is found in the writings of the prophets Isaiah, Jeremiah, Ezekiel, Nahum, Habakkuk, Zechariah and Malachi to describe the Word God had laid on their hearts.[9] This apparently is what the Thyatiran mystic Jezebel wanted the church to think was happening with her. Instead Jesus told John, who would be the last prophet, that he was going to make the mystic suffer until she repented and then he would kill her followers.

And, finally, here are some very interesting directions to Jeremiah from God concerning how he should answer the people of Judah who asked about the "burden" of the Lord:

And when this people, or the prophet, or a priest, shall ask thee, saying, "What is the burden of the Lord?" thou shalt then say unto them, "What burden? I will even forsake you, saith the Lord." And as for the prophet, and the priest, and the people that shall say, "The burden of the Lord," I will even punish that man and his house. Thus shall ye say everyone to his neighbor, and everyone to his brother, "What hath the Lord answered?" and, "What hath the Lord spoken?" And the burden of the Lord shall ye mention no more: for every man's word shall be his burden; for ye have perverted the words of the living God,

---

[9] See Isaiah 13:1, 14:28, 15:1, 17:1, 19:1, 21:1, 21:11, 21:13, 22:1, 23:1, and 30:27. See also Ezekiel 12:10, Nahum 1:1, Habakukk 1:1, Zechariah 9:1, Zechariah 12;1 and Malachi 1:1.

*of the Lord of hosts our God. Thus shalt thou say to the prophet, "What
hath the Lord answered thee?" and, "What hath the Lord spoken?" But
since ye say, "The burden of the Lord"; therefore thus saith the Lord;
Because ye say this word, "The burden of the Lord", and I have sent
unto you, saying, Ye shall not say, "The burden of the Lord."*

                                                    – Jeremiah 23:33-38

There are two more things that fall under the category of false teaching
besides the many already mentioned:

1. One is the error of twisting Scripture to make it mean what we want it
   to mean.

There is danger that comes from teaching directly from the Scriptures
when the Word of God is interpreted to make it say what you want. Once
again, Satan is the original twisted scripture artist. For example, Satan
twisted Psalm 91:11-12 to make it say that Jesus should jump off one
of the highest locations of the temple mount so that angels could catch
him. Jesus, knowing that the Truth of God must be found in the fullness
of Scripture and not in one particular verse, refuted Satan with Scripture.
This idea is what Psalm 119:160 means when it says:

The sum of your Word is Truth. (ESV, NAS, Amplified, Rotherhams)

The doctrines of Scripture stand together to reveal the Truth of God, so
there is no room for an individual to slice out a portion of the Word and
create his own personal interpretation of what Truth is. Peter addresses
this issue when he explains that even the prophets who spoke and
recorded the Word of God were not given the freedom to interpret it
however they wanted – nor were they allowed to add their own views to it.
The Scriptures mean what they mean and our responsibility is to learn the
knowledge they communicate.

*Knowing this first of all, that no prophecy of Scripture comes from
someone's own interpretation. For no prophecy was ever produced by
the will of man.*   – 2 Peter 1:20-21, ESV

Peter identifies the problem best when he explains that some people were
ignorantly twisting Paul's letters to mean something that neither Paul nor
God (who inspired Paul) meant. The result, as always, was disastrous:

[Paul] writes the same way in all his letters, speaking in them of these matters. His letters contain some things that are hard to understand, which ignorant and unstable people distort, as they do the other Scriptures, to their own destruction. — 2 Peter 3:15-16

2. The last problem to mention here also involves those who teach Scripture. This problem does not come from those who twist Scriptures to their own desired ends, but from those who know accurately and clearly what the Word of God says. Remember the Word of God is a seed. It is sown into the hearts and minds of people. It begins to grow and produce fruit when it is heard and understood. But, James clearly identifies a problem among even those who do not accept false teaching, do not listen to mystics, do not fall into religious rituals, do not fall for asceticism, and do not twist Scripture. Instead, these people hear the Word and know the Truth – but they simply do not do it. They choose to disobey what they know to be right.

Of course, this should not be surprising since it happens all the time in the natural world. Children disobey when they know very clearly what they should do. Adults know what the speed limit is but freely choose to ignore the signs. Very few people are locked up in prison for doing things that they actually thought were right. Likewise, Christians can sit under good Bible teaching, hear correct interpretation, receive instruction on application and living a fruitful life and simply choose not to do it. Yes, the Word of God is the seed that produces righteousness and so we must faithfully sow that seed into the souls of men. But it is not magic.

Jack may have traded his cow for magic beans that miraculously grew to a tremendous height overnight, but that is a different story than what we find in the biblical account. We teach the Truth. We sow the Word of God. But, we do not have magic seeds. The man who hears, understands and believes the Word of God is going to have to stand up and execute the plan. The Bible teacher sows the Word of God, which is the power of God in hearts filled with faith and in the hands of the obedient.

Do not merely listen to the word, and so deceive yourselves. Do what it says. — James 1:22

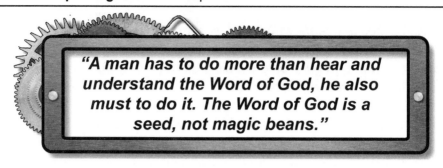

"A man has to do more than hear and understand the Word of God, he also must to do it. The Word of God is a seed, not magic beans."

It is important to know that God does use false teaching by allowing it to test the hearts of his people. A person who follows false teaching ultimately does so because he wants to follow false teaching and walk away from God and his Truth:

> *If a prophet, or one who foretells by dreams, appears among you and announces to you a miraculous sign or wonder, and if the sign or wonder of which he has spoken takes place, and he says, "Let us follow other gods" (gods you have not known) "and let us worship them," you must not listen to the words of that prophet or dreamer. The Lord your God is testing you to find out whether you love him with all your heart and with all your soul. It is the Lord your God you must follow, and him you must revere.* — Deuteronomy 13:1-4

Only men who have already rejected the Truth will search for and be willing to follow a lie – that is, a counterfeit reality. Scripture even says that God sends delusions to lead astray and judge those who have already rejected his Truth. As John writes, *"their going showed that none of them belonged to us"* (1 John 2:19).

> *The coming of the lawless one will be in accordance with the work of Satan displayed in all kinds of counterfeit miracles, signs and wonders, and in every sort of evil that deceives those who are perishing. They perish because they refused to love the truth and so be saved. For this reason God sends them a powerful delusion so that they will believe the lie and so that all will be condemned who have not believed the truth but have delighted in wickedness.* — 2 Thessalonians 2:9-12

> *Therefore, dear friends, since you have been forewarned, be on your guard so that you may not be carried away by the error of the lawless and fall from your secure position. But grow in the grace and knowledge of our Lord and Savior Jesus Christ.* — 2 Peter 3:17-18

Judes Top 20 List of Characteristics of False Teachers

1. Dreamers (their spiritual truth is not reality)
2. Those who pollute their own body
3. Rejecters of the Apostles' teaching
4. Slanderers of celestial beings
5. Those who speak abusively against the special revelation available in the Scripture (things not understood) and against natural revelation revealed to all men (things understood)
6. Ones who take the way of Cain (who kill truth with man's religion, false worldviews and human effort)
7. Those who rush for profit into Balaam's error (who use their talents and gifts for their own profit)
8. People who are like those destroyed in Korah's rebellion (who reject and overthrow God's established spiritual leadership)
9. Blemishes at your love feasts (deceivers who are still in church and leading churches)
10. Shepherds who feed only themselves (these do not teach the people – but they do collect money from the people)
11. Clouds without rain, blown by wind (their teaching has no truth, but is driven by popular opinion and considered to be culturally relevant)
12. Autumn trees, twice dead (these are both barren with no fruit at the end of summer, and uprooted)
13. Wild waves of the sea (they are all appearance with no shape, substance or lasting impact)
14. Wild waves of the sea foaming up their shame (the only thing the false teachers can leave behind is the pollution of their souls, similar to ocean waves leaving the trash of the oceans on the beach)
15. Wandering stars (people cannot use these teachers for life's navigational purposes because they are not stable; and if they do trust them they will get confused and lost)
16. Grumblers
17. Faultfinders
18. Those who follow their own evil desires, not the Word of Truth or the Spirit of God
19. Those who boast and promote themselves, instead of the Word of God and Jesus Christ
20. Those who flatter others for their own advantage (if you are a friend or a partner in ministry, that too is for their advantage)

These are found in Jude verses 8-16. Here are the verses in full:

> *In the very same way, on the strength of their dreams these ungodly people pollute their own bodies, reject authority and heap abuse on celestial beings. But even the archangel Michael, when he was disputing with the devil about the body of Moses, did not himself dare to condemn him for slander but said, "The Lord rebuke you!" Yet these people slander whatever they do not understand, and the very things they do understand by instinct—as irrational animals do—will destroy them. Woe to them! They have taken the way of Cain; they have rushed for profit into Balaam's error; they have been destroyed in Korah's rebellion. These people are blemishes at your love feasts, eating with you without the slightest qualm—shepherds who feed only themselves. They are clouds without rain, blown along by the wind; autumn trees, without fruit and uprooted—twice dead. They are wild waves of the sea, foaming up their shame; wandering stars, for whom blackest darkness has been reserved forever. Enoch, the seventh from Adam, prophesied about them: "See, the Lord is coming with thousands upon thousands of his holy ones to judge everyone, and to convict all of them of all the ungodly acts they have committed in their ungodliness, and of all the defiant words ungodly sinners have spoken against him." These people are grumblers and faultfinders; they follow their own evil desires; they boast about themselves and flatter others for their own advantage.*

So, just how dangerous is the temptation to false teaching?

Peter writes in his second letter that the word of God is so important that, *"I will always remind you of these things, even though you know them and are firmly established in the truth you now have"* (2 Peter 1:12). Peter then goes on to explain that even though he lived and traveled with Jesus, and saw miracles and other amazing things, the most important thing is the word of God. Peter explains that even though he could tell stories about when *"we were eyewitnesses"* to the transfiguration and *"we ourselves heard this voice that came from heaven when we were with him"*, there is something more important, something more secure, something more certain – that is, the words of the prophets recorded in the written word of God. It is to these that people should listen:

We were eyewitnesses of his majesty.... We ourselves heard this voice that came from heaven when we were with him on the sacred mountain. And we have the word of the prophets made more certain, and you will do well to pay attention to it.   *— 2 Peter 1:16-19*

In chapter one of this same letter, Peter tells his readers that even though they know the Truth, he will continue to remind them of what they already know and, in fact, are already firmly established in. And, even though he could amaze them with sermon after sermon of stories and accounts of Jesus' miracles, he will not do it. Instead, he will always bring them back to the "word of the prophets". After promising this, Peter warns them that, just as people in the Old Testament had to deal with false prophets speaking alongside true prophets, people of the church will also have false teachers who will have to be heard, analyzed and separated from the teachers of the Truth:

There were also false prophets among the people, just as there will be false teachers among you.   *— 2 Peter 2:1*

Peter then gives a long, detailed description of what these false teachers will look like. Here is my list of eighteen traits Peter mentions. This list is followed by Peter's actual words, so that you can read them for yourself and decide who these false teachers are today. Think more deeply and seriously, if you can, than simply naming Benny Hinn and Harold Camping – although I would certainly say they qualify. There are many more out there, and they are probably much closer to home. (I will confess that my fear continues to be that, without constant and careful self-scrutiny, I myself could be or become a false teacher.)

False teachers will:
1. Secretly introduce destructive heresies
2. Deny the sovereign Lord who bought them
3. Cause their followers to live shameful lives and Christianity to be mocked
4. Exploit people by taking offerings after telling stories they make up
5. Be bold and arrogant and not fear slandering or speaking about things they are ignorant of, including the spiritual world
6. Blaspheme in matters they do not understand
7. Openly sin for the sake of personal pleasure

8. Allow their openly sinful pleasures to become blots and blemishes on you, even while they associate with you

9. Constantly look at others with eyes of adultery and so never really stop sinning long enough to be in fellowship with God

10. Seduce unstable Christians who do not know the Word of God

11. Be trained and practiced experts in the art of greed

12. Leave the straight way to follow the example of Balaam, which means they will use their talents and gifts, not to serve people, but for financial gain

13. Be empty and useless – do not expect to learn anything useful from them, for they are springs without water, gifted teachers without truth

14. Refuse to take a stand on any issue, because they are mists driven by a storm (or, their opinions are driven by the winds of culture and popular opinion)

15. Have only empty words – words void of doctrine and truth

16. Pour out boastful words, constantly promoting themselves and their ministry/business, instead of promoting the Word of God and Jesus Christ

17. Entice recent converts who are ready to leave the ways of the world in order to renew their minds to truth; this will result in their spiritual lives being destroyed.

18. Speak as if their words will bring freedom, peace, satisfaction, happiness – but they themselves are still in bondage to the world and are still seeking sin, lust, wealth, fame, etc.

We who are in the church and the Christian world must be very careful!

Here is the actual text of 2 Peter 2:1-3; 10-18.:

But there were also false prophets among the people, just as there will be false teachers among you. They will secretly introduce destructive heresies, even denying the sovereign Lord who bought them – bringing swift destruction on themselves. Many will follow their shameful ways and will bring the way of truth into disrepute. In their greed these teachers will exploit you with stories they have made up. Their condemnation has long been hanging over them, and their destruction has not been sleeping....This is especially true of those who follow the corrupt desire of the sinful nature and despise authority. Bold and arrogant, these men are not afraid to slander celestial beings; yet even angels, although they are stronger and more powerful, do not bring slanderous accusations against such beings in the presence of the Lord. But these men blaspheme in matters they do not understand. They are like brute beasts, creatures of instinct, born only to be caught and destroyed, and like beasts they too will perish. They will be paid back with harm for the harm they have done. Their idea of pleasure is to carouse in broad daylight. They are blots and blemishes, reveling in their pleasures while they feast with you. With eyes full of adultery, they never stop sinning; they seduce the unstable; they are experts in greed – an accursed brood! They have left the straight way and wandered off to follow the way of Balaam son of Beor, who loved the wages of wickedness. But he was rebuked for his wrongdoing by a donkey – a beast without speech – who spoke with a man's voice and restrained the prophet's madness. These men are springs without water and mists driven by a storm. Blackest darkness is reserved for them. For they mouth empty, boastful words and, by appealing to the lustful desires of sinful human nature, they entice people who are just escaping from those who live in error.

Section Three
The Ten Concepts in Scriptural Context

Teachers Be Careful How You Build
Disqualified for the Prize?
The Spirit Removes the Veil
Teaching Matures the Believer for New Life
The Three Phases: Made Holy, Cleansed with the Word, Presented
Blameless

Growth in Knowledge and Insight = Fruit
Bearing Fruit and Growing
Full Riches of Complete Understanding
Struggle, Sequence and Results of Teaching
Phase One: Image in Mirror; Phase Two: the Man
Peter's First Discourse on the Word
Peter's Second Discourse on the Word
Peter's Third Discourse on the Word
John Describes the System
Stop Neglecting Your Gift: Read, Preach, Teach the Word
Paul Instructs Timothy to Use his Gift of Teaching
Parable of the Sower
A Study of the Word of God
How the Word of God Relates
God's Word through Time

Chapter Nineteen:
1 Corinthians 3:10-16 – Teachers Be Careful How You Build

By the grace God has given me, I laid a foundation (the Gospel) as a wise builder, and someone else is building on it. But each one should build with care (because each has been entrusted). For no one can lay any foundation other than the one already laid (the Gospel), which is Jesus Christ. If anyone builds on this foundation using gold, silver, costly stones, (the building blocks of the spiritual mind), wood, hay or straw (the doctrines and deceptions of demons), their work will be shown for what it is, because the Day will bring it to light. It will be revealed with fire, and the fire will test the quality of each person's work. If what has been built survives, the builder (who was entrusted with the work) will receive a reward (often called "crowns" in Scripture). If it is burned up, the builder will suffer loss but yet will be saved—even though only as one escaping through the flames. Don't you know that you yourselves are God's temple and that God's Spirit dwells in your midst? If anyone destroys God's temple, God will destroy that person; for God's temple is sacred, and you together are that temple.

– 1 Corinthians 3:10-16

Chapter Twenty:
1 Corinthians 9:26-27 – Disqualified for the Prize?

Therefore I do not run like someone running aimlessly; I do not fight like a boxer beating the air. No, I strike a blow to my body and make it my slave so that after I have preached to others, I myself will not be disqualified for the prize.   *– 1 Corinthians 9:26-27*

Chapter Twenty-One:
2 Corinthians 3:7-4:18 – The Spirit Removes the Veil

The ministry of the Holy Spirit is an absolute necessity for revealing the Word to the believer. This crucial ingredient has not been the focus of this book, even though the Holy Spirit is of supreme importance in breathing the Word to the writers of Scripture (2 Timothy 3:16), revealing the Word to the Apostles (Ephesians 3:5; 1 Corinthians 2:10), and empowering the ministers and teachers of the Word (Acts 1:8 and 1 Corinthians 12:4, 28). Even the ability to hear (Revelation 2:7), know (Isaiah 11:2), understand (Ephesians 1:17), and have faith in the Word of God comes from the Holy Spirit. The culmination of events during the first and second phases of salvation – the new birth (John 3:5-8) and the production of fruit (Romans 8:23; Galatians 5:22-23) – is credited to the work of the Holy Spirit. The Holy Spirit also actively guides us into Truth (John 16:13) and away from false teaching (1 John 2:20-21; 26-27). Resisting the Holy Spirit's work as he assists us in hearing, understanding, teaching, producing fruit, and avoiding error can prevent or misdirect the effectiveness of the Word of God in our lives (Ephesians 4:30; 1 Thessalonians 5:19).

Now if the ministry that brought death, which was engraved in letters on stone, came with glory, so that the Israelites could not look steadily at the face of Moses because of its glory, transitory though it was, will not the ministry of the Spirit be even more glorious? If the ministry that brought condemnation was glorious, how much more glorious is the ministry that brings righteousness! For what was glorious has no glory now in comparison with the surpassing glory. And if what was transitory came with glory, how much greater is the glory of that which lasts! Therefore, since we have such a hope, we are very bold. We are not like Moses, who would put a veil over his face to prevent the Israelites from seeing the end of what was passing away. But their minds were made dull, for to this day the same veil remains when the old covenant is read. It has not been removed, because only in Christ is it taken away. Even to this day when Moses is read, a veil covers their hearts. But whenever anyone turns to the Lord, the veil is taken away. Now the Lord is the Spirit, and where the Spirit of the Lord is, there is freedom. And we all, who with unveiled faces contemplate the Lord's glory, are being transformed into his image with ever-increasing glory, which

comes from the Lord, who is the Spirit.
Therefore, since through God's mercy we have this ministry, we do
not lose heart. Rather, we have renounced secret and shameful ways;
we do not use deception, nor do we distort the word of God. On the
contrary, by setting forth the truth plainly we commend ourselves to
everyone's conscience in the sight of God. And even if our gospel is
veiled, it is veiled to those who are perishing. The god of this age has
blinded the minds of unbelievers, so that they cannot see the light
of the gospel that displays the glory of Christ, who is the image of
God. For what we preach is not ourselves, but Jesus Christ as Lord,
and ourselves as your servants for Jesus' sake. For God, who said,
"Let light shine out of darkness," made his light shine in our hearts
to give us the light of the knowledge of God's glory displayed in the
face of Christ. But we have this treasure in jars of clay to show that
this all-surpassing power is from God and not from us. We are hard
pressed on every side, but not crushed; perplexed, but not in despair;
persecuted, but not abandoned; struck down, but not destroyed. We
always carry around in our body the death of Jesus, so that the life
of Jesus may also be revealed in our body. For we who are alive are
always being given over to death for Jesus' sake, so that his life may
also be revealed in our mortal body. So then, death is at work in us, but
life is at work in you. It is written: "I believed; therefore I have spoken."
Since we have that same spirit of faith, we also believe and therefore
speak, because we know that the one who raised the Lord Jesus
from the dead will also raise us with Jesus and present us with you to
himself. All this is for your benefit, so that the grace that is reaching
more and more people may cause thanksgiving to overflow to the glory
of God. Therefore we do not lose heart. Though outwardly we are
wasting away, yet inwardly we are being renewed day by day. For our
light and momentary troubles are achieving for us an eternal glory that
far outweighs them all. So we fix our eyes not on what is seen, but on
what is unseen, since what is seen is temporary, but what is unseen
is eternal.   – 2 Corinthians 3:7 – 4:18

Chapter Twenty-Two:
Ephesians 4:12-25 – Teaching Matures Believer for the New Life

Teachers help prepare and mature the body of Christ, which then produces good works:

So Christ himself gave the apostles, the prophets, the evangelists, the pastors and teachers, to equip his people for works of service, so that the body of Christ may be built up until we all reach unity in the faith and in the knowledge of the Son of God and become mature, attaining to the whole measure of the fullness of Christ. Then we will no longer be infants, tossed back and forth by the waves, and blown here and there by every wind of teaching and by the cunning and craftiness of people in their deceitful scheming. Instead, speaking the truth in love, we will grow to become in every respect the mature body of him who is the head, that is, Christ. From him the whole body, joined and held together by every supporting ligament, grows and builds itself up in love, as each part does its work. So I tell you this, and insist on it in the Lord, that you must no longer live as the Gentiles do, in the futility of their thinking. They are darkened in their understanding and separated from the life of God because of the ignorance that is in them due to the hardening of their hearts. Having lost all sensitivity, they have given themselves over to sensuality so as to indulge in every kind of impurity, and they are full of greed. That, however, is not the way of life you learned when you heard about Christ and were taught in him in accordance with the truth that is in Jesus. You were taught, with regard to your former way of life, to put off your old self, which is being corrupted by its deceitful desires; to be made new in the attitude of your minds; and to put on the new self, created to be like God in true righteousness and holiness. Therefore each of you must put off falsehood and speak truthfully to your neighbor.

Chapter Twenty-Three:
Ephesians 5:25-26 – The Three Phases: Made Holy, Cleansed with the Word, Presented Blameless

The complete system is described in Ephesians 5:25-26:

> *Christ loved the church and gave himself up for her to make her holy, cleansing her by the washing with water through the word, and to present her to himself as a radiant church, without stain or wrinkle or any other blemish, but holy and blameless.*

Notes:
1. **Phase one is the Gospel** – "Gave Himself" to "make her holy"
2. **Phase Two is maturity and fruit** – "washing with water through the word"
3. **Phase Three is the Crown** – "present her to himself" a "radiant church," "without stain or wrinkle or blemish, but blameless" (To be blameless after phase two – this is the goal.)

Chapter Twenty-Four:
Philippians 1:9-11 – Growth in Knowledge and Insight = Fruit

And this is my prayer: that your love may abound more and more in knowledge and depth of insight, so that you may be able to discern what is best and may be pure and blameless for the day of Christ, filled with the fruit of righteousness that comes through Jesus Christ—to the glory and praise of God.

In this passage, Paul is expressing to the Philippians his desire for their lives as Christians in this world, from the time they became saints (born-again believers in Christ) and "until the day of Christ". During this period of life as a Christian on earth, the goal of the believer is to:

1. Mature and grow in Christ, and have the nature of God abound more and more in their lives
2. Increase in the knowledge of and insight into God's Word, which is the Truth; God's Word reveals God's nature, God's will, God's desire, God's plan, God's attitude, and God's power; knowledge of the Word also brings hope, faith, empowerment and understanding (and many other things as well); knowledge of the Word enables the Christian "to discern what is best" (Philippians 1:10) and to "test and approve what God's will is" (Romans 12:2)
3. Gain this empowerment to know and to have faith do God's word, which will result in being "filled with the fruit of righteousness" in the period between the point of salvation (phase one) and glorification (phase three)
4. Produce a fruitful life and be found pure and blameless on the day they stand before Jesus Christ (2 Corinthians 5:10); those who grow in the knowledge of the Word of God and attain the ability to discern how to think, speak and act like God will succeed
5. Make the effort to grow, because success is not guaranteed; not all Christians will achieve the goal of being "filled with the fruit of righteousness" since doing so requires more than merely believing there is a God and having faith in Jesus his Son for salvation (phase one); success in phase two is achieved by knowing God's Word – not "knowing" like the Gnostics, but instead, having a knowledge that leads to the ability to discern, recognize, and identify Truth from

falsehood, reality from deception, God from gods, holiness from sin, etc; it is the renewing of the formerly corrupt mind and soul

Without growing in the knowledge of God, the born-again believer will be left to live his life as a new creature in Christ without really knowing who God is, who he is, what he is to do, how he will be evaluated, etc. Instead, he will be left to find the answers to these questions by reasoning from the darkness of a pagan past or by replacing pagan reasoning with imaginative mystical logic based on cultural remains of Christian lore, tradition and fragmented pieces of Christian scripture or recycled theology.

Chapter Twenty-Five:
Colossians 1:5-14 – Bearing Fruit and Growing

... the faith and love that spring from the hope stored up for you in heaven and about which you have already heard in the true message of the gospel that has come to you. In the same way, the gospel is bearing fruit and growing throughout the whole world—just as it has been doing among you since the day you heard it and truly understood God's grace. You learned it from Epaphras, our dear fellow servant, who is a faithful minister of Christ on our behalf, and who also told us of your love in the Spirit. For this reason, since the day we heard about you, we have not stopped praying for you. We continually ask God to fill you with the knowledge of his will through all the wisdom and understanding that the Spirit gives, so that you may live a life worthy of the Lord and please him in every way: bearing fruit in every good work, growing in the knowledge of God, being strengthened with all power according to his glorious might so that you may have great endurance and patience, and giving joyful thanks to the Father, who has qualified you to share in the inheritance of his holy people in the kingdom of light. For he has rescued us from the dominion of darkness and brought us into the kingdom of the Son he loves, in whom we have redemption, the forgiveness of sins.

Chapter Twenty-Six:
Colossians 2:2-3:16 – Full Riches of Complete Understanding

My goal is that they may be encouraged in heart and united in love, so that they may have the full riches of complete understanding, in order that they may know the mystery of God, namely, Christ, in whom are hidden all the treasures of wisdom and knowledge. I tell you this so that no one may deceive you by fine-sounding arguments…. So then, just as you received Christ Jesus as Lord, continue to live your lives in him, rooted and built up in him, strengthened in the faith as you were taught…. See to it that no one takes you captive through hollow and deceptive philosophy, which depends on human tradition and the elemental spiritual forces of this world rather than on Christ…. God made you alive with Christ. He forgave us all our sins, having canceled the charge of our legal indebtedness, which stood against us and condemned us; he has taken it away, nailing it to the cross…. Since you died with Christ to the elemental spiritual forces of this world, why, as though you still belonged to the world, do you submit to its rules: "Do not handle! Do not taste! Do not touch!"? These rules, which have to do with things that are all destined to perish with use, are based on merely human commands and teachings. Such regulations indeed have an appearance of wisdom, with their self-imposed worship, their false humility and their harsh treatment of the body, but they lack any value in restraining sensual indulgence. Since, then, you have been raised with Christ, set your hearts on things above, where Christ is, seated at the right hand of God. Set your minds on things above, not on earthly things. For you died, and your life is now hidden with Christ in God. When Christ, who is your life, appears, then you also will appear with him in glory. Put to death, therefore, whatever belongs to your earthly nature: sexual immorality, impurity, lust, evil desires and greed, which is idolatry. Because of these, the wrath of God is coming. You used to walk in these ways, in the life you once lived. But now you must also rid yourselves of all such things as these: anger, rage, malice, slander, and filthy language from your lips. Do not lie to each other, since you have taken off your old self with its practices and have put on the new self, which is being renewed in knowledge in the image of its Creator…. Therefore, as God's chosen people, holy and dearly loved, clothe yourselves with compassion, kindness, humility, gentleness and patience…. And over all these virtues put on love, which binds them all together in perfect unity. Let the peace of Christ rule in your hearts, since as members of one body you were called to peace.

Chapter Twenty-Seven:
Hebrews 5 and 6 – Struggle, Sequence and Results of Teaching

We have much to say about this, but it is hard to make it clear to you because you no longer try to understand (also, because you are slow to learn). In fact, though by this time you ought to be teachers, you need someone to teach you the elementary truths of God's word all over again. You need milk, not solid food! Anyone who lives on milk, being still an infant, is not acquainted with the teaching about righteousness. But solid food is for the mature, who by constant use have trained themselves to distinguish good from evil.   *– Hebrews 5:11-14*

Therefore let us move beyond the elementary teachings about Christ and be taken forward to maturity, not laying again the foundation of repentance from acts that lead to death, and of faith in God, instruction about cleansing rites, the laying on of hands, the resurrection of the dead, and eternal judgment. And God permitting, we will do so. It is impossible for those who have once been enlightened, who have tasted the heavenly gift, who have shared in the Holy Spirit, who have tasted the goodness of the word of God and the powers of the coming age and who have fallen away, to be brought back to repentance. To their loss they are crucifying the Son of God all over again and subjecting him to public disgrace. Land that drinks in the rain often falling on it and that produces a crop useful to those for whom it is farmed receives the blessing of God. But land that produces thorns and thistles is worthless and is in danger of being cursed. In the end it will be burned. Even though we speak like this, dear friends, we are convinced of better things in your case—the things that have to do with salvation.   *– Hebrews 6:1-9*

Chapter Twenty-Eight:
James 1:18-25 – Phase One: Image in Mirror; Phase Two: the Man

James teaches about the saving and transforming power of the Word in James 1:18-25:

> *He chose to give us birth through the word of truth, that we might be a kind of firstfruits of all he created…. Therefore, get rid of all moral filth and the evil that is so prevalent and humbly accept the word planted in you, which can save you. Do not merely listen to the word, and so deceive yourselves. Do what it says. Anyone who listens to the word but does not do what it says is like someone who looks at his face in a mirror and, after looking at himself, goes away and immediately forgets what he looks like. But whoever looks intently into the perfect law that gives freedom, and continues in it—not forgetting what they have heard, but doing it—they will be blessed in what they do.*

The Word is the seed that causes the new birth. It is engrafted into you at the new birth, but we must also meekly receive it and allow it to renew our minds.

Chapter Twenty-Nine:
1 Peter 1:9-15 – Peter's First Discourse on the Word

… for you are receiving the end result of your faith, the salvation of your souls. Concerning this salvation, the prophets, who spoke of the grace that was to come to you, searched intently and with the greatest care, trying to find out the time and circumstances to which the Spirit of Christ in them was pointing when he predicted the sufferings of the Messiah and the glories that would follow. It was revealed to them that they were not serving themselves but you, when they spoke of the things that have now been told you by those who have preached the gospel to you by the Holy Spirit sent from heaven. Even angels long to look into these things. Therefore, with minds that are alert and fully sober, set your hope on the grace to be brought to you when Jesus Christ is revealed at his coming. As obedient children, do not conform to the evil desires you had when you lived in ignorance. But just as he who called you is holy, so be holy in all you do; for it is written: "Be holy, because I am holy."

Chapter Thirty:
1 Peter 1:22-2:3 – Peter's Second Discourse on the Word

Now that you have purified yourselves by obeying the truth so that you have sincere love for each other, love one another deeply, from the heart. For you have been born again, not of perishable seed, but of imperishable, through the living and enduring word of God. For,
"All people are like grass,
and all their glory is like the flowers of the field;
the grass withers and the flowers fall,
but the word of the Lord endures forever."
And this is the word that was preached to you. Therefore, rid yourselves of all malice and all deceit, hypocrisy, envy, and slander of every kind. Like newborn babies, crave pure spiritual milk, so that by it you may grow up in your salvation, now that you have tasted that the Lord is good.

Chapter Thirty-One:
2 Peter 1:2-2:1 – Peter's Third Discourse on the Word

Grace and peace be yours in abundance through the knowledge of God and of Jesus our Lord. His divine power has given us everything we need for a godly life through our knowledge of him who called us by his own glory and goodness. Through these he has given us his very great and precious promises, so that through them you may participate in the divine nature, having escaped the corruption in the world caused by evil desires. For this very reason, make every effort to add to your faith goodness; and to goodness, knowledge; and to knowledge, self-control; and to self-control, perseverance; and to perseverance, godliness; and to godliness, mutual affection; and to mutual affection, love. For if you possess these qualities in increasing measure, they will keep you from being ineffective and unproductive in your knowledge of our Lord Jesus Christ. But whoever does not have them is nearsighted and blind, forgetting that they have been cleansed from their past sins.

Therefore, my brothers and sisters, make every effort to confirm your calling and election. For if you do these things, you will never stumble, and you will receive a rich welcome into the eternal kingdom of our Lord and Savior Jesus Christ. So I will always remind you of these things, even though you know them and are firmly established in the truth you now have. I think it is right to refresh your memory as long as I live in the tent of this body, because I know that I will soon put it aside, as our Lord Jesus Christ has made clear to me. And I will make every effort to see that after my departure you will always be able to remember these things. For we did not follow cleverly devised stories when we told you about the coming of our Lord Jesus Christ in power, but we were eyewitnesses of his majesty. He received honor and glory from God the Father when the voice came to him from the Majestic Glory, saying, "This is my Son, whom I love; with him I am well pleased." We ourselves heard this voice that came from heaven when we were with him on the sacred mountain. We also have the prophetic message as something completely reliable, and you will do well to pay attention to it, as to a light shining in a dark place, until the day dawns and the morning star rises in your hearts.

Above all, you must understand that no prophecy of Scripture came about by the prophet's own interpretation of things. For prophecy never had its origin in the human will, but prophets, though human, spoke from God as they were carried along by the Holy Spirit. But there were also false prophets among the people, just as there will be false teachers among you. They will secretly introduce destructive heresies, even denying the sovereign Lord who bought them—bringing swift destruction on themselves.

Note what Peter is saying in this passage:

1. Faith = being born again
2. Goodness = receiving the new nature
3. Knowledge = study
4. Self-control =putting off of the old self
5. Perseverance = continuing and enduring
6. Godliness = Fruit times 30
7. Kindness = Increasing to 60 times
8. Love = Fullness of 100 times

Chapter Thirty-Two:
1 John 1:1-7 – John Describes the System

John addresses this same system in John 1:1-7:

That which was from the beginning, which we have heard, which we have seen with our eyes, which we have looked at and our hands have touched—this we proclaim concerning the Word of life. The life appeared; we have seen it and testify to it, and we proclaim to you the eternal life, which was with the Father and has appeared to us. We proclaim to you what we have seen and heard, so that you also may have fellowship with us. And our fellowship is with the Father and with his Son, Jesus Christ. We write this to make our joy complete. This is the message we have heard from him and declare to you: God is light; in him there is no darkness at all. If we claim to have fellowship with him and yet walk in the darkness, we lie and do not live out the truth. But if we walk in the light, as he is in the light, we have fellowship with one another, and the blood of Jesus, his Son, purifies us from all sin.

Chapter Thirty-Three:
1 Timothy – Stop Neglecting Your Gift: Read, Preach, Teach the Word

As I urged you when I went into Macedonia, stay there in Ephesus so that you may command certain people not to teach false doctrines any longer or to devote themselves to myths and endless genealogies. Such things promote controversial speculations rather than advancing God's work—which is by faith. The goal of this command is love, which comes from a pure heart and a good conscience and a sincere faith. Some have departed from these and have turned to meaningless talk. They want to be teachers of the law, but they do not know what they are talking about or what they so confidently affirm. We know that the law is good if one uses it properly. We also know that the law is made not for the righteous but for lawbreakers and rebels, the ungodly and sinful, the unholy and irreligious, for those who kill their fathers or mothers, for murderers, for the sexually immoral, for those practicing homosexuality, for slave traders and liars and perjurers—and for whatever else is contrary to the sound doctrine that conforms to the gospel concerning the glory of the blessed God, which he entrusted to me. — 1 Timothy 1:3-11*

Timothy, my son, I am giving you this command in keeping with the prophecies once made about you, so that by recalling them you may fight the battle well, holding on to faith and a good conscience, which some have rejected and so have suffered shipwreck with regard to the faith. Among them are Hymenaeus and Alexander.... — 1 Timothy 1:18-20

This is good, and pleases God our Savior, who wants all people to be saved and to come to a knowledge of the truth.... And for this purpose I was appointed a herald and an apostle—I am telling the truth, I am not lying—and a true and faithful teacher of the Gentiles. — 1 Timothy 2:3, 4, 7

I am writing you these instructions so that, if I am delayed, you will know how people ought to conduct themselves in God's household, which is the church of the living God, the pillar and foundation of the truth. — 1 Timothy 3:14-15

The Spirit clearly says that in later times some will abandon the faith and follow deceiving spirits and things taught by demons. Such teachings come through hypocritical liars, whose consciences have been seared as with a hot iron. They forbid people to marry and order them to abstain from certain foods, which God created to be received with thanksgiving by those who believe and who know the truth. For everything God created is good, and nothing is to be rejected if it is received with thanksgiving, because it is consecrated by the word of God and prayer. If you point these things out to the brothers, you will be a good minister of Christ Jesus, nourished on the truths of the faith and of the good teaching that you have followed. Have nothing to do with godless myths and old wives' tales; rather, train yourself to be godly. — 1 Timothy 4:1-7

Command and teach these things. —1 Timothy 4:11

Until I come, devote yourself to the public reading of Scripture, to preaching and to teaching. Do not neglect your gift! — 1 Timothy 4:13

Be diligent in these matters; give yourself wholly to them, so that everyone may see your progress. Watch your life and doctrine closely. Persevere in them, because if you do, you will save both yourself and your hearers. — 1 Timothy 4:15

The elders who direct the affairs of the church well are worthy of double honor, especially those whose work is preaching and teaching. — 1 Timothy 5:17

… so that God's name and our teaching may not be slandered. — 1 Timothy 6:1

These are the things you are to teach and insist on. — 1 Timothy 6:2

Have nothing to do with godless myths and old wives' tales; rather, train yourself to be godly. For physical training is of some value, but godliness has value for all things, holding promise for both the present life and the life to come. This is a trustworthy saying that deserves full acceptance. That is why we labor and strive, because we have put our hope in the living God, who is the Savior of all people, and especially of those who believe. Command and teach these things. Don't let anyone look down on you because you are young, but set an example for the believers in speech, in conduct, in love, in faith and in purity. Until I come, devote *yourself to the public reading of Scripture, to preaching and to teaching. Do not neglect your gift, which was given you through prophecy when the body of elders laid their hands on you. Be diligent in these matters; give yourself wholly to them, so that everyone may see your progress. Watch your life and doctrine closely. Persevere in them, because if you do, you will save both yourself and your hearers.*   — 1 Timothy 4:8-16

These are the things you are to teach and insist on. If anyone teaches otherwise and does not agree to the sound instruction of our Lord Jesus Christ and to godly teaching, they are conceited and understand nothing. They have an unhealthy interest in controversies and quarrels about words that result in envy, strife, malicious talk, evil suspicions and constant friction between people of corrupt mind, who have been robbed of the truth and who think that godliness is a means to financial gain. But godliness with contentment is great gain…. But you, man of God, flee from all this, and pursue righteousness, godliness, faith, love, endurance and gentleness. Fight the good fight of the faith.   — 1 Timothy 6:2-6,11

Timothy, guard what has been entrusted to your care. Turn away from godless chatter and the opposing ideas of what is falsely called knowledge, which some have professed and in so doing have departed from the faith.   — 1 Timothy 6:20

Chapter Thirty-Four:
2 Timothy – Paul Instructs Timothy to Use his Gift of Teaching

I am reminded of your sincere faith…. For this reason I remind you to fan into flame the gift of God, which is in you.   *– 1 Timothy 1:5, 6*

What you heard from me, keep as the pattern of sound teaching, with faith and love in Christ Jesus. Guard the good deposit that was entrusted to you—guard it with the help of the Holy Spirit who lives in us.
– 2 Timothy 1:13-14

You know that everyone in the province of Asia has deserted me, including Phygelus and Hermogenes.   *– 2 Timothy 1:15*

And the things you have heard me say in the presence of many witnesses entrust to reliable people who will also be qualified to teach others.
– 2 Timothy 2:2

Keep reminding God's people of these things. Warn them before God against quarreling about words; it is of no value, and only ruins those who listen. Do your best to present yourself to God as one approved, a worker who does not need to be ashamed and who correctly handles the word of truth. Avoid godless chatter, because those who indulge in it will become more and more ungodly. Their teaching will spread like gangrene. Among them are Hymenaeus and Philetus, who have departed from the truth. They say that the resurrection has already taken place, and they destroy the faith of some.   *– 2 Timothy 2:14-18*

But mark this: There will be terrible times in the last days. People will be lovers of themselves, lovers of money, boastful, proud, abusive, disobedient to their parents, ungrateful, unholy, without love, unforgiving, slanderous, without self-control, brutal, not lovers of the good, treacherous, rash, conceited, lovers of pleasure rather than lovers of God—having a form of godliness but denying its power.

Have nothing to do with such people. They are the kind who worm their way into homes and gain control over gullible women, who are loaded down with sins and are swayed by all kinds of evil desires, always learning but never able to come to a knowledge of the truth. Just as Jannes and Jambres opposed Moses, so also these teachers oppose the truth. They are men of depraved minds, who, as far as the faith is concerned, are rejected. But they will not get very far because, as in the case of those men, their folly will be clear to everyone.

You, however, know all about my teaching, my way of life, my purpose, faith, patience, love, endurance, persecutions, sufferings —what kinds of things happened to me in Antioch, Iconium and Lystra, the persecutions I endured. Yet the Lord rescued me from all of them. In fact, everyone who wants to live a godly life in Christ Jesus will be persecuted, while evildoers and impostors will go from bad to worse, deceiving and being deceived. But as for you, continue in what you have learned and have become convinced of, because you know those from whom you learned it, and how from infancy you have known the Holy Scriptures, which are able to make you wise for salvation through faith in Christ Jesus. All Scripture is God-breathed and is useful for teaching, rebuking, correcting and training in righteousness, so that the servant of God may be thoroughly equipped for every good work.   – 2 Timothy 3:1-17

In the presence of God and of Christ Jesus, who will judge the living and the dead, and in view of his appearing and his kingdom, I give you this charge: Preach the word; be prepared in season and out of season; correct, rebuke and encourage—with great patience and careful instruction. For the time will come when people will not put up with sound doctrine. Instead, to suit their own desires, they will gather around them a great number of teachers to say what their itching ears want to hear. They will turn their ears away from the truth and turn aside to myths. But you, keep your head in all situations, endure hardship, do the work of an evangelist, discharge all the duties of your ministry.   – 2 Timothy 4:1-5

Get Mark and bring him with you, because he is helpful to me in my ministry. I sent Tychicus to Ephesus. When you come, bring the cloak that I left with Carpus at Troas, and my scrolls, especially the parchments.
                                                        – 2 Timothy 4:11-13

The Lord stood at my side and gave me strength, so that through me the message might be fully proclaimed and all the Gentiles might hear it.
                                                        – 2 Timothy 4:17

Chapter Thirty-Five:
Mysticism

Throughout this book, "mysticism" has been categorized and described as a substitute for Truth – as a deceptive imitation. The reason for this is that the Paul and other writers of Scripture portray personal mystical experience in a negative light when compared with the Truth of the divinely originated Word of God. Paul says:

> *Do not let anyone who delights in false humility and the worship of angels disqualify you for the prize. Such a person goes into great detail about what he has seen, and his unspiritual mind puffs him up with idle notions. He has lost connection with the Head.*   – Colossians 2:18-19

God rebukes the mystics of Ezekiel's day when he says through his true prophet:

> *Woe to the foolish prophets who follow their own spirit and have seen nothing! You have not gone up to the breaks in the wall to repair it for the house of Israel so that it will stand firm in the battle on the day of the Lord. Their visions are false and their divinations a lie. They say, "The Lord declares," when the Lord has not sent them; yet they expect their words to be fulfilled. Have you not seen false visions and uttered lying divinations when you say, "The Lord declares," though I have not spoken?*   – Ezekiel 13:3-9

God speaks in the same vein in Jeremiah when he says:

> *Do not listen to what the prophets are prophesying to you; they fill you with false hopes. They speak visions from their own minds, not from the mouth of the Lord…. I did not send these prophets, yet they have run with their message; I did not speak to them, yet they have prophesied…. I have heard what the prophets say who prophesy lies in my name. They say, "I had a dream! I had a dream!" How long will this continue in the hearts of these lying prophets, who prophesy the delusions of their own minds?*   – Jeremiah 23:16, 21, 25

According to the Collins English Dictionary (HarperCollins Publishers 2003), mysticism can be described in three ways:

1. Belief in or experience of a reality surpassing normal human understanding or experience, especially a reality perceived as essential to the nature of life
2. In Christian religious writings (Theology), a system of contemplative prayer and spirituality aimed at achieving direct intuitive experience of the divine
3. Obscure or confused belief or thought

These definitions, taken together, describe something that is a spiritual experience beyond human ability, which is accepted as a direct experience of God, but which can also result in obscure or confused doctrine. Indeed, mysticism must exist in the Christian experience at some level, but is there a definable limit to its appropriateness? Should it be limited according to its historical place in time and/or space? By the spiritual office of the one who experiences it? Or, is it right and wise to limit it by the spiritual condition (i.e., maturity) of the recipient? Should the size of the intended audience be considered as a factor? Can a mystical message be given to just one person to share with everyone in a larger group?

Without question, the Bible supports the reality of mystical experience for mankind – particularly for believers. To help navigate our way through the subject of appropriate "mysticism" we could begin by identifying three subcategories: revelation, illumination and application. All three come under the heading in theology called the "Ministry of the Holy Spirit." In the past the Holy Spirit moved the writers of Scripture through revelation. Today the Holy Spirit illuminates our understanding of those Scriptures when we study them in the context in which they were written. Also, today we are empowered by the Holy Spirit to live a Christian life that produces the fruits and gifts of the Spirit in our lives. This would be the subcategory of "mysticism" just identified as "application." If today's Christian wants a mystical experience then let it be an experience with the Holy Spirit illuminating their understanding of the written Word of God and the Holy Spirit applying the nature of Christ in their lives as the fruit and gifts of the Spirit. There are several reasons a positive form of mystical experience is expected, and even necessary, for a healthy biblical theology and a productive Christian life.

1. When we truly understand the Gospel message of salvation or the revealed written Word of God, we are described as having "heard" the Word of God because of the testimony of the Holy Spirit in our hearts:

   a. "When the Counselor comes, whom I will send to you from the Father, the Spirit of Truth who goes out from the Father, he will testify about me. And you also must testify, for you have been with me from the beginning." (John 15:26)

   b. "'No eye has seen, no ear has heard, no mind has conceived what God has prepared for those who love him' but God has revealed it to us by his Spirit." (1 Corinthians 2:9-10)

   c. "No one knows the thoughts of God except the Spirit of God. We have not received the spirit of the world but the Spirit who is from God, that we may understand what God has freely given us." (1 Corinthians 2:11-12)

   d. "He who has an ear, let him hear what the Spirit says to the churches." (Revelation 2:7, 11, 17, 29; 3:6, 13, 22)

2. We are mystically (supernaturally) regenerated (re-created, born again) by the Holy Spirit, as Paul wrote to Titus:

   a. "He saved us, not because of works done by us in righteousness, but according to his own mercy, by the washing of regeneration and renewal of the Holy Spirit." (Titus 3:5)

   b. "No one can see the kingdom of God unless he is born again.... No one can enter the kingdom of God unless he is born of water and the Spirit. Flesh gives birth to flesh, but the Spirit gives birth to spirit." (John 3:3, 5, 6)

3. To understand the message of the Word of God the believer must be illuminated by the Spirit of God:

   a. "When he, the Spirit of Truth, comes he will guide you into all Truth.... He will bring glory to me by taking from what is mine and making it known to you." (John 16:13-14)

   b. "The Counselor, the Holy Spirit, whom the Father will send in my name, will teach you all things and will remind you of everything I have said to you." (John 14:26)

4. The "calling" of God in the heart of a believer for service (gifting) is a form of mysticism:
   a. "Those who are led by the Spirit of God are sons of God." (Romans 8:14)

5. We have the testimony of God in our hearts and know with assurance what God has revealed to us:
   a. "God's testimony is greater because it is the testimony of God, which he has given about his Son. Anyone who believes in the Son of God has this testimony in his heart." (1 John 5:9-10)
   b. "The Spirit himself testifies with our spirit that we are God's children." (Romans 8:16)
   c. "Because you are sons, God sent the Spirit of his Son into our hearts, the Spirit who calls out: 'Abba, Father.' So you are no longer a slave, but a son." (Galatians 4:6)

6. Jesus said that "out of his heart will flow rivers of living water" when he referred to the Holy Spirit flowing through our lives. This is a description of the manifestation of super-human character, good works, spiritual gifts and fruits of righteousness (John 7:37-39).
   a. "Now to each one the manifestation of the Spirit is given for the common good." (1 Corinthians 12:7)
   b. "God also testified to it by signs, wonders and various miracles, and gifts of the Holy Spirit distributed according to his will." (Hebrews 2:4)

7. Upon being regenerated by the Holy Spirit (born again, phase one), the believer is permanently and eternally indwelt by the Holy Spirit:
   a. "I will ask the Father, and he will give you another Counselor to be with you forever – the Spirit of Truth." (John 14:16)
   b. "You know him, for he lives with you and will be in you." (John 14:17)
   c. "God's Spirit lives in you." (1 Corinthians 3:16)
   d. "Having believed, you were marked in him with a seal, the promised Holy Spirit, who is a deposit guaranteeing our inheritance." (Ephesians 1:13-14)

8. Even a natural man, fully of this world, can be influenced by a mystical experience with the Holy Spirit. This is called "conviction":
   a. "When he comes, he will convict the world of guilt in regard to sin and righteousness and judgment." (John 16:8)
   b. "By the waters of Meribah they angered the Lord, and trouble came to Moses because of them; for they rebelled against the Spirit of God." (Psalm 106:32-33)

The context of the above verses is very important for correctly understanding "good" versus "bad" mysticism. In most of them, having the Word of God available in the soul or mind of the believer is a prerequisite for the mystical experience. The Word always precedes the Spirit. Before the world or the church or the believer can experience the ministry of the Spirit of God, they must have first experienced the ministry of the Word of God.

In Romans 8, Paul writes first about how those "who live in accordance with the spirit have their minds set on what the Spirit desires" (verse 5) and then explains that, "the mind controlled by the Spirit is life and peace" (verse 6), before he writes this:

For if you live according to the sinful nature, you will die; but if by the Spirit you put to death the misdeeds of the body, you will live, because those who are led by the Spirit of God are sons of God.

– Romans 8:13-14

The context of Romans 8 is a mind "set on" – or renewed to – the Word of God, for the Spirit of God to use. This mind, "set on what the Spirit desires" (the Word of God), is contrasted with those "who live according to the sinful nature [and] have their minds set on what that nature desires" (Romans 8:5).

The problem with "being led by the Spirit," "hearing the voice of God," "receiving a revelation," or any of the other mystical experiences I had in mind as I wrote this book, is that they can either result from neglect of the Word of God, or result in neglect of the Word of God.

The Scriptures clearly teach that:
- The Spirit of God moves in our world among unbelievers to convict them of the Truth of the Word
- The man who places faith in the Truth of the Gospel experiences a mystical relationship while hearing the Gospel
- The believer is placed in a mystical relationship with the Spirit of God who lives in him and who unites the believer mystically to Jesus Christ
- During phase two the believer is indwelt by the Holy Spirit who will work, and speak in and through that believer

But, we must keep in mind that all of this is necessarily preceded by the hearing, understanding and accepting of the revelation of the Word of God. In other words, if a person has not heard, understood, known, believed and applied the Word of God, any mystical experience they claim to have had is not a result of the Spirit of God. There is no doubt in my mind that it may be mystical or spiritual, but just because something is supernatural does not mean it is true, righteous, holy, or from God.

As we have noted, the Scriptures clearly state that many false prophets, spirits and teachings have gone out into the world and even into the church – none of which are from God. And, this is not even taking into consideration the imaginations and diluted consciences of men void of the Word of God, or those who consciously ignore the Truth of God's biblical revelation.

It is more convenient to "receive" a subjective message or teach relative "insight" than to understand, present and deal with absolute Truth – or the subsequent harsh, unbending reality of the world God created, and in which we live. Imagination is always easier than reality. It is easier to watch a movie than it is to produce one.

And so, in our biblically illiterate modern Western culture (like many, many other cultures worldwide), it is easier to "hear God" or be "spiritually led" than to learn and understand the Truth. Thus, the lazy, illiterate, blind mystics lead the lazy illiterate, blind masses. This is, to borrow a phrase, the blind leading the blind.

Part of the problem is that a mystical interpretation of Scripture is a deviant form of hermeneutics. When a mystic seeks for the meaning of a passage of Scripture by "allowing the Spirit to lead them" without taking the basic principles of proper hermeneutics into account, they are in error. Truly serious and accurate Bible interpretation requires more than the guidance of the Holy Spirit. The books of the Bible are historical documents written with real words that have real and absolute meanings – not only for the people in the cultures to which the Word of God was written, but also for us today. And so, to correctly understand them, we have to take them into account.

In other words, proper hermeneutics of divinely inspired Scripture must take into consideration the historical setting, the exegetical meaning, the literal translation of the words in the text, and categorical comparison of similar subject matter throughout the rest of Scripture. The bad news for the mystic is that this is a lot of work. It requires a tremendous amount of insight into natural history, linguistics, and basic theology.

The point? It is so much easier for the mystic to simply "hear God" or "let the Spirit reveal" the meaning of a passage of Scripture. And, even more so if the passage is difficult or seems to contradict what the mystic wants to believe or teach. Allegorical interpretation and the spiritualization of words, events and characters in the Bible are very helpful ways for a mystic to avoid any kind a reasonable hermeneutic responsibility. Accordingly, you will often hear the mystic begin a presentation of their pathetic scriptural insight by saying, "The Lord as shown to me...."

These people would do well to recall Peter's words:

> Above all, you must understand that no prophecy of Scripture came about by the prophet's own interpretation. For prophecy never had its origin in the will of man.   – 2 Peter 1:20-21

John tells his readers to "test the spirits to see whether they are from God." But realize, the only way for a believer to test or evaluate a mystic (or a true teacher!) is to know some portion of the Truth by which to compare the teaching. In a scripturally illiterate culture, the standard for this test is not the Word of God, but the hearer's emotions or previous worldview.

Dear friends, do not believe every spirit, but test the spirits to see
whether they are from God, because many false prophets have gone
out into the world. — 1 John 4:1

A mystic who teaches this kind of people – ones who can only judge
based on emotion, human worldview or minimal Bible knowledge (which
may itself be corrupted in its interpretation) – are destined to enter an
erroneous cycle of hearing, evaluating and confirming bad doctrine,
leading ultimately into a descending spiral of doctrinal corruption
and chaos.

The bottom line is this: Your relationship with the Holy Spirit is worthless
without the Word of God. This is not due to any fault of the Spirit of God,
but is entirely due to the weakness and corruption of the unregenerate
human mind and sin nature in man. In other words, you must understand
and be living in the Truth to benefit from the Spirit's presence.

Any revelation or insight that comes from the Spirit of God today is for
the receiver's private guidance or personal confirmation. While it is
hard to imagine, it is impossible for the Holy Spirit to reveal anything for
public proclamation or public instruction now that has not already been
revealed in the written Word of God in Scripture. That is to say, there
are no Apostles in this age receiving new revelation from God for public
proclamation, since if this were to happen, the accuracy or completeness
of the written Word of God would be in question, and we would be forced
to choose between accepted Scripture and mystic apostles.

I have become its servant by the commission God gave me to present
to you the word of God in its fullness – the mystery that has been kept
hidden for ages and generations, but is now disclosed to the saints.
— Colossians 1:25-26

In reading this, then, you will be able to understand my insight into
the mystery of Christ, which was not made known to men in other
generations as it has now been revealed by the Spirit to God's holy
apostles and prophets. — Ephesians 3:4-5

*I warn everyone who hears the words of the prophecy of this book:
If anyone adds anything to them, God will add to him the plagues
described in this book. And if anyone takes words away from this book
of prophecy, God will take away from him his share in the tree of life
and in the holy city, which are described in this book.*

– Revelation 22:18-19 (96 AD)

*I will not impose any other burden on you; only hold on to what you
have until I come.* *– Revelation 2:24-25*

Chapter Thirty-Six:
Psalm 119, A Study of the Word of God

The 176 verses of Psalm 119 are divided into twenty-two groups of eight verses each (22 x 8 = 176). The twenty-two groups, or strophes, are each headed with one of the twenty-two letters of the Hebrew alphabet – and every one of the eight verses in each strophe begins with the same Hebrew letter. For example, the strophe consisting of verses 1-8 are headed with the first letter of the Hebrew alphabet, aleph, and each of those eight verses begins with aleph.

Every Hebrew letter is a symbol representing a picture, and the name of each letter has a meaning corresponding to the ancient image it models.

There are ten synonyms used to refer to the Word of God – the revelation of Truth that God has given to man – in this Psalm. These ten words are:

1. Law (torah) – used 25 times; means direction or instruction
2. Word (dabar) – used 20 times; is a general term for God's revelation
3. Promise ('imrah) – used 19 times; used to capture the lure of the Word
4. Commands (miswah) – used 21 times; indicates the absolute nature of God's Word
5. Decrees (huqqim) – used 21 times; "things inscribed" such as recorded law
6. Laws (mispot) – used 19 times; means a binding law
7. Precepts (piqqudim) – used 21 times; refers to a legal order to do or not do something
8. Statutes ('edah) – used 22 times; a declaration of God's will which becomes conduct
9. Way (derek) – used 11 times; refers to walking in God's Word in life
10. Path ('orah) – used 5 times; also refers to walking in God's Word

The writer of this Psalm describes several conflicts he faces because of his commitment to the Word of God and his desire to follow the Word of God:

1. The need for steadfastness to walk in God's ways
2. Inner sinful desires
3. Persecution by officials
4. Mocking by men
5. Pressure to forsake his commitment

א Aleph   (Verses 1-8)

The letter aleph is a symbol of two ox heads yoked together to represent strength or leadership. The word aleph means "to learn".

1 Blessed are those whose ways are blameless,
who walk according to the law of the Lord.
2 Blessed are those who keep his statutes
and seek him with all their heart—
3t hey do no wrong
but follow his ways.
4 You have laid down precepts
that are to be fully obeyed.
5 Oh, that my ways were steadfast
in obeying your decrees!
6 Then I would not be put to shame
when I consider all your commands.
7 I will praise you with an upright heart
as I learn your righteous laws.
8 I will obey your decrees;
do not utterly forsake me.

The conflict described in verses 1-8 arose from the psalmist's desire to be steadfast in his obedience, like the men he describes as blameless, walking in the law, keeping the statutes and seeking God (1-3). The writer desires to be like these men, but he knows that he is weak and not far along in the process of becoming like them. He desires to obey, and seeks help. The help sought here, and throughout Psalm 119, comes from the Word of God. He vows to "consider all [God's] commands," and "learn [God's] righteous laws". In this way, he will be able to "obey [God's] decrees", as long as God continues to be with him and help him.

ב **Beth**   (Verses 9-16)

The letter beth is a symbol for a house or a tent, and means "house". It represents being in God's will by creating the image of a home with a wife and kids, or of the house of God, which is the Temple. In other words, we find the Word and we live there. We hear ("I have hidden"), understand ("teach me") and continue in God's Word ("I rejoice…I meditate…I delight").

> *9 How can a young person stay on the path of purity?*
> *By living according to your word.*
> *10 I seek you with all my heart;*
> *do not let me stray from your commands.*
> *11 I have hidden your word in my heart*
> *that I might not sin against you.*
> *12 Praise be to you, Lord;*
> *teach me your decrees.*
> *13 With my lips I recount*
> *all the laws that come from your mouth.*
> *14 I rejoice in following your statutes*
> *as one rejoices in great riches.*
> *15 I meditate on your precepts*
> *and consider your ways.*
> *16 I delight in your decrees;*
> *I will not neglect your word.*

The conflict of verses 9-16 is the writer's desire to avoid sin – to not stray, but remain pure (1-3). The solution is fivefold:

1. Take in – or hear – the Word of God ("hidden your word in my heart" – 11)
2. Understand the Word of God that was taught ("teach me your decrees" – 12)
3. Speak the Word of God that is understood ("with my lips I recount all the laws" – 13)
4. Follow and do the Word of God ("I rejoice in following your statutes" – 14)
5. Continue in the Word of God that you already know ("I meditate on your precepts" – 15)

ג Gimel   (Verses 17-24)

The letter gimel is a pictograph of a camel's neck. The word means to "recompense" or "benefit", and the benefit or goodness in this Psalm comes when God gives understanding to the psalmist so he can see and understand the Word.

> 17 Be good to your servant while I live,
>   that I may obey your word.
> 18 Open my eyes that I may see
>   wonderful things in your law.
> 19 I am a stranger on earth;
>   do not hide your commands from me.
> 20 My soul is consumed with longing
>   for your laws at all times.
> 21 You rebuke the arrogant, who are accursed,
>   those who stray from your commands.
> 22 Remove from me their scorn and contempt,
>   for I keep your statutes.
> 23 Though rulers sit together and slander me,
>   your servant will meditate on your decrees.
> 24 Your statutes are my delight;
>   they are my counselors.

In verses 17-24 the psalmist identifies himself as a "stranger on earth" who lives among arrogant men (sadly, including rulers) who have rejected God's Word and so are accursed. These men cannot help the psalmist with counsel for his life and would rather treat him, like they do God's Word, with scorn and contempt.

The psalmist thus turns to God's Words, saying of them, "they are my counselors". The psalmist seeks goodness from God (17), but not in the form of physical blessings. What the psalmist prays instead is that God would "Open my eyes that I may see wonderful things in your law" (18), because he knows that when his eyes are opened he will be empowered to "obey [God's] word". This empowerment through understanding that leads to obedience is called "good" because it prevents the psalmist from becoming like the arrogant, accursed men who treat God's Truth with contempt – and then in its place, promote their own ways and counselors.

⊤ Daleth   (Verses 25-32)

The letter daleth is a symbol of an open door, or a curtain of a tent. In the early days of Israel, doors were hinged in the top corner and this is reflected in the symbol. The word refers to letting something in or finding your way into God. The bent shape of the daleth can also represent a person who is bent over in need. It is said that the "ear" of the letter is leaning toward the letter gimmel, listening for the approach of goodness and loving-kindness.

> 25 I am laid low in the dust;
>   preserve my life according to your word.
> 26 I gave an account of my ways and you answered me;
>   teach me your decrees.
> 27 Cause me to understand the way of your precepts,
>   that I may meditate on your wonderful deeds.
> 28 My soul is weary with sorrow;
>   strengthen me according to your word.
> 29 Keep me from deceitful ways;
>   be gracious to me and teach me your law.
> 30 I have chosen the way of faithfulness;
>   I have set my heart on your laws.
> 31 I hold fast to your statutes, Lord;
>   do not let me be put to shame.
> 32 I run in the path of your commands,
>   for you have broadened my understanding.

The psalmist is troubled because of both his physical ("laid low in dust") and mental condition ("soul is weary with sorrow"). Yet he knows the answer to his physical problem is in the promises of God's Word ("preserve me according to your Word"), and his weary, sorrowful soul can be strengthen by that same Word ("strengthen me according to your word"). In each case, after stating his problem the psalmist asks God to teach him. First, he says "teach me your decrees" and then, "teach me your law". He states that he has chosen to be faithful by setting his "heart on [God's] laws" and holding "fast to [God's] statutes". These eight verses end with the author rejoicing that, because God has "broadened my understanding" of his Word, he has been enabled to "run in the path of [God's] commands". So, the man who was physically low and mentally weary regained his strength and began to run, because God had opened the door of his understanding of the Word – just like he had asked.

ה He   (Verses:33-40)

This letter represents a window, a lattice or a house with a window.
It suggests the letting in of light or revelation.

> 33 Teach me, Lord, the way of your decrees,
>   that I may follow it to the end.
> 34 Give me understanding, so that I may keep your law
>   and obey it with all my heart.
> 35 Direct me in the path of your commands,
>   for there I find delight.
> 36 Turn my heart toward your statutes
>   and not toward selfish gain.
> 37 Turn my eyes away from worthless things;
>   preserve my life according to your word.
> 38 Fulfill your promise to your servant,
>   so that you may be feared.
> 39 Take away the disgrace I dread,
>   for your laws are good.
> 40 How I long for your precepts!
>   In your righteousness preserve my life.

The psalmist asks for the light of the Word of God to enter his soul when
he says, "teach me", "give me understanding", "direct me", "turn my
heart", and "turn my eyes". Two things he recognizes as blocking the
entrance of the light of the Word are "selfish gain" and "worthless things".
Worthless things would refer to false teachings, false gods, worldly
philosophies, etc. Here we see that the Word of God, understood in the
heart of a man, removes disgrace and preserves life.

ו Waw   (Verses 41-48)

The letter waw is an image of a hook, a nail, or a peg. It symbolizes the
hooks of silver fastened to posts that held the curtains of the tabernacle
and other tents in place. The letter waw represents something you
depend on, such as the Word of God. In these verses, the psalmist
focuses on how he can trust God's Word. Since he can depend on it to be
true, he will speak of God's Word even before kings. The psalmist, like the
Apostle Paul, knows that he will never be ashamed or let down by God's
Word (Romans 1:16) because the Word of God has the power to do what
it claims to be able to do.

41 *May your unfailing love come to me, Lord,*
  your salvation, according to your promise;
42 *then I can answer anyone who taunts me,*
  for I trust in your word.
43 *Never take your word of truth from my mouth,*
  for I have put my hope in your laws.
44 *I will always obey your law,*
  for ever and ever.
45 *I will walk about in freedom,*
  for I have sought out your precepts.
46 *I will speak of your statutes before kings*
  and will not be put to shame,
47 *for I delight in your commands*
  because I love them.
48 *I reach out for your commands, which I love,*
  that I may meditate on your decrees.

God's Word tells us of the salvation that comes from God (which is also called the "unfailing love" of God's covenant). It appears that the psalmist is enduring the "taunts" of men for having trusted in the promise of salvation found in God's Word. Still, he fully counts on experiencing that salvation. He says with Paul, I "will not be put to shame". Because he has sought God's Truth, the psalmist knows the Truth and "will walk about in freedom". Jesus said the same thing when he promised: "You will know the truth, and the truth will set you free" (John 8:32).

ז Zayin   (Verses 49-56)

The letter zayin describes a weapon – most likely, a sword. The word zayin derives from a root word meaning "sustenance" or "nourishment". It includes the concept that to survive and provide for yourself, there are times you must fight and defend yourself, especially in the area of Truth and spiritual warfare.

49 *Remember your word to your servant,*
  for you have given me hope.
50 *My comfort in my suffering is this:*
  Your promise preserves my life.
51 *The arrogant mock me unmercifully,*

but I do not turn from your law.
52 I remember, Lord, your ancient laws,
  and I find comfort in them.
53 Indignation grips me because of the wicked,
  who have forsaken your law.
54 Your decrees are the theme of my song
  wherever I lodge.
55 In the night, Lord, I remember your name,
  that I may keep your law.
56 This has been my practice:
  I obey your precepts.

The psalmist recognizes that the Word of God provides him with hope (49) in the midst of mocking by the arrogant (51) and the wicked (53). The promises of the Word of God nourish the psalmist with comfort and provide a defensive weapon for the preservation of his life (50). The ancient laws are said to also supply comfort (52). The arrogant and wicked attack this believer's stance on the Truth, yet he remains faithful (50-52). The arrogant have rejected God's Word and become wicked, but the indignation of the psalmist preserves his heart. The psalmist continues the practice of remembering the Truth wherever he spends his nights, so the Truth continues to provide his shelter in the night (53-56).

ת Heth   (Verses 57-64)
The letter heth is a symbol of a hedge, a fence, or an enclosure – that is, protection. The image may be of stacked stones that surround and protect.

57 You are my portion, Lord;
  I have promised to obey your words.
58 I have sought your face with all my heart;
  be gracious to me according to your promise.
59 I have considered my ways
  and have turned my steps to your statutes.
60 I will hasten and not delay
  to obey your commands.
61 the wicked bind me with ropes,
  I will not forget your law.

62 At midnight I rise to give you thanks
  for your righteous laws.
63 I am a friend to all who fear you,
  to all who follow your precepts.
64 The earth is filled with your love, Lord;
  teach me your decrees.

The Lord is the portion (57) located inside the parameters of the wall of protection provided by the Truth. The psalmist promises to stay inside these parameters and obey God's Word. God's statues (the Word) are the steppingstones that guide the writer (59). Even if the wicked physically restrain him he will not forget God's law (61). Everyone who fears the Lord and follows his Word is within the same enclosure, or sphere of protection and fellowship, as the psalmist, and so is considered his friend (63).

The entire earth is enclosed with God's Word (64), so there is nowhere anyone can go that God has not already established his Truth and reality. The wicked may bind this writer (61), but God's word is there to provide a greater hedge of protection for him since he:

1. Has made the Lord his portion (57)
2. Has promised to obey God's Word (57)
3. Has sought God's face with all the understanding of his inner being (58)
4. Has analyzed his lifestyle and adjusted it to correspond to God's statutes (59)
5. Does not delay in obeying God's commands (60)
6. Refuses to forget God's law in the face of physical opposition (61)
7. Desires to be taught the decrees of God (64)

ט Teth   (Verses 65-72)

The letter teth was patterned on two rolls, curves, or snakes and may look like something that is twisted or knotted together. It represents the paradox of good and evil, such as how a person could choose to respond to God or circumstances in a good or evil way. The word teth means"to stand up or bow down", in reference to a relationship with God.

65 Do good to your servant
   according to your word, Lord.
66 Teach me knowledge and good judgment,
   for I trust your commands.
67 Before I was afflicted I went astray,
   but now I obey your word.
68 You are good, and what you do is good;
   teach me your decrees.
69 Though the arrogant have smeared me with lies,
   I keep your precepts with all my heart.
70 Their hearts are callous and unfeeling,
   but I delight in your law.
71 It was good for me to be afflicted
   so that I might learn your decrees.
72 The law from your mouth is more precious to me
   than thousands of pieces of silver and gold.

The very nature of God's Word creates a paradox. The Word of God is holy and good, and yet it can benefit both the obedient and the disobedient – both the blessed and the afflicted. The psalmist recounts his experience of this principle in verses 67 and 71 when he says,

Before I was afflicted I went astray, but now I obey your word… It was good for me to be afflicted so that I might learn your decrees.

The Word of God speaks to all people, but the results depend on each individual's heart. Some hearts are calloused and unfeeling, but the psalmist's heart was soft and responded with delight to God's Word (70). Likewise, affliction draws some toward a desire for the Truth; yet for others, affliction releases bitterness and the arrogance of their heart (69). Although confusing, all of this is good because it provides the opportunity to learn what God is teaching (68). For those who respond positively to the Truth, there will be benefits more "precious… than thousands of pieces of silver and gold" (72).

Yodh   (Verses 73-80)

Yodh is a symbol of a cupped or bent hand. The image may also be of a closed fist or a hand that is holding something. It indicates power or guidance.

> 73 *Your hands made me and formed me;*
>   *give me understanding to learn your commands.*
> 74 *May those who fear you rejoice when they see me,*
>   *for I have put my hope in your word.*
> 75 *I know, Lord, that your laws are righteous,*
>   *and that in faithfulness you have afflicted me.*
> 76 *May your unfailing love be my comfort,*
>   *according to your promise to your servant.*
> 77 *Let your compassion come to me that I may live,*
>   *for your law is my delight.*
> 78 *May the arrogant be put to shame for wronging me without cause;*
>   *but I will meditate on your precepts.*
> 79 *May those who fear you turn to me,*
>   *those who understand your statutes.*
> 80 *May I wholeheartedly follow your decrees,*
>   *that I may not be put to shame.*

The psalmist uses the fact that he has been made and formed by God as the basis for asking God to help him understand his Word (73). He is a man in affliction caused by other men who unjustly come against him (78) and who are the enemies of Truth since they reject the Word of God and in their arrogance advance their own plans and the world's views. In this unjust affliction the psalmist realizes that the creator who formed him with His hands still holds him and has allowed this undeserved affliction through the hands of men (75-76). He counts on God's unfailing love and compassion to comfort him and allow him to live (76-77). The result will be that other men who fear God will rejoice when they see the psalmist's deliverance by the hand of God (74). The arrogant who oppose God's Word will be put to shame (78), while those who renew their minds by meditating on God's Word will continue to find comfort in the midst of their afflictions (78, 75, 76).

⊃ Kaph   (Verses 81-88)

The letter kaph shows the palm or hollow of a hand and represents a hand, bowl, plate or anything designed to receive. By association, it can mean asking, weakness or reaching out to receive.

> 81 *My soul faints with longing for your salvation,*
>   *but I have put my hope in your word.*
> 82 *My eyes fail, looking for your promise;*
>   *I say, "When will you comfort me?"*
> 83 *Though I am like a wineskin in the smoke,*
>   *I do not forget your decrees.*
> 84 *How long must your servant wait?*
>   *When will you punish my persecutors?*
> 85 *The arrogant dig pits to trap me,*
>   *contrary to your law.*
> 86 *All your commands are trustworthy;*
>   *help me, for I am being persecuted without cause.*
> 87 *They almost wiped me from the earth,*
>   *but I have not forsaken your precepts.*
> 88 *In your unfailing love preserve my life,*
>   *that I may obey the statutes of your mouth.*

The psalmist is still suffering at the hands of men who have rejected the authority of the Word of God (84). They are arrogant, and persecute the man whose hope is in the Word (85). They use laws and logic contrary to God's law to prove the godly man and his godly ways are in error, and so conclude that the ways of God are unprofitable and inappropriate for mankind.

In the face of this attack, the persecuted man puts his hope in God's Word, but still finds himself weak, and asks for help from God (81). His soul (mind, emotions, intellect, will) faint and his eyes (physical effort) fail (81-82) as he waits for God's promises to manifest (82, 84). Just as a wineskin in the smoke (83) holds onto its content in the midst of a blinding odor that stings the eyes, the psalmist sees himself as struggling to hold to his commitment to the Truth in his soul while persevering against the blinding, painful odor of worldly philosophy. He waits with his hands open and his soul reaching out to be filled by God.

ל Lamedh   (Verses 89-96)

Lamedh is an ox goad that is used to get an ox moving. It can mean learning or teaching. When Jesus said to Paul, "It is hard for you to kick against the goads," he may have been referring to Paul coming against the Scriptural teaching concerning the Messiah with a traditional Jewish understanding of the Messiah. The word also refers to correction, learning and the fear of God. Lamedh is the tallest and the middle letter of the Hebrew alphabet, so it appears to tower over the other letters as central and most important.

> 89 Your word, Lord, is eternal;
>   it stands firm in the heavens.
> 90 Your faithfulness continues through all generations;
>   you established the earth, and it endures.
> 91 Your laws endure to this day,
>   for all things serve you.
> 92 If your law had not been my delight,
>   I would have perished in my affliction.
> 93 I will never forget your precepts,
>   for by them you have preserved my life.
> 94 Save me, for I am yours;
>   I have sought out your precepts.
> 95 The wicked are waiting to destroy me,
>   but I will ponder your statutes.
> 96 To all perfection I see a limit,
>   but your commands are boundless.

The tallest letter of the Hebrew alphabet is used to head a set of verses that attest to the established, eternal and enduring Truth of God's Word (89). Understanding of the Word is essential, since all things are based on it (90-91), and without it, we perish in both time and eternity (92-93).

God has revealed himself in the Scriptures, but also in his created universe. Because this general revelation is available in nature, all mankind can seek, study and apply many of God's eternal principles (90-91), and this understanding is of utmost importance. Throughout the psalmist's life the precepts of God's eternal Truth have preserved him (93). The last verse in this section makes a distinction between created things that are limited and the eternal ("boundless") Truth of God (96).

Knowing, understanding, and applying this boundless Truth in a universe with limits, delivers us and preserves our life in time and in eternity when the wicked seek to destroy it (95). This is the greatest Truth.

ת Mem   (Verses 97-104)

The letter mem symbolizes waves of water, and refers to a large body of water such as a sea or ocean. The idea of water rising out of a spring to form a body of water is symbolic of wisdom rising out of the Word of God to fill a man's soul and words with wisdom, as in Proverbs 18:4: "The words a man speaks are deep waters, A flowing stream, a fountain of wisdom."

> 97 Oh, how I love your law!
>   I meditate on it all day long.
> 98 Your commands are always with me
>   and make me wiser than my enemies.
> 99 I have more insight than all my teachers,
>   for I meditate on your statutes.
> 100 I have more understanding than the elders,
>   for I obey your precepts.
> 101 I have kept my feet from every evil path
>   so that I might obey your word.
> 102 I have not departed from your laws,
>   for you yourself have taught me.
> 103 How sweet are your words to my taste,
>   sweeter than honey to my mouth!
> 104 I gain understanding from your precepts;
>   therefore I hate every wrong path.

The source of wisdom, insight and understanding is the Word of God (97-100). It is a spring of water that fills the sea of the psalmist's soul. When he meditates on the law, God's commands are always with him (97-98), and the wisdom which springs from the Word fills his soul to make him wiser than his enemies (98), give him more insight than his teachers (99), and provide him with more understanding than the elders (110).

The psalmist does not mean he is too arrogant to learn from others; nor is he implying that he is wiser – with more insight and understanding

– in his own self or by his own ability. He is simply making a humble acknowledgement that the source of eternal wisdom is not men ("enemies"), nor even the great teachers and elders of Israel. Instead, his wisdom comes from the Word of God itself.

Men are to fill their souls with the Word of God as the rivers fill the sea. The soul filled with the Word of God produces obedience:

"I obey your precepts" (100)
"I have kept my feet from every evil path" (101)
"I have not departed from your laws" (102)
"I gain understanding from your precepts therefore I hate every
wrong path" (104)

ℷ Nun   (Verses 105-112)

The letter nun comes from the image of a fish, tadpole or snake, and means "to propagate, to increase", "offspring", and "prosperity". A fish represents life and activity. It also includes the idea of faithfulness and rewards for faithfulness.

105 Your word is a lamp for my feet,
a light on my path.
106 I have taken an oath and confirmed it,
that I will follow your righteous laws.
107 I have suffered much;
preserve my life, Lord, according to your word.
108 Accept, Lord, the willing praise of my mouth,
and teach me your laws.
109 Though I constantly take my life in my hands,
I will not forget your law.
110 The wicked have set a snare for me,
but I have not strayed from your precepts.
111 Your statutes are my heritage forever;
they are the joy of my heart.
112 My heart is set on keeping your decrees
to the very end.

The psalmist recognizes that in order to preserve his life in a world of suffering and snares (107, 110), he must be committed (106) to walking in the light of the Word of God (105). To this end, he has taken and confirmed a vow to follow God's laws (106). Not only will faithfulness to the Word protect him during his time on earth, but faithfulness to the end (112) will ensure him eternal rewards ("heritage forever" – 111).

O Samekh   (Verses 113-120)

The letter samekh is a prop, support, fulcrum or lever, and it has a meaning of leaning upon something or supporting yourself with something. Leverage and support give stability. The closed circle also represents a shield used for protection. And, it is a visual image of the eternal spiraling of God's Truth and ever-increasing glory.

> 113 I hate double-minded people,
>   but I love your law.
> 114 You are my refuge and my shield;
>   I have put my hope in your word.
> 115 Away from me, you evildoers,
>   that I may keep the commands of my God!
> 116 Sustain me, my God, according to your promise, and I will live;
>   do not let my hopes be dashed.
> 117 Uphold me, and I will be delivered;
>   I will always have regard for your decrees.
> 118 You reject all who stray from your decrees,
>   for their delusions come to nothing.
> 119 All the wicked of the earth you discard like dross;
>   therefore I love your statutes.
> 120 My flesh trembles in fear of you;
>   I stand in awe of your laws.

Trusting in a false worldview, like leaning on a splintered staff, will cause chaos and end in disaster. And this is exactly what happens to the double-minded man (113). Only those who are committed to God's Truth will experience God as their refuge and shield (114), and God is well able to shelter and shield those who hope in his Word. The psalmist wants nothing to do with double-minded evildoers (115) because their ways will neutralize the leverage and support (116, 117) that God's promises and decrees provide on this earth. The double-minded philosophies of man provide no true support or assistance, but instead splinter and collapse like weak levers, which should be rejected and discarded (118-119). It is an awesome thing to understand the looming danger of worthless worldviews when compared to the awesome potential of God's word in our temporal world (120).

ע Ayin   (Verses 121-128)

The letter ayin was made to resemble a pair of eyes or a fountain. The reference is to a means of expression, such as how the eyes are a fountain of the body that express sorrow or pain. The eyes that see represent understanding, which is necessary for obedience. The eyes anticipate obedience.

> 121 *I have done what is righteous and just;*
>   *do not leave me to my oppressors.*
> 122 *Ensure your servant's well-being;*
>   *do not let the arrogant oppress me.*
> 123 *My eyes fail, looking for your salvation,*
>   *looking for your righteous promise.*
> 124 *Deal with your servant according to your love*
>   *and teach me your decrees.*
> 125 *I am your servant; give me discernment*
>   *that I may understand your statutes.*
> 126 *It is time for you to act, Lord;*
>   *your law is being broken.*
> 127 *Because I love your commands*
>   *more than gold, more than pure gold,*
> 128 *and because I consider all your precepts right,*
>   *I hate every wrong path.*

In this strophe, the psalmist is praying for discernment so he can understand the Word (125), and he asks for a revelation of the Truth, so that he will be able to live in obedience to it. In fact, he makes a point of telling God, it is "time for you to act" (126), because he realizes that it is due to his lack of understanding that he breaks the law of God.

The psalmist waits for this teaching, and continues to ask for even more understanding and discernment in order to improve his level of obedience. Since the psalmist has lived in obedience to the Word of God to the best of his ability (121), he confidently anticipates God's help in this regard.

Deliverance is based on obedience, and obedience requires teaching and understanding. The psalmist knows that his inability to see or understanding the Word of God is causing him to be oppressed.

פ Pe   (Verses 129-136)

The letter pe is a symbol of a mouth with a tongue and refers to speech of man or the mouth of God speaking forth his Word in judgment. Since the Pe (speech, word) follows the Ayin (eye, understanding) in the alphabet the order of these two letters indicates it is necessary to understand the Word of God before you start to express the Word of God. Pe means the man is now expressing with his mouth what he understands.

129 *Your statutes are wonderful;*
    therefore I obey them.
130 *The unfolding of your words gives light;*
    it gives understanding to the simple.
131 *I open my mouth and pant,*
    longing for your commands.
132 *Turn to me and have mercy on me,*
    as you always do to those who love your name.
133 *Direct my footsteps according to your word;*
    let no sin rule over me.
134 *Redeem me from human oppression,*
    that I may obey your precepts.
135 *Make your face shine on your servant*
    and teach me your decrees.
136 *Streams of tears flow from my eyes,*
    for your law is not obeyed.

Understanding leads to obedience since sanctification comes from knowing the Truth (129). What the eye can see (or, the mind understand), the mouth can manifest (or, the person can follow) (130-131). The

Psalmist recognizes that the understanding of God's Word enables him to overcome personal sin (133). God's presence brings teaching and understanding (135) that will help overcome the sorrow of failing to obey God's Word (136).

צ Tsadhe   (Verses 137-144)

Tsadhe is a symbol of a reaping hook, a sickle, or a fish hook, and it indicates that the harvest is coming.

> 137 *You are righteous, Lord,*
> *and your laws are right.*
> 138 *The statutes you have laid down are righteous;*
> *they are fully trustworthy.*
> 139 *My zeal wears me out,*
> *for my enemies ignore your words.*
> 140 *Your promises have been thoroughly tested,*
> *and your servant loves them.*
> 141 *Though I am lowly and despised,*
> *I do not forget your precepts.*
> 142 *Your righteousness is everlasting*
> *and your law is true.*
> 143 *Trouble and distress have come upon me,*
> *but your commands give me delight.*
> 144 *Your statutes are always righteous;*
> *give me understanding that I may live.*

Indeed the harvest, or final judgment, is coming. In the end, it will be the Word that still stands. The psalmist says the Word of God is:

1. Right (137)
2. Righteous (138)
3. Fully trustworthy (138)
4. Thoroughly tested (140)
5. Everlasting (142)
6. True (142)
7. Always righteous (144)

Here and now, the "enemies ignore" God's Word (138), and the psalmist is "lowly and despised" (141). Even though "trouble and distress have come upon" him (143), the psalmist loves and is zealous for God's Word (140), which gives him great delight (143). In the end, Truth will prevail, and so he asks for even more wisdom and strength (144).

ק Qoph (Verses 145-152)

The letter qoph is a symbol of an axe or the back of the head and refers to "coming around", as in a circle of space (such as the motion created by the swing of an axe) or "a space of time". It can also refer to the back of one's mind.

> 145 I call with all my heart; answer me, Lord,
>   and I will obey your decrees.
> 146 I call out to you; save me
>   and I will keep your statutes.
> 147 I rise before dawn and cry for help;
>   I have put my hope in your word.
> 148 My eyes stay open through the watches of the night,
>   that I may meditate on your promises.
> 149 Hear my voice in accordance with your love;
>   preserve my life, Lord, according to your laws.
> 150 Those who devise wicked schemes are near,
>   but they are far from your law.
> 151 Yet you are near, Lord,
>   and all your commands are true.
> 152 Long ago I learned from your statutes
>   that you established them to last forever.

The psalmist compares the Word of God to the full circle of time represented by the Hebrew letter qoph in verse 152 when he says, "Long ago I learned from your statues, that you established them to last forever." Since the psalmist had "learned...long ago" that the Word of God was eternal, he was able to develop a lifestyle that included:

1. Calling on God with all his heart (145)
2. Rising before dawn to cry for help (147)
3. Meditating on the Word throughout the night (148)

While the psalmist spends his life committed to the Word of God, there are others near him who are far from it. These people spend their time devising evil schemes and laws based on worldly philosophies and human opinion (150). However, in the long run, when life and history have come full circle, the Word of God will prove true (152).

ר **Resh**   (Verses 153-160)

The letter resh was made to resemble the front of a man's head, and represents something that comes first, something that is the leader, or the first thing on one's mind.

> 153 *Look on my suffering and deliver me,*
>   *for I have not forgotten your law.*
> 154 *Defend my cause and redeem me;*
>   *preserve my life according to your promise.*
> 155 *Salvation is far from the wicked,*
>   *for they do not seek out your decrees.*
> 156 *Your compassion, Lord, is great;*
>   *preserve my life according to your laws.*
> 157 *Many are the foes who persecute me,*
>   *but I have not turned from your statutes.*
> 158 *I look on the faithless with loathing,*
>   *for they do not obey your word.*
> 159 *See how I love your precepts;*
>   *preserve my life, Lord, in accordance with your love.*
> 160 *All your words are true;*
>   *all your righteous laws are eternal.*

What separates the righteous from the wicked are the things they think about (155, 157, 158). The first thing on the psalmist's mind is the Word of God, which has been his guide and enables him to confidently wait for God's deliverance (153), defense (154) and preservation (154, 156). The psalmist is walking in the compassion (156) and love (159) of God, because he has not forgotten God's law (153), nor has he wavered from God's statutes (157).

ש Sin   (Verses 161-168)

The letter sin symbolizes a tooth – not the front teeth, but a tooth that is used for chewing, such as a molar. It also represents the sharpening of swords, arrows – or even the tongue.

> 161 *Rulers persecute me without cause,*
> *but my heart trembles at your word.*
> 162 *I rejoice in your promise*
> *like one who finds great spoil.*
> 163 *I hate and detest falsehood*
> *but I love your law.*
> 164 *Seven times a day I praise you*
> *for your righteous laws.*
> 165 *Great peace have those who love your law,*
> *and nothing can make them stumble.*
> 166 *I wait for your salvation, Lord,*
> *and I follow your commands.*
> 167 *I obey your statutes,*
> *for I love them greatly.*
> 168 *I obey your precepts and your statutes,*
> *for all my ways are known to you.*

Rulers chew up the psalmist with persecution (161). Yet the psalmist fears the power of the Word of God more (161) and rejoices in its promises of victory (162). Seven times a day the writer sharpens the edge of the sword of the Word of God with praise (164). Those who meditate, or chew, on the Word are empowered to keep their souls in God's "great peace" (165) and enabled to walk in the light, so that "nothing can make them stumble" (165).

Following false ways or giving up in midst of persecution because of fear are always an option, but instead, the psalmist "trembles" at God's word – not because of temptation or persecution (161). This fear of God's Word causes him to obey all God's precepts and statues, because, as he says, "all my ways are known to you" (168). He knows there can be no hiding from God.

Chapter Thirty-Seven:
God's Word Through Time

The Force of the Word of God throughout Time

Exodus 9:20 – *"Those officials of Pharaoh who **feared the Word** of the Lord hurried to bring their slaves and their livestock inside."*

Numbers 15:31 – *"Because he has despised the Lord's Word and **broken his commands**, that person must surely be cut off; his guilt remains on him."*

Numbers 20:24 – *"Aaron will be gathered to his people. He will not enter the land I give the Israelites, because both of you **rebelled against my command** at the waters of Meribah."*

Deuteronomy 4:1,2,6 – *"Hear now, O Israel, the **decrees and laws** I am about to **teach you**. Follow them so that you may live and may go in and take possession of the land…Do not add to what I command you and do not subtract from it, but keep the commands…Observe them carefully, for this will show your wisdom and understanding to the nations, who will hear about all these decrees…"*

Deuteronomy 30:14 – *"No, the **word is very near you**; it is in your mouth and in your heart so you may obey it."*

Deuteronomy 33:9 – *"(Aaron) **watched over your word** and **guarded your covenant**. He **teaches your precepts** to Jacob and your law to Israel…Bless all his skills, O Lord, and be pleased with the work of his hands. Smite the loins of those who rise up against him; strike his foes till they rise no more."*

Joshua 1:8 – *"Do not let this **Book of the Law** depart from **your mouth; meditate on it** day and night, so that you may be careful to **do everything written in it**. Then you will be prosperous and successful."*

First Samuel 15:23, 26 – *"Because you have **rejected the Word of the Lord**, he has rejected you as king…You have **rejected the Word of the Lord**, and the Lord has rejected you as king over Israel!"*

First Kings 8:56 – *"Praise be to the Lord, who has given rest to his people Israel just as he promised. **Not one Word has failed** of all the good promises he gave through his servant Moses."*

Second Chronicles 6:17 – *"And now, O Lord, God of Israel, let **your Word** that you promised your servant David **come true."***

Second Chronicles 34:21 – *"Go and inquire of the Lord for me and for the remnant in Israel and Judah about what is written in this book that has been found."*

Psalm 17:4 – *"By the Word of your **lips** I **have kept** myself from the ways of the violent."*

Psalm 33:4 – *"The **Word of the Lord is right and true**; he is faithful in all he does."*

Psalm 56:4, 10 – *"In God, whose **Word I praise**, in God I trust; I will not be afraid. What can mortal man do to me?...In God, whose **Word I praise**, in the Lord, whose **Word I praise** – in God I trust."*

Psalm 103:20 – *"Praise the Lord, you his angels, you mighty ones who do his bidding, who obey his Word."*

Psalm 106:24 – *"They **did not believe his promise**. They grumbled in their tents and **did not obey** the Lord."*

Psalm 107:20 – *"He sent forth his **Word** and **healed** them; he **rescued** them from the grave."*

Psalm 130:5 – *"I wait for the Lord, my soul waits, and **in his Word I put my hope."***

Psalm 138:2 – *"You have **exalted above all things** your name and **your Word."***

Psalm 147:15, 18, 19 – *"He **sends his command** to the earth; his **Word runs swiftly."***

Psalm 147:18 – *He **sends his Word** and **melts them**; he stirs up his breezes, and the waters flow."*

Psalm 147:19 – *"He has **revealed his Word** to Jacob, his **laws** and **decrees** to Israel. He has done this for no other nation; they do not know his laws."*

Proverbs 7:1-2 – *"My son, **keep my words** and **store up my commands** within you. Keep my commands and you will live; **guard my teachings as the apple of your eye."***

Isaiah 1:10 – *"**Hear the Word of the Lord**, you rulers of Sodom; **listen to the law** of our God, you people of Gomorrah!"*

Isaiah 5:24 – *"Therefore, as tongues of fire lick up straw and as dry grass sinks down in the flames, so their roots will decay and their flowers blow away like dust; for they have **rejected the law** of the Lord Almighty and **spurned the Word** of the Holy One of Israel."*

Isaiah 8:20 – *Why consult the dead on behalf of the living? To the **law** and to **the testimony**! If they **do not speak according to this Word**, they have **no light** of dawn."*

Isaiah 28:13-15 – *"So then, the **Word of the Lord** to them will become: Do and do, do and do, rule on rule, rule on rule; a little here, a little there – so that they will go and fall backward, be injured and snared and captured…for we (scoffers) have **made a lie our refuge** and **falsehood our hiding place**."*

Isaiah 30:8-12 – *"Go now, **write it on a tablet** for them, **inscribe it on a scroll**, that for the days to come it may be an everlasting witness. These are rebellious people, deceitful children, children **unwilling to listen** to the Lord's **instruction**. They say to the seers, 'See **no more visions!**' and to the prophets, 'Give us **no more visions of what is right!**' Tell us pleasant things, **prophesy illusions. Leave this way, get off this path**, and **stop confronting us** with the Holy One of Israel!' Therefore, this is what the Holy One of Israel says: 'Because you have **rejected this message**, relied on oppression and depended on deceit, this sin will become for you like a high wall, cracked and bulging, that collapses suddenly, in an instant.' "*

Isaiah 40:8 – *"The grass withers and the flowers fall, but the **Word of our God stands forever.**"*

Isaiah 55:10-11 – *"As the rain and the snow come down from heaven, and do not return to it without watering the earth and making it bud and flourish, so that it yields seed for the sower and bread for the eater, **so is my Word** that goes out from my mouth: It will not return to me empty, but will accomplish what I desire and achieve the purpose for which I sent it."*

Jeremiah 15:16 – *"When **your words** came, I ate them; they were my joy and my heart's delight, for I bear your name, O Lord God Almighty."*

Jeremiah 15:19 – *The Lord said to Jeremiah, "If you repent, I will restore you that you may serve me; if you utter worthy, not worthless, words, you will be my spokesman. Let this people turn to you, but you must not turn to them."*

Jeremiah 17:15 - *The rebellious people kept saying to Jeremiah, "Where is the Word of the Lord? Let it now be fulfilled?"*

Jeremiah 19:3 – *"**Hear the Word of the Lord**, O kings of Judah and people of Jerusalem. This is what the Lord Almighty, the God of Israel, says: 'Listen! I am going to bring a disaster on this place that will make the ears of everyone who hears of it tingle.'"*

Jeremiah 23:10-32 – *"The <u>prophets follow an evil course</u> and <u>use their power unjustly.</u> Both prophet and priest are <u>godless</u>; even <u>in my temple I find their wickedness</u>…Among the prophets of Samaria I saw this repulsive thing: They <u>prophesied by Baal</u> and <u>led my people Israel astray.</u> And among the prophets of Jerusalem I have seen something horrible: They <u>commit adultery</u> and <u>live a lie.</u> They <u>strengthen the hands of evildoers</u>, so that <u>no one turns from his wickedness</u>…This is what the Lord Almighty says concerning the (false) prophets: 'I will make them eat bitter food and drink poisoned water, because from the prophets of Jerusalem <u>ungodliness has spread throughout the land</u>… Do not listen to what the prophets are prophesying to you; they <u>fill you with false hopes.</u> They speak <u>visions from their own minds</u>, not from the mouth of the Lord. They keep saying to those who despise*

Mark 7:13 – *"Thus you **nullify the Word of God** by your tradition that you have handed down. And you do many things like that."*

Mark 13:31 – *"Heaven and earth will pass away, but **my Words will never pass away.**"*

Luke 6:47 – *"I will show you what he is like who comes to me and **hears my words and puts them into practice**. He is like a man building a house, who dug down deep and laid the foundation on rock. When a flood came, the torrent struck that house but could not shake it. Because it was well built. But the one who hears my words and does not put them into practice is like a man who built a house on the ground without a foundation. The moment the torrent struck that house, it collapsed and its destruction was complete*

Luke 8:11 – ***"The seed is the Word of God."***

John 1:1-4 – ***"In the beginning was the Word**, and the **Word was with God**, and the **Word was God**. He was with God in the beginning. Through him all things were made; without him nothing was made that has been made. In him was **life**, and that life was the **light** of men."*

John 1:14, 16 – *"The **Word became flesh** and made his dwelling among us…**grace** and **Truth** came through Jesus Christ."*

John 6:33 – *"For the **bread of God** is he who comes down **from heaven** and **gives life** to the world."*

John 6:63 – *"**The words** I have spoken to you **are spirit** and **they are life**."*

John 10:35 – *"The **Scripture cannot be broken.**"*

John 17:17 – *"Sanctify them by the Truth; **your Word is Truth**."*

Acts 4:2 – *"They were greatly disturbed because the **apostles were teaching the people** and proclaiming in Jesus the resurrection of the dead."*

Acts 4:4 – *"Many who **heard the message believed**, and the number of men grew to about five thousand."*

Acts 4:29,31

Acts 5:20 – *"Go, stand in the temple courts and* **tell the people the full message** *of this new life."*

Acts 5:42 – *"Day after day, in the temple courts and from house to house,* **they never stopped teaching and proclaiming** *the good news that Jesus is the Christ."*

Acts 6:2, 4 *"So the Twelve gathered all the disciples together and said,* **'It would not be right for us to neglect the ministry of the word of God** *in order to wait on tables…We will turn this responsibility over to them and will* **give our attention to prayer and the ministry of the word."**

Acts 6:2 – **"It would not be right for us to neglect the ministry of the Word of God** *in order to wait on tables."*

Acts 6:3-4 – *"We will turn this responsibility over to them and will* **give our attention to prayer and the ministry of the Word."**

Acts 6:7 – **So the Word of God spread.** *The number of disciples in Jerusalem increased rapidly, and a large number of priests became obedient to the faith."*

Acts 11:1 – *"The apostles and the brothers throughout Judea heard that the* **Gentiles also head received the Word of God."**

Acts 12:24 – *"The* **Word of God** *continued to increase and spread."*

Acts 13:7 – *The proconsul, an intelligent man, sent for Barnabas and Saul because he wanted to hear the* **Word of God.**"

Acts 13:26 – *"Brothers, children of Abraham, and you God-fearing Gentiles, it is to us that this* **message of salvation** *has been sent."*

Acts 13:48 – *"When the Gentiles heard this, they were glad and* **honored the Word of the Lord."**

Acts 18:11 – *"So Paul stayed for a year and a half, **teaching them the Word of God.**"*

Acts 19:20 – *"In this way the **Word of the Lord spread widely** and grew in power."*

Acts 20:32 – *"Now I commit you to God and to **the Word of his grace**, which can build you up [Phase Two] and give you an inheritance [Phase Three] among all those who are sanctified [Phase Two]."*

Romans 10:8 – *" 'The **Word is near you**; it is in your mouth and in your heart,' that is, the **Word of faith we are proclaiming.**"*

Romans 10:17 – *"Faith comes from **hearing the message**, and the message is heard through the **Word of Christ.**"*

2 Corinthians 2:17 – *"Unlike so many, we **do not peddle the Word of God for profit**. On the contrary, in Christ we speak before God with sincerity, like men sent from God."*

2 Corinthians 4:2 – *"We have renounced secret and shameful ways [False Teaching]; we do not use deception, nor do we distort the Word of God [Doctrines of Demons]. On the contrary, be **setting forth the Truth** [Word of God] plainly we commend ourselves to every man's conscience in the sight of God."*

Colossians 1:25 – *"I have become its servant by the commission God gave me to present to you **the Word of God in its fullness** – the mystery that has been kept hidden for ages and generations, but is now disclosed to the saints."*

Titus 1:3 – *"At his appointed season **he brought his Word to light** through the preaching entrusted to me by the command of God our Savior."*

Hebrews 1:3 – *"The Son is the radiance of God's glory and the exact representation of his being, **sustaining all things by his powerful word.**"*

Hebrews 4:2 – *"For we also have had the **gospel preached** to us, just as they did; but **the message they heard** was of no value to them, because those who **heard** did not combine it with faith."*

Hebrews 4:12 – *"The **Word of God is living and active**. Sharper than any double-edged sword, it penetrates even to dividing soul and spirit, joints and marrow; it judges the thoughts and attitudes of the heart."*

Hebrews 6:5 – *"Who have tasted the goodness of the **Word of God**."*

Hebrews 11:3 – *"By faith we understand that the universe was formed at **God's command**, so that what is seen was not made out of what was visible."*

Hebrews 13:7 – *"Remember your leaders, who **spoke the Word of God** to you. Consider the outcome of their way of life [Phase Two] and imitate their faith…Do not be carried away by all kinds of strange teachings [False Doctrine]."*

James 1:18 – *"He chose to give us birth through the **Word of Truth**."*

James 1:21 – *"Humbly **accept the Word planted in you**, which can save you."*

First Peter 1:23 – *"You have been born again, not of perishable seed, but of imperishable, through the living and enduring **Word of God**."*

First Peter 1:25 – *" 'The **word of the Lord** stands forever.' And this is **the Word** that was preached to you."*

First Peter 2:2 – *"Like newborn babies, crave **pure spiritual milk**, so that by it you may grow up in your salvation, now that you have tasted that the Lord is good."*

Second Peter 3:16 – *"…ignorant and unstable **people distort, as they do the other Scriptures**, to their own destruction."*

First John 1:1 – *"…this we proclaim concerning the Word of life."*

Revelation 22:7 – *"Blessed is he who keeps the words of the prophecy in this book."*